D1324601

Windows
on Luke

an anthology to amplify the
Gospel readings for Year C
of the Lectionary

Ronald W. Dale

Kevin Mayhew

First published in 2000 by
KEVIN MAYHEW LTD
Buxhall
Stowmarket
Suffolk IP14 3BW

0 1 2 3 4 5 6 7 8 9

ISBN 1 84003 602 8
Catalogue No 1500374

Front cover: *St Luke,* relief from the north side of the basilica (marble)
12th-13th century. San Marco, Venice.
Reproduced by courtesy of Bridgeman Art Library, London

Cover design by Jaquetta Sergeant
Edited by Helen Elliot
Typesetting by Elisabeth Bates

Printed and bound in Great Britain

About the author

The Reverend Ron Dale entered the ministry after seven years in the electrical wholesale business and two years as a military dog handler in Libya. He has worked on a variety of Methodist circuits as pastor, superintendent and preacher, combining this with part-time teaching, industrial chaplaincy, broadcasting with the BBC regional network in Birmingham, Derby, Devon, Cornwall and the Channel Islands, prison chaplaincy and a considerable involvement with ecumenical work. He is married with two adult children.

Contents

Foreword

I have greatly enjoyed researching and planning *Windows on Luke,* the final volume of a trilogy on what are called the Synoptic Gospels of Matthew, Mark, and Luke. *The Revised Common Lectionary,* on which the other three-year lectionaries are based, takes us through each of the Synoptics, in a three-yearly cycle, with the Gospel of John being used for the main Christian festivals, such as Christmas and Easter.

Having now completed this project, I am firmly convinced of the value of each Gospel for a 'rounded' picture of Christ and his redemptive ministry. Each Gospel window sheds its light from a different angle, revealing distinct but complementary aspects of the person and teaching of Jesus.

So for me, Matthew is the great teaching Gospel, with the Sermon on the Mount of critical importance. I found Mark, almost from the beginning, concerned with conflict and opposition to Jesus and his Gospel, with misunderstanding about his person, his message and the mighty works which led finally to his rejection and death. Nevertheless, Mark has Good News for the blind and the leper, for those who were in one way or another made to feel outsiders.

Luke is the great theologian whose themes touch on Church and Synagogue; picturing a universal Church hopefully meeting a universal need of God, offered in his only Son. Who can forget the wonderful parables, unique to Luke: the Prodigal Son, and the Good Samaritan? Who can fail to be struck by Luke's depiction of Jesus elevating the status of women, as with the 'bad' woman who bathed the feet of Jesus with her tears and dried them with her hair, finding through her actions pardon, dignity and a new status?

But John gives us a very different portrayal of Christ. His Gospel deliberately uses the same words as Genesis 1: 'In the beginning . . .' going on to describe Jesus by saying, 'All creation took place through him, and none took place without him' (J. B. Phillips). Christ is the Logos, the Word of God made flesh, who comes to pitch his tent amongst us, full of grace and truth. The Law was given through Moses, but grace and truth, glory and love, are given through Christ: in his life, teaching, healing, death and resurrection.

Living with all four Gospels for the last few years has been a very enriching experience. I hope that you will find priceless treasure within these pages, both for yourself and for sharing with others.

RON DALE, 2000

First Sunday of Advent

Luke 21:25-36

The inexplicable arrival of Jesus Christ . . . has to take place within the individual human heart and soul, till Christ comes again into the life of every person, and until eschatology so becomes personalised.

Waiting

A tourist wandering along the shores of Lake Como, in northern Italy, happened to come to the castle known as Villa Asconati, and even at first glance he realised that it was one of the most gracious buildings of its kind he had ever seen. Presently a very old but friendly gardener, opening the gate, invited the tourist to look round; so the two walked along paths, under trees and amid lawns and flowers, and no matter where they went everything was immaculate in spite of the curious fact that quite obviously the castle was deserted. No one sat at a window. Nobody walked in the grounds. No servants appeared. No dog barked. After some conversation, the tourist enquired when the owner had last been in residence.

'Twelve years ago,' replied the gardener.

'I suppose he writes?'

'Never.'

'Then who gives you your instructions?'

'His agent in Milan.'

'Does the agent come sometimes?'

'Oh, no, the agent never comes.'

'But surely somebody visits the place?'

The old gardener shook his head. 'Nobody, ' he said sadly. 'Nobody ever sees the gardens except an occasional traveller like yourself.'

For a while the tourist said nothing. Captivated as he was by the exquisite lawns, each perfect, the flowers, the borders in which he could not find even a single weed, he was puzzled. Moreover, he was aware of a hint of mystery and, still more, of a feeling that he had unconsciously walked into the middle of a parable. 'But,' said he at last, 'you keep everything here beyond all reproach as if you are expecting the master to come tomorrow.'

Several years have passed since the tourist made that observation, but to this day he recalls the light which kindled in the old gardener's eyes, the excitement which brought a flush to his cheeks, the quiver in his voice as he cried passionately, 'Today, sir! . . . may it be TODAY!'

H. L. Gee
Telling Tales

He is coming

The response put into the mouth of God by the prophet Malachi is to say: 'Yes, the Lord whom you seek will suddenly come to his temple.' He *is* going to intervene. He is coming. 'But who can endure the day of his coming, and who can stand when he appears?' The unpalatable fact is that God is not to be called in to be a fairy godmother. If he comes and when he comes, he will come as himself. An uncomfortable God. A God who is more demanding in his holiness than ever we thought. A God of justice indeed.

We are told that his first task will be to purify the sons of Levi, the leaders of the Church, the priesthood. Malachi uses the simile of the silver refiner to illustrate his point. It is a striking and moving picture. For the purifying process takes place under great heat, which causes the mixed contents of the refiner's cauldron to bubble and boil, as the lead oxide separates from the pure silver. The dross then rises to the surface and at a certain temperature becomes translucent so that the silver becomes like a mirror. The refiner sits by his cauldron and keeps looking in until the process is complete and he can see his face mirrored in the now purified metal. God refines his people, often through the fires of testing, until he can see his own image reflected in us. Then we shall be pure and more ready to serve him acceptably and, as Malachi puts it, 'The the offering of Judah and Jerusalem will be pleasing to the Lord as in the days of old'.

John B. Taylor
Preaching on God's Justice

The meaning of the Second Coming

Can we come to any general conclusions about the meaning of the Parousia of Jesus Christ? It seems that there are four possible lines of approach.

(a) *A definite event in history.* We may regard the Parousia of Jesus Christ as one definite event, which will take place at some unknown time in the future. We may look for the Second Coming of Jesus Christ as an event in history, even if it is the event to end history. Lines of argument to support this view are not lacking. It may be said that, so far as there is an orthodox view of the Second Coming, this is the orthodox view. It well fits in with the whole biblical view of history. It would be the New Testament counterpart, or rather the New Testament fulfilment, of the Old Testament picture of the Day of the Lord. In the historical Second Coming of Jesus Christ the Old Testament expectation of the Day of the Lord would find its true consummation and completion. It might be well said that the historical Second Coming of Jesus Christ is the essential corollary of his resurrection and his ascension and exaltation. The resurrection vindicated every claim of Jesus Christ, and the Second Coming would be the universal demonstration of the universal and eternal lordship of Jesus Christ. An historical Second Coming would conserve the great Christian and biblical truth that history is going somewhere towards a goal, that there is a plan and a purpose in events, that history is not circular and repetitive, not pointless and purposeless, not on the way to slow extinction, but that it has a consummation in the mind of God. It is further to be said that there is little doubt that, in the thought of the Early Church, the Second Coming was to be an historical event involving the Christians and all mankind. The arguments for the Second Coming as a future, definite event are strong; but nonetheless it remains true that the evidence for this kind of Second Coming is not nearly so strong in the Gospels as at first sight it appears, and it may well be that we shall have to seek some other line of approach.

(b) *The Holy Spirit is the Second Coming of Jesus*. It is possible to argue that the Second Coming of Jesus Christ has happened in the coming of the Holy Spirit. To all intents and purposes this would mean that the events of Pentecost constitute the Second Coming of Jesus Christ. There is at least something of this conception in the thought of the fourth Gospel. 'I will not leave you comfortless,' says the Christ of the fourth Gospel, 'I will come to you' (John 14:18), and that coming was definitely in the coming of the Holy Spirit. 'If a man love me, he will keep my words: and my Father will love him, and we will come unto him, and make our abode with him' (John 14:23). There is no doubt that the fourth Gospel does see the coming of the Spirit as the coming of Jesus Christ into an individual's life. This would be in the most literal sense to spiritualise the whole idea of the Second Coming. Jesus Christ would then be the Person who came once in the flesh, and who came again in the Holy Spirit, and who continues to come.

(c) *All was completed in Jesus*. It is possible to approach the whole conception of the Second Coming along the lines of what is known as realised eschatology. To do that is to say that the whole process of eschatological events has already been realised in Jesus Christ. In him the victory over all evil has finally been won; the powers of darkness and the spirits of evil have finally been defeated. In him the kingdom has been fully realised and did fully come.

There is a sense in which this is emphatically true. In the life and death of Jesus Christ something did happen to break the power of sin. The Lord's Prayer sets two petitions side by side: 'Thy kingdom come', and 'Thy will be done in earth as it is in heaven'. If we apply the ordinary principles of Hebrew parallelism to these two phrases we may say that the kingdom of heaven is a society in which God's will is as perfectly done on earth as it is in heaven. And, if that is so, then the kingdom was fully and finally realised in Jesus Christ, because in him and by him God's will was perfectly done. On this view the Second Coming is no longer a necessary event, because the whole eschatological process and ideal has found its consummation and realisation and completion in Jesus Christ.

This idea found its most epigrammatic and succinct expression in the famous dictum that D-day (the day of the allied invasion of Europe) is now past, and V-day (the day of victory) must of necessity follow.

Stated, as it were, in theory, there is great attraction in that way of putting things. But one cannot evade the feeling that it does not fit the facts. In point of fact the forces of evil are not subdued, and in point of fact human nature is not changed, and in point of fact sin is not defeated.

The D-day, V-day analogy suffers from one basic defect; the fact is that the process of salvation, God's offer of salvation, the way in which an individual is saved, cannot properly be likened to a campaign. When a war has been waged, and when victory has been won, every member of the victorious nation shares in that victory, whether they like it or not. The nation as a whole is released from danger; the nation as a whole is no longer threatened; the nation as a whole enjoys the benefits of that victory. Individuals cannot even opt out of that victory; they are members of a victorious nation.

Now the whole point of the benefits of salvation in Christ is that they have to be appropriated. Assuredly no one can either merit them or achieve them, but they must appropriate them. A much closer analogy is the discovery of some cure whereby a fatal illness can be cured and overcome. Even if there be such a cure, the person suffering from that illness can find no cure until he or she accepts the cure and submits to the treatment and appropriates the benefits which are now available for them. Christ's victory is a victory which has to be appropriated. We, therefore, suggest that there is still another way in which to approach the whole matter of the Parousia, the Second Coming, of Jesus Christ.

Appropriate it (.

(d) *Personalised eschatology*. There is the way which, we suggest, may be described by the phrase 'personalised eschatology'. It is possible to think of the whole eschatological process, and, in particular, of the Second Coming of Jesus Christ, as happening within the individual heart and soul.

The coming of Jesus Christ in the flesh was an event in history. But it is an event which is different from any other event which ever happened in history. It makes no difference to a person's present life in this world or to their eternal welfare in any other world, if they never think of, or if they totally disregard, the historical event of the Battle of Hastings. It does not essentially affect the individual, even if they are quite unaware that that battle was ever fought. No one would ever dream of sending missionaries to the ends of the earth to tell people that William of Normandy landed in Sussex in England in the year 1066. But we do seek to bring the news to all humankind that Jesus Christ was born into Palestine. We do so because we believe that the coming into the world of Jesus Christ was an event that has its direct value for everyone.

Now, if someone is unaware of the coming of Christ, they have to be told of it. If they disregard it, they have to be brought to see its supreme importance. And, therefore, it is literally true to say that Jesus Christ has to come again into every individual life. The shattering change, the inbreak of God, the inexplicable arrival of Jesus Christ, the whole eschatological process has to take place within the individual human heart and soul, till Christ comes again into the life of every person, and until eschatology so becomes personalised.

The Parousia of Christ, his Second Coming, is not a subject on which anyone would wish, or indeed has any right, to dogmatise. But it may well be that the whole picture of it in scripture is a vivid, dramatic, symbolic representation of a process which must take place within the individual human heart, so that the whole eschatological process, and the Second Coming of Christ, become personalised in each person's being.

William Barclay
Great Themes of the New Testament

Second Sunday of Advent

Luke 3:1-6
Luke 1:68-79 (Benedictus)

There is no Advent without preparation.

Luke 1:68-79: The introduction to the song makes two important statements: first, Zechariah is filled with the Holy Spirit; and second, what he says is identified as prophecy. In this characterisation, Zechariah joins Elizabeth (1:41-45), Mary (1:46-55) and Simeon (2:27-32), as well as Jesus, the apostles and early Christian prophets. In fact, for Luke, a primary role of the Holy Spirit is inspiring speech, and this speech, defined as prophetic, joins the Christian movement with Judaism, where God also works through prophetic words. The Benedictus itself falls into two units: verses 68-75 and 76-79. The first unit praises God not for sending John but for raising up 'a mighty saviour for us; that is, Jesus. Full of Old Testament allusions, these verses are distinctly Jewish, similar to canonical psalms that praise God as deliverer (Psalms 34; 67; 103; 113). The Dead Sea Scrolls contain similar psalms of praise and thanksgiving. Israel's eschatological hopes will be fulfilled, promises will be kept, the covenant with Abraham will be remembered, and all enemies will be overthrown.

The second unit (verses 76-79) speaks of John, but even here the focus is on Jesus, for John 'will go before the Lord to prepare his ways' (verse 76). The song provides a concise summary of what John will do and what Jesus will do, drawing heavily on Malachi 3:1-2; 4:5-6 and on Isaiah 9:2; 42:7. However, we must keep in mind that throughout the passage, the true object of praise is God: 'Blessed be the Lord God of Israel' (verse 68). In the ministry of John, God comes to us. That advent prepares us for the fuller advent in Jesus of Nazareth.

Luke 3:1-6: On this Second Sunday of Advent, all four writers of the scripture texts look to the day of the Lord, each having in mind an advent of God. Their understandings of the coming of the Lord differ, but they are of one mind in the conviction that there is no advent without preparation. In that faith the father of John the Baptist praises God, the prophet looks to the coming of God's messenger who will purify Israel, the apostle ministers in anticipation, and the evangelist introduces John, the voice crying in the wilderness.

John, the son of Zechariah who prepares the way for Jesus, is himself of unusual birth and a gift from God (Luke 1:5-25, 57-80), for Luke understands that not only the Lord's coming but also the preparation for that coming are the initiatives of a gracious God.

. . . Our Gospel for today begins, then, with a list of names and titles – how preachers hate lists! – but does it matter? Perhaps Luke was a history buff, but is it important to anyone else? The answer is yes. Luke, by setting the preparation for the advent of Jesus Christ in the context of world history and the universal purpose of God, says that the Gospel belongs to all people. The Gospel is not the Church's possession to be subsequently carried to others. The Gospel is for the world before it is ever uttered, by John, by Jesus, or by the Church. This is God's gift to God's creation.

Fred B. Craddock
Preaching Through the Christian Year: 'C'

'He shall not judge by what his eyes see, or decide by what his ears hear.' Which is wonderful if you are oppressed or discriminated against or victimised. But what about the rest of us? Is this bit of Bible, this Advent hope, this Christmas good news, anything for us? Why should I want to hear that God will judge fairly? Why should I want to hear that God will judge at all?

To tell the truth, most of the time I don't want to hear that! But it is part of the Christian message, and it is particularly and traditionally part of the Advent message. God coming as judge. Christians who take that seriously – and I'm not sure that you can be a Christian if you don't take it seriously – react in one of two ways to that idea.

First there are those who face God, the coming judge, with fear and despair. They are those who know that they are, in the old words, 'wicked and unprofitable servants'; who know that when the eyes of the just judge are turned on them, they will tremble and be right to tremble. They are those who know that even their best acts are tainted with mixed motives and that secretly, deep down, they put themselves first every single time, whatever the world says about their selflessness and care for others. These are they who know that their prayers are shallow, their love for their

15

neighbour extremely conditional and their trust in God merely prudential. They are those who know that God is a jealous God, loving the right and hating the wrong, who desires mercy, not sacrifice, and whose will will be done.

And to that extent I hope you are among them.

Yet I hope you do not fear the judgement of God. For there is something else. The second group are those who know the depth of their own sin, but also know the depth of the love of God and the sacrifice of the cross. Christian faith at its best understands the judgement of the Messiah like this. Christ, coming to us as judge, sees us with terrible clarity and sees us whole. Christ's love so wishes our joy that it is ruthless against everything in us that diminishes our joy. The one who judges us most finally will be the one who loves us most fully. The worst sentence love can pass is that we behold the suffering which love has endured for our sake: and that is also our acquittal. The justice and mercy of this judge are ultimately one.

Come, thou long-expected Jesus, born to set thy people free. From our sins and fears release us; let us find our rest in thee. Amen.

Andrew R. C. McLellan
Preaching for These People

Third Sunday of Advent

Luke 3:7-18

Advent is not a time of casual waiting. It is a demanding piece of work.

Kaj Munk was a pastor of the church in Denmark. He became the spiritual force behind the Danish resistance to Hitler at the time of the Nazi occupation. In January 1944, they took him away one night and shot him like a dog in the field, but his life and death continued to inspire the Danes in their struggle for freedom. To me, Kaj Munk is one of the great men in the recent history of the Christian Church. He reminded his fellow pastors of what they needed in a world where the choices were becoming more stark, more painful, more unavoidable day by day. 'What is therefore the task of the preacher today? Shall I answer: faith, hope and love? That sounds beautiful. But I would rather say: courage. No, even that is not challenging enough to be the *whole* truth . . . Our task today is recklessness . . . For what we as a Church lack is most assuredly not psychology or literature. We lack a holy rage. . .'

A holy rage. The recklessness that comes from the knowledge of God and humanity. The ability to rage when justice lies prostrate on the streets and when the lie rages across the face of the earth. A holy anger about things that are wrong in the world. To rage against the ravaging of God's earth and the destruction of God's world. To rage when little children must die of hunger while the tables of the rich are sagging with food. To rage against the senseless killing of so many and against the madness of militarism. To rage at the lie that calls the threat of death and the strategy of destruction 'peace'. To rage against the complacency of so many in the Church who fail to see that we shall live only by the truth, and that our fear will be the death of us all . . . To restlessly seek that recklessness which will challenge and to seek to change human history until it conforms to the norms of the kingdom of God.

'And remember,' says Kaj Munk, 'the signs of the Christian Church have always been the lion, the lamb, the dove and the fish. But *never* the chameleon.' And remember too: the Church is the chosen people of God. But the chosen shall be known by their choices.

Allan Boesak, 'The Reuben Option'
Sermon from *Walking on Thorns: The Call to Christian Discipleship*

Into this world of lyrical poetry, says our Gospel, pushes the unkempt, unwelcome figure of John the Baptiser. You remember him. He is dressed in a hair shirt. He eats wild honey and such other gifts that he can forage in the rough. He comes in anger and demand, threat and insistence. He speaks really only one word: Repent! Recognise the danger you are in and change.

In the Gospel narrative, John embodies the best and the last of the old tradition of Torah demand. He has this deep sense of urgency about the world, but it is not an urgency of newness. It is an urgency of threat and danger and jeopardy, one that we ourselves sense now about our world. He comes first in the story. He comes before Jesus. He is the key player in the Advent narrative.

When Jesus appears on the scene, John the Baptiser immediately acknowledges the greatness of Jesus, greater than all that is past – greater than John, greater than all ancient memories and hopes. When Jesus comes into the narrative, John quickly, abruptly, without reservation, says of Jesus, 'He must increase, I must decrease.'

. . . If John embodies all that is old and Jesus embodies all that is new, take as your Advent work toward Christmas that enterprise: decrease/increase. Decrease what is old and habitual and destructive in your life, so that the new life-giving power of Jesus may grow large with you. Decrease what is greedy, what is frantic consumerism, for the increase of simple, life-giving sharing. Decrease what is fearful and defensive, for the increase of life-giving compassion and generosity. Decrease what is fraudulent and pretence, for the increase of life-giving truth-telling in your life, truth-telling about you and your neighbour, about the sickness of our society and our enmeshment in that sickness. Decrease what is hateful and alienating for the increase of healing and forgiveness, which finally are the only source of life.

Advent basks in the great promises. In the meantime, however, there are daily disciplines, day-to-day exercises of Advent, work that requires time and intentionality, that has nothing to do with the busyness that the world imposes upon us. God will do much to bring the promises to fruition. But God will not do our work of redeciding our life. There is for us, only us, the staggering possibility of choosing real life and turning away from the killing in which we are much practised.

Advent is not for sitting around, but it is for pondering and noticing, embracing, renouncing and receiving. We watch while we notice the increase of gospel living, of sharing, of growing in compassion, of generosity, of hope, of truth-telling, in healing and in forgiveness. Such newness.

As the gifts of the Gospel embodied in Jesus may increase for us, something peculiar and cosmic happens in our midst. We begin to hear the rustle of new heaven and new earth, new Jerusalem and new Atlanta, and it does not now sound so outrageous in its coming. . .

Advent is not a time of casual waiting. It is a demanding piece of work. It requires that we attend to both the outrageousness of God and the daily work of decreasing. The outcome of such an Advent goes like this. Listen:

They shall not hurt or destroy
in all my holy mountain, says the Lord.

That will be some newness! Some Christmas! Some Gospel!

Walter Brueggemann
The Threat of Life

*the American theologian, has a
terrific passage — worth
quoting in full —*

Wrath, anger, indignation

God's attitude to sin is described in both OT and NT in terms borrowed from the human passion of anger, indignation and wrath. It is not to be thought of as an irrational, irresponsible action on the part of God, but rather as the manifestation, sometimes suddenly and immediately experienced, of that aversion to sin which is part of his character. It is especially called forth for presumptuous sin, and it shows itself in the severe punishment and even utter destruction of the offender.

It has been the custom to distinguish between the OT as emphasising the divine wrath, and the NT as emphasising the divine mercy and love, but such a sharp distinction is unwarranted. The OT is the story of God's steady anger against sin in every form, whether within Israel or outside, coupled with his forbearance to execute the fierceness of his anger (Hosea 11:9), that is, to wipe out Israel entirely by allowing her to pay the proper penalty for her sin. The extreme example of both God's wrath and his forbearance is to be seen in Exodus 32:7-14, the story of the golden calf, especially since it was a saying of the Rabbis that in every sin there is something of the golden calf. God's wrath waxed hot against the people because of this crowning apostasy, but, at the pleading by Moses, he 'repented of the evil which he said he would do' to them. In his wrath he remembered mercy (Habakkuk 3:2).

The NT shows everywhere the same twin attitude on the part of God, an intense anger against sin, and great forbearance towards the sinner. It is by his grace that he is full of forbearance, for though he is strong and firm in his judgement against sin, it is not his will that any should perish, but rather that they should turn to him and live. Nevertheless, there does come at length the Day of Wrath, which is the day of God's final and irrevocable judgement against sin and all unrepentant sinners. This Day of Wrath is spoken of in the Gospels, in the Epistles and in the Apocalypse; and the NT nowhere says that mercy has the last word. God's last word is of condemnation and destruction of sin and stubborn sinners on the one hand, and of full pardon and restoration to the divine favour to all who truly repent and have faith in him.

Article by N. H. Snaith
in *A Theological Word Book of the Bible,*
ed. Alan Richardson, DD

Fourth Sunday of Advent

Luke 1:39-45 (46-55)

I wish you joy . . .
and tender love
from all.

Joy that was not?

Describing a local farmer called Prospect Smiler, Laurie Lee says, 'Few men I think can have been as unfortunate as he, for on the one hand he was a melancholic with a loathing for mankind, on the other, some paralysis had twisted his mouth into a permanent and radiant smile. So everyone he met, being warmed by this smile, would shout him a happy greeting. And beaming upon them with his sunny face he would curse them all to hell.'

Laurie Lee
Cider with Rosie

I wish you joy,
love with your friends,
happiness in your work,
fortune with your salary,
pleasure in your walks,
well-being in your dwelling,
health in your body,
beauty in yourself,
delight in all,
kindness from your friends,
excellence in all you do,
courage to do all well,
determination to get things right,
and tender love from all.

Katie Mitchell, aged 14
My Wish for You

To the Editor of Lloyd's Evening Post

On 15 October Wesley 'walked up to Knowle, a mile from Bristol, to see the French prisoners'. He found they had only a few foul thin rags to cover them. 'I was much affected, and preached in the evening on Exodus 23:9'. £18 was collected and next day it was made up to £24. Clothes were bought, and carefully distributed to the most needy. The Corporation sent mattresses and blankets. Contributions were set on foot in London and other places; and from that time the prisoners 'were pretty well provided with all the necessaries of life'.

Sir,
Since I came to Bristol, I heard many terrible accounts concerning the French prisoners at Knowle, as that 'they were so wedged together that they had no room to breathe'; that 'the stench of the rooms where they lodged was intolerable'; that 'their food was only fit for dogs'; that 'their meat was carrion, their bread rotten and unwholesome'; and that, 'in consequence of this inhuman treatment, they died in whole shoals'.

Desiring to know the truth, I went to Knowle on Monday, and was showed all the apartments there. But how was I disappointed!
(1) I found they had large and convenient space to walk in, if they chose it, all the day.
(2) There was no stench in any apartment which I was in, either below or above. They were all sweeter and cleaner than any prison I have seen either in England or elsewhere.
(3) Being permitted to go into the larder, I observed the meat hanging up, two large quarters of beef. It was fresh and fat, and I verily think as good as I ever desire to eat.
(4) A large quantity of bread lay on one side. A gentleman took up and cut one of the loaves. It was made of good flour, was well baked and perfectly well-tasted.
(5) Going thence to the hospital, I found that even in this sickly season, there are not thirty persons dangerously ill out of twelve or thirteen hundred.
(6) The hospital was sweeter and cleaner throughout than any hospital I ever saw in London. I think it my duty to declare these things, for clearing the innocence and the honour of the English nation.

Yet one thing I observed with concern. A great part of these men are almost naked; and winter is now coming upon them in a cold prison and a colder climate than most of them have been accustomed to. But will not the humanity and

generosity of the gentlemen of Bristol prevent or relieve this distress? Did they not make a notable precedent during the late war? And surely they are not weary of well-doing? Tuesday night *we* did a little according to our power; but I shall rejoice if this be forgotten through the abundance administered by their liberality in a manner which they judge most proper. Will it not be both for the honour of their city and country, for the credit of our religion, and for the glory of God, who knows how to return it sevenfold into their bosom?
I am
Your humble servant.

Letter by John Wesley, dated 20 October 1759
The Letters of John Wesley: Volume 4

Stanford in G is one of the most beautiful settings of the Magnificat there could be. I often used to think of Charles Villiers Stanford seated at the organ of Trinity, Cambridge – first as organist, then as Professor of Music. The gifts of the Spirit were so manifest in the beauty of what he wrote that it was right that at the end he should be buried next to Henry Purcell in Westminster Abbey.

But I have often wondered what picture of the Virgin Mary was in his mind when he composed his Magnificat in G. Some think he had in mind an Old Master: Mary, the Virgin, sitting at her spinning wheel, singing sweetly as she spun. Perhaps, but by itself *that* picture of the Virgin Mary and the Magnificat simply will not do . . .

Mary was the wife of a working carpenter. Her song is one of revolution, in which she prophesies her son will cast down those in power, send the rich empty away, and fill the hungry with good things. Any setting of the Magnificat which induces slumber and acquiescence is to be questioned. Thomas Hancock, one of the outstanding clergy of the nineteenth century, wrote, 'The Magnificat is the inspired summary of the tendency and direction of the future social history of humankind'.

Eric James
A Time to Speak

Christmas Day – First Proper

Luke 2:1-14 (15-20)

In the infant Jesus, four apparent opposites meet together: incarnation with redemption; birth with death; motherhood with virginity; humanity with the divine.

Christmas carols

There is nothing like Christmas carols to evoke the spirit of the season. Whether heard in the shopping mall or in the sanctuary, the traditional songs trigger emotions buried deep within our souls.

Because we learn Christmas carols during childhood, they provide an emotional 'safe place' in our constantly changing world, as well as fashion a theological portrait of Jesus.

Sister Gillian Leslie ODC, of Norwich, England, offers insight into the theological formation created by Christmas carols when she writes in the November/December 1995 issue of *Living Pulpit*: 'What I refer to as the theology of the Christmas carol can, I think, be summarised briefly in terms of four recurring themes. In the infant Jesus, four apparent opposites meet together: incarnation with redemption; birth with death; motherhood with virginity; humanity with the divine. It is the paradox of their union in the nativity of this one child that, consciously or unconsciously, we take on our lips in our Christmas liturgies.'

G. Curtis Jones and Paul H. Jones
500 Illustrations: Stories from Life for Preaching & Teaching

The burning babe

As I in hoary winter's night
stood shivering in the snow,
surprised I was with sudden heat
which made my heart to glow;
and lifting up a fearful eye
to view what fire was near,
a pretty babe all burning bright
did in the air appear;
who, scorched with excessive heat,
such floods of tears did shed,

as though his floods should quench his flames,
which with his tears were bred:
'Alas!' quoth he, 'but newly born
in fiery heats I fry,
yet none approach to warm their hearts
or feel my fire but I.
My faultless breast the furnace is;
the fuel, wounding thorns;
love is the fire, and sighs the smoke;
the ashes, shames and scorns;
the fuel Justice layeth on,
and mercy blows the coals,
the metal in this furnace wrought
are men's defiled souls:
for which, as now on fire I am
to work them to their good,
so I will melt into a bath
and wash them with my blood.'
With this he vanished out of sight
and swiftly shrunk away,
and straight I called unto mind
that it was Christmas Day.

Robert Southwell (1561?-95)

December 25, I went with my wife and family to London to celebrate Christmas Day. Mr Gunning preaching in Excester Chapell on 7 Mich 2. Sermon ended, as he was giving us the holy Sacrament, the Chapell was surrounded by soldiers. All the Communicants and Assembly surpris'd and kept prisoners by them, some in the house, others carried away. It fell to my share to be confined to a roome in the house, where yet were permitted to dine with the master of it, the Countesse of Dorset, Lady Hatton and some others of quality who invited me. In the afternoon came Colonel Whaly, Goffe and others from Whitehall to examine us one by one, and some they committed to the Martial, some to Prison.

When I came before them they tooke my name and aboad, examined me, why contrarie to an Ordinance made that none should any longer observe the superstitious time of the Nativity (so esteem'd by them) I durst offend, and particularly be at Common Prayers, which they told was but the

Masse in English, and particularly pray for Charles Stuart, for which we had no scripture. I told them we did not pray for Charles Stuart but for all Christian Kings, Princes and Governors. They replied, in so doing we prayed for the K. of Spain too, who was their Enemie and a Papist, with other frivolous and insnaring questions, with much threatening, and finding no colour to detaine me longer, with much pitty of my Ignorance, they dismiss'd me. These were men of high flight, and above Ordinances; and spake spitefull things of our B. Lord's nativity; so I got home late the next day blessed be God. These wretched miscreants held their muskets against us as we came up to receive the Sacred Elements, as if they would have shot us at the Altar, but yet suffering us to finish the Office of Communion, as perhaps not in their Instructions what they should do in case they found us in that Action.

John Evelyn: Diary – 25 December 1657
ed. Guy de la Bédoyère

Christmas Day – Second Proper

Luke 2: (1-7) 8-20

*All doubts,
suspicions,
conscientious
scruples and
struggles, regrets,
anxieties, have
eventually
vanished. Now
there is only
delight.*

Let me tell you of another of the presents I've enjoyed this year. It arrived in a cardboard tube, quite a while before Christmas, from a friend of mine, Ralph Deppen, who was Archdeacon of Chicago when I first met him in the 1960s, and who now lives in retirement in Los Angeles. Art and artists have always meant a great deal to him; and it was a splendid idea of his to send me, as a present, a print of a painting in the Norton Simon Foundation Gallery in Pasadena. It's by Giovanni Battista Gaulli, sometimes called Baciccio, who was a pupil of the Baroque master Bernini. I'm afraid I'd never heard of him before.

The subject of the painting is most unusual. It's Joseph holding the Christ-child in his arms. His strong, gentle hands support the infant, and hold him tenderly close. The child reaches up to play with Joseph's flowing beard. The two brightly lit figures of Joseph and the infant are set against a dark background. But within the darkness, the columns of a building can be discerned, suggesting that the painting may be alluding to the circumcision of Christ, and his presentation in the temple, or perhaps the columns may hint symbolically of the whole House of Israel, or it may be that the darkness is the darkness of all that lies ahead for Jesus: for the child Jesus.

But, in the foreground, it's a supremely joyous painting. The brown drapery of Joseph and the white swaddling clothes of the babe curve and fold like joyous waves. Joseph's face radiates delight in the child, and the face of the child, looking up and into Joseph's face, is also suffused with delight.

I have to say, that painting has tremendously helped me this Christmas and New Year. I don't think I've ever thought before so much about Joseph. I've known, of course, that betrothal in Jewish law – indeed, the mere possibility that one party believed himself or herself to be betrothed to the other – constituted a relationship that prevented marriage to any other, and a betrothed girl became a widow if her fiancé died. After betrothal, a man was legally the husband. I've known that as a good Jew, Joseph might have shown what a zealous Jew he was if he branded Mary with public disgrace. But he rose above that. The thought – the possibility – of bringing Mary into the glare of publicity clearly passed through Joseph's mind.

. . . What struck me about that painting I've received is how wonderfully it depicts the faith of Joseph. All doubts, suspicions, conscientious scruples and struggles, regrets, anxieties, have eventually vanished. Now there is only delight: delight in the child Jesus, whom Mary has mothered and whom Joseph has agreed to father – in the sense of seeing to his upbringing – so that it wouldn't be long before people would say: 'Is not this Joseph's son?'

In one of his longer poems, entitled *For the Time Being*, and which he subtitles *A Christmas Oratorio*, W. H. Auden reflects on this subject of what he calls 'The Temptation of St Joseph', and he gives to the chorus, in this verbal oratorio, some pretty sharp thoughts on the situation. The chorus says:

Joseph, you have heard
what Mary says occurred;
yes, it may be so.
Is it likely? No.

And, a little later, the chorus butts in again:

Mary may be pure,
but, Joseph, are you sure?
How is one to tell?
Suppose, for instance . . . Well . . .

And then, a third time, the chorus has its say:

Maybe, maybe not.
But, Joseph, you know what
your world, of course, will say
about you anyway.

Joseph himself says:

All I ask is one
important and elegant proof
that what my Love had done
was really at your will
and that your will is Love.

The Angel Gabriel replies:

No, you must believe;
be silent, and sit still.

. . . Already twice this year in chapel, I have gathered an infant in my arms at a baptism and sprinkled water upon it . . . I think I almost know what was in Joseph's heart and mind as he looked on the face of the infant Jesus. I almost know what Baciccio was trying to paint.

In these days since Christmas, I've finished reading the remarkable autobiography of Nelson Mandela, which he has called *Long Walk to Freedom*. In it he describes most movingly how his second youngest daughter, Zeni, and her husband Prince Thumbumuzi of Swaziland, came to visit him in prison on Robben Island, and brought with them their new-born child. Having been in prison so many years, Mandela hadn't in fact seen his now grown-up daughter since she was about her own baby daughter's age. Mandela's son-in-law hands him in prison his tiny granddaughter, whom Mandela says he did not let go of for the entire visit. And he writes: 'To hold a new-born baby, so vulnerable and soft, in my rough hands, hands that for too long held only picks and shovels, was a profound joy. I don't think a man was ever happier to hold a baby than I was that day.' Mandela was Joseph that day; and he named the child 'Zaziwe' – which means 'Hope'.

Eric James
A Time to Speak

Christmas Day – Third Proper

John 1:1-14

It raises the question as to what we are looking for at Christmas, and indeed in the incarnation of our Lord.

Shadowlands – the play or the film – will have refreshed the acquaintance of many of us with C. S. Lewis, the Oxbridge professor of English and writer of children's tales, and, of course, theology. Few probably know that C. S. Lewis regarded George MacDonald as his 'master'. He calls him that in the anthology he assembled of MacDonald's writings. MacDonald was a Scottish poet and novelist. He briefly became a Congregationalist minister. He not only influenced C. S. Lewis, but also G. K. Chesterton and Auden . . .

I simply want to read you a poem of MacDonald's and share with you a few thoughts on it. Here's the poem – MacDonald called it *That Holy Thing*:

They were all looking for a king
to slay their foes, and lift them high:
thou cam'st, a little baby thing
that made a woman cry.

Son of Man, to right my lot
naught but thy presence can avail;
yet on the road thy wheels are not,
nor on the sea thy sail!

My fancied ways why should'st thou heed?
Thou com'st down thine own secret stair,
com'st down to answer all my need –
yea, every bygone prayer.

I don't want to make a meticulous analysis of the whole of that poem, but I think you'll agree the beginning is particularly striking:

They all were looking for a king
to slay their foes, and lift them high . . .

It refers, of course, to the Jewish people. But it raises the question for all of us, as to what we are looking for at Christmas, and indeed in the incarnation of our Lord, not least *this* Christmas. '*They* were all looking for a king . . .' What are *we* looking for? What lies behind all this massive output of Christmas shopping, decorations, Christmas cards and carol services?

MacDonald continues:

thou cam'st, a little baby thing
that made a woman cry.

Well, one more baby to add to all the babies of the world wouldn't, of course, make any significant difference. So there's a huge weight upon that word *'thou'*: *'thou* cam'st, a little baby thing'. What we Christians believe, what we proclaim, is almost all in that one word 'thou': in that one *word*: the Word made flesh.

But I say again: one more baby to add to all the babies of the world wouldn't have made any significant difference. There's no answer to what the world is looking for simply in a baby: in the Word made merely a baby. Yet Christmas starts there. It must. There's no answer in a person that doesn't begin in a baby; and a baby is manifestly weak, helpless and vulnerable.

'They were all looking for a king . . .' I said that the poem refers to the Jewish people; but at the end of this particular week, and in this particular place, the scene of the Coronation itself, we can't quite so easily pass over that first line, and that first phrase, 'They were all looking for a king . . .', without saying that it surely does have some reference to most of us. What were a thousand million people doing, the world over, when in 1981 they were glued to their television sets to watch the Royal Wedding? What was going on [that] Monday evening when so many millions of us watched Princess Diana on TV? Someone phoned me – an American, from Los Angeles – at eight o'clock Tuesday morning, to say *they'd* watched the programme. The royalty subject must surely have a profound symbolic power that touches some of our own depths, our own needs: our need, for instance, of cherished symbols, not just of abstract symbols, but of living persons – people like us; yet not like us; our need of symbols of transcendence: of glory, of what is royal and regal about our humanity, in down-to-earth terms. And, of course, that, not least, is what Christmas is – in part – about. 'And glory shone around.'

'They were all looking for a king . . .' I suggest that our regard for royalty, for earthly royalty, may in fact surprise in us deep, unfulfilled needs and desires, which in the end can only be met through 'God in man made manifest'. They were *all* looking for a king . . . is perhaps more profoundly true than sometimes we're willing to admit.

Eric James
Sermon entitled 'George MacDonald at Christmas', preached at Westminster Abbey in 1995.

Winter birth

The winter is the childhood of the year. Into this childhood of the year came the child Jesus; and into this childhood of the year must we all descend. It is as if God spoke to us according to our need: My son, my daughter, you are growing old and cunning; you must grow a child again, with my son, this blessed birth-time. You are growing old and careful; you must become a child. You are growing old and distrustful; you must become a child. You are growing old and petty, and weak and foolish; you must become a child – my child – like the baby there, that strong sunrise of faith and hope and love, lying in his mother's arms in the stable.

George MacDonald: 'Adela Cathcart'
Quoted in *The Wind and the Stars: Through the Year with George MacDonald*

Christer the Son

> *God, who at sundry times, and in divers manners,*
> *spake in time past unto the fathers by the prophets,*
> *hath in these last days spoken unto us by his Son.*
> (Hebrews 1:1)

Two critical remarks:

1. 'Sundry times' – more literally, sundry portions – sections, not of time, but of the matter of the revelation. God gave his revelation in parts, piecemeal, as you teach a child to spell a word – letter by letter, syllable by syllable – adding all at last together. God had a Word to spell – his own Name. By degrees he did it. At last it came entire. The Word was made flesh.

2. 'His Son', more correctly, 'a Son' – for this is the very argument. Not that God now spoke by Christ, but that whereas once he spoke by prophets, now by a Son. The filial dispensation was the last.

F. W. Robertson
Sermons on Biblical Subjects

First Sunday of Christmas

Luke 2:41-52

Jesus now claims for himself that special relation to God that was symbolised in his dedication as an infant.

Early occasions

> *And when he was twelve years old,*
> *they went up to Jerusalem after the custom of the feast.*

Oh, vicar, thank you terribly for asking after Joey;
his progress all the term has been phenomenally showy;
the school report was wonderful, and even on vacation,
he's feverishly busy with unending occupation:
he's working on the radio to make it pre-selective,
and reading criminology, to be a great detective;
and while his scholarship exam is pending a decision,
he's mastering the principles of modern television.
He understands the mysteries of synchrony and scanning,
and here's a little sketch of apparatus that he's planning.
He made a lovely aeroplane with accurate dihedral,
and built a perfect replica of Exeter Cathedral;
he's classified a thousand trains, observed on
    railway stations,
and catalogued the foreign stamps of ninety-seven nations!
He'd join your confirmation class, but Dad and I
    have banned it;
You see, we feel *he's just a bit too young to understand it.*

S. J. Forrest
'Unconfirmed Marvel', from *What's the Use?*

Jesus now claims for himself that special relation to God that was symbolised in his dedication as an infant. Up to this point all the signs of Jesus' unusual nature or mission have been to or through others: the angel, Mary, Elizabeth, shepherds, Simeon, and Anna; but now Jesus claims it for himself (Luke 2:49).

. . . In summary, three statements can be made in reflection on this vignette from Jesus' boyhood, the only record about Jesus between infancy and manhood. First, Luke wants it understood that Jesus was nurtured in a context of obedience and worship. He was from birth to death the true Israelite, unwavering in his observance of the demands of home, synagogue and temple. Second, at age 12 there were in him vague stirrings of his own uniqueness. The circle of his awareness and sense of obligation is beginning to widen beyond the home in Nazareth. Third, Jesus' move towards God is not without its tensions in the family. Even though Jesus returned home with Mary and Joseph and was obedient to them (2:51), three expressions in the story register the tension: 'Child, why have you treated us like this?' (verse 48); 'Look, your father and I have been searching for you in great anxiety' (verse 48); 'But they did not understand what he said to them' (verse 50). Even so, the tension here does not approach that reported by Mark (3:31-35) on the occasion of Jesus' mother and brothers coming for him, having heard that he was beside himself (3:21). The truth that Mark states explicitly and Luke certainly implies in today's lection is clear: family loves and loyalties have their life and place under the higher love and loyalty to God.

Fred B. Craddock
Preaching Through the Christian Year: 'C'

Second Sunday of Christmas

John 1:(1-9) 10-18

Jesus is different. Despite all parallels in detail, the historical Jesus in his wholeness turns out to be completely unique – in his own time and in ours.

In the year 42 or 41 *before* Jesus' birth, at the beginning of the fifteen years of grievous civil war following on the murder of Caesar, the Roman poet Virgil in his famous *Fourth Eclogue* announced the birth of a world saviour. Was this an expression of hope in Caesar's great nephew and adopted son Octavius and his house? In any case, when Octavius finally returned to Rome in the year 29, as sole ruler, after the victory over Antony and Cleopatra, his first official act was to close the temple of Janus, the double-faced god of war. And 'Augustus Divi Filius' – 'son of the divine one' (of Caesar, elevated after his death to be a state god), translated in the Greek East as 'Son of God' – did everything possible to realise the hopes nourished by Virgil of the Utopia of an imminent reign of peace: Pax Romana, Pax Augusta, sealed with the consecration of the gigantic Ara Pacis Augustae, the Augustan altar of peace, in the year 9 BC. In the same year (according to the famous inscription found in 1890 in Priene in Asia Minor and later elsewhere) the 'gospel' (*euangelion*, 'good news') of the birthday of the 'Saviour' and 'God' who had now appeared – Caesar Augustus – was proclaimed in the East to the whole world: the saviour who had brought to the broken world new life, happiness, peace, fulfilment of ancestral hopes, salvation.

Hans Kung
On Being a Christian

Jesus apparently cannot be fitted in anywhere: neither with the rulers nor with the rebels, neither with the moralisers nor with the silent ascetics. He turns out to be provocative, both to right and to left. Backed by no party, challenging on all sides: 'The man who fits no formula.' He is neither a philosopher nor a politician, neither a priest nor a social reformer. Is he a genius, a hero, a saint? Or a religious reformer? But is he not more radical than someone who tries to reform, reshape things? Is he a prophet? But is a 'last' prophet, who cannot be surpassed, a prophet at all? The normal typology seems to break down here. He seems to have something of the most diverse types (perhaps more of the prophet and reformer than of the others), but for that very reason does not belong to any one of them. He is on a different plane: apparently closer than the priests to God, freer than the ascetics in regard to the world, more moral than the moralists, more revolutionary than the revolutionaries. Thus he has depths and vastnesses lacking in others. It is obviously difficult for friends and enemies to understand him, still less wholly to penetrate his personality. Over and over again it becomes clear that *Jesus is different*. Despite all parallels in detail, the historical Jesus in his wholeness turns out to be completely unique – in his own time and ours.

. . . To sum it up briefly, Jesus was not someone brought up at court as Moses apparently was, nor a king's son like Buddha. But neither was he a scholar and politician like Confucius nor a rich merchant like Muhammad. The very fact that his origins were so insignificant makes his enduring significance all the more amazing.

Hans Kung
On Being a Christian

Our life together

No one has ever seen God; the only Son, who is in the bosom of the Father, he has made him known.
(John 1:18)

Christian living is in response to an action of God, whereby men are known, are called, and are engaged in service. An equally important truth is that Christian life is life lived together. It is a people who are known and called and engaged to serve . . .

In the text which we are considering, the point is explicitly made that God can never be seen, and that he can only be known. God can never be object to our vision or to our knowledge. He is always subject who makes himself known by the ways in which he establishes relationships. We get to know him by the ways in which he relates himself to us and the ways in which he relates us to one another. What is it that God has done, on the basis of which we are able to say, 'He has made himself known'? The evangelist says: 'Through Moses, God gave us the law; now, through Jesus Christ, he has given us himself.' The gift of law means that God has defined the limitations of man's freedom, determined the boundaries of his life and detailed the obligations which he must fulfil. Now, within this very life, so defined and delimited, he himself has entered as companion to man, leading man into an experience of the graciousness of truth. The law is also truth. But it is truth which is stern. In Jesus truth was gracious . . .

The evangelist says that this revelation of God as gracious truth came through the Son. In a later passage in the Gospel we read, 'No man comes to the Father but by me' (John 14:6). Jesus is the way to the Father, because he is the Son of the Father. He represents what it means to be the Father's son. 'To those who accepted him,' the evangelist says, 'he gave authority to become the children of God' (John 1:12). Why is such authority or permission necessary? Because the prodigal cannot just walk into his father's house. He has to be forgiven, and the forgiveness has to be authoritatively declared. It is not enough that sins are forgiven in the sense that the guilt is taken away or that the consequences of sin are cancelled. Forgiveness means, fundamentally, restoration to the Father and to the life of the whole family. This is why the experience of forgiveness in Jesus Christ has its peculiar connotation. It is more than a transaction between God and the sinner. The flock is a scattered flock, until every lost sheep is found. The chain cannot be worn until all the ten coins are hanging on it. One lost coin means a useless chain. The prodigal son has to be restored not only to the father, but also to the home. The father's forgiveness of the boy who has come back has serious consequences and imposes obligations on the brother who never went away (Luke 15:3-32). When John says therefore, 'No man has ever seen God; the only Son who is in the bosom of the Father, he has made him known', he is pointing to the nature of the life together which is involved in Christian living . . . Jesus makes God known by loving us. We make God known by loving one another.

D. T. Niles
The Power at Work Among Us

The Epiphany

Matthew 2:1-12

It seems perfectly fitting that the most learned should come: it seems just as fitting that the unlettered should come. With equal ease they can all come to Jesus.

The Bible contains two very distinct and very diverse elements. It opens and closes on a note of *sublimity*. This epic of creation at the beginning of my Bible: this apocalypse of splendour at the end: here I discover a quality so magnificent, so transcendent, so sublime that it can never be explained or expounded in any human speech. The eye is blinded by excess of light. We are in the realm of the infinite and the incomprehensible.

Yet, side by side with this, I detect the note of *simplicity*. There are passages, such as the twenty-third Psalm and the fourteenth [chapter] of John, that little children love to lisp.

I see that the Magi – the savants and scientists and academicians of the East – represent that first element of sublimity; and the shepherds, who rank as the very lowliest type of unskilled labour, represent that second element, the element of simplicity. But in neither case is there the slightest incongruity in their pilgrimage to Bethlehem. Sublimity and simplicity keep there a natural tryst. It seems perfectly fitting that the most learned should come: it seems just as fitting that the unlettered should come. High or low, Oriental or Occidental, sage or simpleton – Bethlehem is the rendezvous for them all. With equal ease they can all come to Jesus, and in no single case however exceptional or abnormal, is there the slightest sense of incongruity in the approach.

F. W. Boreham
I Forgot to Say

Towards the end of his life Marco Polo wrote an account of his travels and included in the material some fabulous stories of a fairy tale style. Maybe this accounts for a supposed record of the Wise Men who presented their gifts to the infant Jesus in the following story, handed down by Marco Polo's three daughters:

Marco Polo discovered, so these ladies averred, that the Three Wise Men were three kings, differing the one from the other as sharply and as strikingly as any three individuals could possibly do. In scarcely one respect did any member of the imposing trio resemble either of his companions.

Gaspar, King of hoary Tarshish, was young and tall, straight as an arrow, and black as ebony. Balthazar, King of ancient Chaldea, was middle-aged and bearded, of medium height, and olive-skinned. Melchior, King of Nubia, was very old, of short stature, withered, infirm, and bent.

If the story, as Fantina, the eldest daughter of Marco Polo, passed it on to her offspring, is to be believed, the travellers had not gone far before ill-fortune overtook them. Gaspar's camel trod upon a viper in the thick undergrowth on the fringe of the desert. The reptile fastened upon the tender part of the animal's foot; in an hour or two the limb was too swollen and inflamed to permit of further progress; and, in the grey of the following dawn, the camel died.

What was to be done? Balthazar and Melchior were as grieved and as troubled as was Gaspar himself. But they pointed out that the star would not stand still in the sky because a snake had killed a camel among the sands. Somebody must follow the celestial guide. Better that two should find the new king than that al three should be whelmed in failure and disappointment.

Gaspar sorrowfully agreed. 'Anyway', he added, his black face brightening with a brave smile, 'I am young and strong; I am accustomed to walking long distances. I will follow the trail of your camels, and, it may be that, in spite of my loss, I, too, may find the king!'

Balthazar and Melchior thereupon bade him a sad farewell and set off by themselves, leaving Gaspar to follow, as best he could, on foot. But, when the day's sun set in splendour over the western horizon, they looked for the star, but for some time failed to discern it. It had become so faint that they had to strain their eyes to detect it. And the next night it vanished altogether.

Mortified and disgusted, they abandoned the quest and started on their return journey. In due course, they met Gaspar struggling cheerfully on. He was surprised to see them and still more astonished when they told their tale.

'Lost the star!' he cried incredulously. 'Why, nonsense! There it is!' And there, surely enough, it was!

They then resolved to journey together, sharing the benefit of the two surviving camels. Sometimes two of them mounted the stronger camel; sometimes Gaspar rode and Balthazar walked beside him; sometimes Balthazar rode the camel while Gaspar resumed his weary trudge; and now and again even Melchior, aged and infirm as he was, insisted on hobbling along on foot while the two younger men rested. But, however they disposed themselves, the star shone brightly on until, in due course, it brought them to the inn in which the young child lay.

And so these pilgrim kings learned that they who follow the star become, in virtue of that circumstance, members one of another. The sorrows of one become the sorrows of all: the privileges of one become the privileges of all. Those who think only of themselves, and who display no sympathy with a less fortunate companion, soon lose the heavenly vision. But when each bravely shares the afflictions of those who have been overtaken by disaster, the star blazes like an oriflamme in the western sky.

It was quite a different experience that intrigued Bellela, Marco Polo's second daughter, and that she most stressed in relating the story to her children. It seems that, whilst resting amidst the shades of a green and hospitable oasis, the three pilgrims began to speculate, as was natural, concerning the appearance of him to whom their celestial guide was leading them. They agreed that he would be stately and regal and grand, noble in bearing and wise in speech. But of what colour?

Gaspar felt certain that he would be black. 'Long before any of your paler civilisations began,' he claimed, 'there dwelt, far back among the forests of the south, black nations of infinite power and inscrutable wisdom. One of these days when the world is wide open, and when the secrets of its remote past are clearly read, humanity will discover with astonishment that vast empires were erected by men of dusky skin whilst the rest of the world was buried in slumber and stagnation. 'I believe,' he concluded, 'that he to whom the star is leading us has come to restore to our peoples their ancient glory!'

Balthazar brushed aside Gaspar's theory with impatience. He was sure that the Divine One to whom they were being led would have a skin of olive-coloured hue. 'Everybody knows,' he insisted, 'that all the world's most famous dreamers and sages and poets have dwelt in the East. And if, or late, the prophetic fires have died down, it is only that they may blaze up again with richer splendour than ever in this heavenly prophet to whom we are being guided.'

'All that you say is true,' exclaimed old Melchior in quiet and unimpassioned tones, 'and yet I feel that you must both be disappointed. Perhaps because my eyes are so soon to close for ever, I seem to scan the years that are coming more clearly than you do. And, looking down the avenue of the centuries-to-be, I see that the white races are to rise to a grandeur and an authority that they have never yet known. And, somehow, I feel that this thing that is just about to happen is the crisis of human destiny, the turning-point of the ages! I believe that we are being led to the creator of a new era – and a white one!'

From quiet reasoning and abstract speculation they soon passed to heated argument and angry contention. Each claimed, for his own section of mankind, virtues and achievements to which the others could never pretend; and each poured upon the others the vials of bitter contempt and withering derision. But, whilst they argued, the shadows lengthened and the dusk fell.

'I have no patience with either of you!' cried Gaspar fiercely, springing to his feet. 'I am sick of your absurdities! I am going to resume the journey. You can come or stay as you will; it is nothing to me!' The others flung their taunts after him; but, they, too, moved toward the camels.

When they were ready to start, however, they each made separately a discovery that filled all three with consternation and dismay. Where was the star? There was no sign of it! And without it how could they proceed?

The catastrophe that had overtaken them filled their hearts with fellow-feeling and with sympathy for one another. In this new situation, they forgot the cruel words that each had spoken, and, secretly ashamed of all that had been said in the course of their wordy warfare, each went out of his way to show kindness and consideration to the others. And as, in their hearts, a new and fonder comradeship was born, the star gradually reappeared in the heavens. They saluted it with gladness, and followed it in peace and mutual goodwill until in due course, it brought them to the little inn at Bethlehem.

But Moreta, the youngest of Marco Polo's daughters, fastened upon a very different aspect of the great adventure, and made the most of it in telling the tale to her children. For, just as the three kings differed in age, in colour, and in outward appearance, so they differed also in relation to their secret thoughts, emotions and aspirations.

Gaspar, the youthful King of Tarshish, set out on his quest hoping that the star would lead him to *a king*. The world, he felt, wanted a master, a sovereign, a ruler, a lord. And, longing for such a lord, Gaspar took with him a tribute of gold, a royal gift. Balthazar, the mature King of Chaldea, hoped that the star would lead him to *a god*. He had lived long enough to realise that behind the seen lies the unseen. And middle age sometimes becomes conscious, at least for a moment, of the dangerous condition into which it has drifted. Balthazar had some such consciousness. Whenever he sought to probe the mysteries of the invisible, his mind became confused. What is God? Where is God? *'Oh, that I knew where I might find him!'* And, thirsting for God as the hart thirsts for the water-brooks, longing for God as blind men long for light, Balthazar answered the challenge of the star. And he took with him a tribute of incense – frankincense – with which to worship.

And Melchior, the aged King of Nubia, longed for *a saviour*. After the fashion of old men, his mind dwelt in the years that were past. And he felt – felt increasingly – that those years were sadly stained, their record tragically smudged. And soon, he realised, he must pass into the great unknown with much of guilt upon his conscience. Was there no priest by whom his iniquity could be absolved, no sacrifice by which his transgression could be removed, no fountain in which his soul could be eternally cleansed? And, hoping fervently that the star might lead him to a saviour – a saviour who, he instinctively felt, must of necessity be a sufferer – he took with him his gift of myrrh.

And so they came to Bethlehem. And when they saw that the star had but led them to a baby in a woman's arms, all three were at first overwhelmed with chagrin and dismay. But as they sat and pondered this strange happening they heard Mary, after the fashion of mothers, singing to her child. And all three listened. 'My soul doth magnify the Lord!' she sang. 'The Lord!' exclaimed Gaspar. 'Then I have found my sovereign, my monarch, my king, my Lord!' And he offered his gold. But Mary sang on. 'And my spirit hath rejoiced in God . . .' she continued. 'In God!' cried Balthazar, his face lighting up. 'Then I have found him – the God for whom my spirit hungered!' And he presented his incense to the babe. But not even yet had Mary finished her song. 'My soul doth magnify the Lord and my spirit hath rejoiced in God my Saviour!' 'My Saviour!' echoed Melchior. 'My Saviour!' And he offered his vase of myrrh.

And so Gaspar found in Jesus the *King* of his desire. And Balthazar found in Jesus the *God* he had so passionately sought. And Melchior found in Jesus the *Saviour* for whom his very soul was aching.

Every man finds in Jesus exactly what he most needs. That is the essence of this Christmas story, and that is the essence of the everlasting Gospel.

F. W. Boreham
Arrows of Desire

First Sunday of Epiphany
The Baptism of the Lord/Ordinary Time 1

Luke 3:15-17, 21-22

When repentance and forgiveness are available, judgement is good news.

The third and last portion of John's message (verses 15-18) is in response to those who would identify him as the Christ. Both Mark (Mark 1:7-8 and Matthew (Matthew 3:11-12) speak of John's messianic preaching, but only the fourth Gospel (John 1:19-28) joins Luke in directly dealing with the question in many minds: is John the Christ? However, all the evangelists faced the issue directly or indirectly. Luke began to do so, as we have seen, when John leaped in his mother's womb as Mary entered the room (1:41). In the text before us, John distinguishes himself from the Christ in three ways: John is not worthy even to be a slave of the mightier one; the Christ will baptise not with water but with the Holy Spirit and with fire (anticipating Pentecost, Acts 2); and the Christ will bring judgement. Luke, here and repeatedly [throughout] the Gospel and Acts, will identify the Holy Spirit as the hallmark of Christianity . . . It does need to be pointed out, however, that the Holy Spirit was a mark of Jesus' work and that of the Church (Luke 24:49; Acts 1:8; 2:38; 10:47 and others) but not of the community created around John the Baptist (Luke3:16; Acts 18:24-28; 19:1-7).

In its present context, 'Spirit and fire' can also be translated 'wind and fire', giving a double meaning to John's words. Wind and fire were symbols for the Holy Spirit, the powerful presence of God (Acts 2:1-4), but also of judgement. Farmers poured wheat from one container to another on a windy day, or tossed the wheat into the air with a fork or shovel so that the chaff would be blown away, leaving the grain clean. The chaff burnt with explosive combustion. To this day, farmers know that a fire in a dry wheat field cannot be contained or controlled. The message is clearly one of judgement, just as in the earlier image, 'The axe is laid to the root of the trees' (Luke 3:9). The preacher should not, however, use John's message as the permission to launch attacks on listeners, without redemptive content. When repentance and forgiveness are available, judgement is good news (Luke 3:18). The primary aim is to save the wheat, not to burn the chaff.

The revelatory drama of Jesus' post-baptismal experience is in three parts. First, 'the heavens were opened'. The expression recalls Isaiah's prayer for heaven to open and for

God to come again as in the Exodus (Isaiah 64:1-4). A new exodus would be the beginning of a new age. Second, the Holy Spirit comes upon Jesus, and therefore marks his ministry (Luke 4:1; Acts 1:1-4). It is difficult to know from what background, if any, the Holy Spirit was associated with a dove. It may have been a connection made by early Christians, but not from Judaism. If Luke's readers were familiar with Hellenistic literature, then they may have recalled stories of birds as harbingers of divine choice or destiny . . . The phrase 'in bodily form', unique to Luke, is especially difficult, since in bodily form is the only way a dove can descend. Perhaps it is Luke's way of asserting the certainty of the experience, not to be confused with thought or feeling alone . . .

The third part of the revelatory drama is the voice from heaven, 'Thou art my beloved Son; with thee I am well pleased' (Luke 3:22). This heavenly attestation reflects Psalm 2:7, used at the coronation of Israel's king as son of God. The two texts join sovereignty and service. There is no justification, however, for pouring into this moment all the implications of Isaiah 42:1, that Jesus here becomes aware that he is to be a suffering servant Messiah . . .

The coming of the Holy Spirit does not make Jesus the Son of God. Luke has told us who Jesus is from the time of the annunciation. The Holy Spirit comes to empower Jesus for his ministry. He will soon be led by the Spirit into the desert (Luke 4:1), and then he will return 'in the power of the Spirit into Galilee' (4:14).

A final word about this text: notice the reference to Jesus praying (verse 21). The prayer life of Jesus is very important to Luke, and, through Luke, for his readers. Jesus will be presented often in prayer, and especially at critical moments, such as when choosing the Twelve, when asking his disciples to say who he is, or on the Mount of Transfiguration (Luke 3:21; 6:12; 9:18-22; 9:28-29; 11:1; 22:32, 41; 23:34, 46). But it is not the prayer life of Jesus alone which concerns Luke as though it were a matter of historical interest. Just as Jesus was praying when the Holy Spirit came upon him, so the Church was in prayer awaiting the promised coming of the Holy Spirit (Acts 1:8, 14), and, after the manner of Jesus, they continued in prayer (Acts 2:42; 3:1; 4:31; 6:4; 12:12; 13:3). There is no reason the Church should think that the Holy Spirit and prayer are data of history and not available for life and ministry until the close of the age. Luke's history is more than history; it is witness.

Fred B. Craddock
Luke: A Bible Commentary for Teaching and Preaching

Second Sunday of Epiphany
Ordinary Time 2

John 2:1-11

When the ruler of the feast had tasted the water that was made wine, and knew not whence it was. (John 2:9)

I just . . . delight to think that the great God is the loving friend, as Jesus showed at that little Cana wedding.

But how could Jesus turn water into wine? Of course he could, because he was God. Will you be surprised if I say he is always doing it, that I have myself seen him doing it dozens of times? I remember one day I was travelling through the Rhône valley in Switzerland when the thought came back to me of this miracle at the wedding. It was pouring with rain. The slopes of the valley were covered with vines. The water was falling heavily on the vineyards. And I thought how in another month the vine gatherers would come and squeeze out the grapes and find that water turned into wine! That is how God gives wine to the world. That is how God gives bread to the world, when the farmer lays in God's earth his few grains of wheat and goes away to return in the autumn and find each little grain changed into sixty or one hundred! And stupid people don't stop to think of these wonderful miracles that God is always doing!

I don't know how Jesus turned water into wine at that wedding. And I don't know how God was doing it that day in the Rhône Valley and in all the countries where I have seen him doing it. I just bow my head in wonder at the greatness of God and delight to think that the great God is the loving friend, as Jesus showed at that little Cana wedding.

J. Paterson Smyth
A Boys' and Girls' Life of Christ

True riches

A man was talking to a monk once and asked what the three knots in his girdle were for. 'They signify poverty, chastity and obedience', was the reply. 'Oh well, if you define chastity as being faithful to one's wife, then I could tie three knots in my belt as well,' said the man. 'I'm married, which is chastity, and the poverty and obedience follow naturally from that!'

Maybe we can leave the chastity and obedience for another occasion – let's talk about poverty. In a couple of hours' time people will be making lots of nice speeches and wishing you all sorts of things. I'm sure they'll be elegantly phrased. They won't be as blunt as I am going to be now. I'm not going to pussyfoot around. My wish for you in the years ahead is that you'll be rich. But rich in particular ways:

First, may you be rich in your affection for each other. May you always feel warm in each other's company. May you always want to go home because of who is there, rather than where it is. May you always be able to exchange glances of common bond across a room, and agree without having to say a word. May you be able to be playful, and find a playmate in each other without being told to stop being silly. May there be a tingle in the shared tablecloth, and even a wonder in the washing-up. May you be so full of affection that it will become a visible thing that others can see – and they will say, 'How rich you are!'

Second, may you be rich in your relationships. We hope that you'll be surrounded by a quiverful of children (to use that wonderful phrase from the Psalms), that in due time your family circle will be extended and your affection enlarged to include some little ones, who in decades to come will thank God for the stable, loving home into which they were born.

Incidentally, to bring up children well, my advice is to give them half as much money and twice as much time as you were going to in the first place.

Let your affection spill over into friendships. Hospitality is a great virtue. You'll remember Dickens' *Christmas Carol*. Who would you rather be? Ebenezer Scrooge, in lonely isolation, counting his money, or Bob Cratchet, surrounded by his family and friends, gathered round the fire? Be a Cratchet! Let warmth, generosity and hospitality be a keynote of your home. And your friends will say, 'Well, we don't know what they've got in the bank, but in all the things that matter they're rich!'

And third, may you be rich in your perceptions. May you be rich in your awareness of what other people don't see, or rather, don't notice:

the mysterious reflections of leaves on still water;
your partner's eyelashes after a bath;

the way a raindrop bends a blade of grass;
the soft tone of a woman's voice when she talks to a baby;
the sunlight glistening on a ladybird;
having a sentence of poetry or a tune ringing in your
    memory like a big bell;
hearing that bit from the Bible, 'God is Love',
    and wondering at the way it works out in the life of Jesus;
the feeling of sacredness and timelessness
    you get in certain places like this.

These riches are under our noses all the time, riches of imagination, perception, depth, growth. Most people don't look very often, and their experience of life is poverty-stricken as a result.

I heard of a wife who saved a thousand pounds over the years, which she spent on some luxury she wanted. This came as a complete surprise to her husband, who couldn't think where she'd kept the money. 'I kept it in the family Bible,' she said. 'I knew it was the one place you'd never look!'

Our lives, our relationships, our families, are full of little treasures not yet discovered. Find them! Get off the tramlines of routine sometimes and look a bit harder at the things you take for granted.

Then you'll be fully alive, and the people who know you well will say, 'We don't know whether the house is paid for or not, but they're rich in spirit'.

So, to sum up my wishes for you: I hope you'll have enough money to get along comfortably. After all, as the saying goes, 'If your outgoings exceed your income, your upkeep will be your downfall'.

But most of all my wish for you is that you'll be rich in the real things that matter – the emotional and spiritual qualities that are at the heart of all good marriages.

May God bless you both.

Frank Pagden
Laughter and Tears

Third Sunday of Epiphany
Ordinary Time 3

Luke 4:14-21

All that Jesus says and does is within the bosom of Judaism.

The importance and value of worship is described in this superb definition by William Temple.

Both for perplexity and for dulled conscience, the remedy is the same. For worship is the submission of all our nature to God. It is the quickening of conscience by his holiness; the nourishment of mind with his truth; the purifying of imagination by his beauty; the opening of the heart to his love; the surrender of will to his purpose – and all of this gathered up in adoration, the most selfless emotion of which our nature is capable and therefore the chief remedy for that self-centredness which is our original sin. Yes – worship in spirit and truth is the way to the solution of perplexity and to the liberation from sin.

But to our superficial souls the divine answer seems to evade the problem precisely because it penetrates to the heart of it. We must wait till there is offered to us in fellowship and communion the eternal God himself.

William Temple
Readings in St John's Gospel

Just as he told of John's imprisonment before he told of Jesus' baptism (Luke 3:19-22), thus leaving the reader with a historical question, so here Luke places the Nazareth visit first because it is first, not chronologically but programmatically. That is to say that this event announces who Jesus is, of what his ministry consists, what his Church will be and do, and what will be the response to both Jesus and the Church.

It is important first of all to allow the passage to remind us of that which Luke never tires of telling: all that Jesus says and does is within the bosom of Judaism. By his faithfulness, Jesus affirms the Sabbath, the scriptures and the synagogue. Jesus not only attends synagogue services regularly but he participates, as all male adults were permitted to do, by reading scripture and commenting upon it. The synagogue services were rather informal, consisting primarily of prayers, reading of scripture, comments, and alms for the poor. This institution of Judaism apparently arose during the exile as a temple surrogate, but of course without altar or priest. Led by laity, the Pharisees being the most prominent among them, the synagogue became the institutional centre of a religion of 'the book', not of 'the altar', and in time became and remains today the dominant form of Judaism. While there was only one temple, synagogues arose everywhere, wherever ten adult males wished to constitute themselves. The synagogue was not only a centre for worship but also a school, a community centre, and a place for administering justice. Among relatives and friends, in the synagogue Jesus is at home.

By reading Isaiah 61:1-2, Jesus not only announces fulfilment of prophecy (verse 21) but defines what his messianic role is. Isaiah 61 is a servant song, and 'anointed me' means 'made me the Christ or Messiah'. When understood literally, the passage says the Christ is God's servant who will bring to reality the longing and the hope of the poor, the oppressed, and the imprisoned. The Christ will also usher in the amnesty, the liberation, and the restoration associated with the proclamation of the year of jubilee (verse 19; Leviticus 25:8-12). At the close of the reading, Jesus said, 'Today this scripture has been fulfilled in your hearing' (verse 21). It is interesting that in Luke's Gospel, the first public word of Jesus as an adult, apart from reading scripture, is 'today'. The age of God's reign is here; the eschatological time when God's promises are fulfilled and God's purpose comes to fruition has arrived; there will be changes in the conditions of those who have waited and hoped. The changes for the poor and the wronged and the oppressed will occur today. This is the beginning of jubilee. The time of God is today, and the ministries of Jesus and of the Church according to Luke and Acts demonstrate that 'today' continued. Throughout these two volumes, 'today' never is allowed to become 'yesterday' or to slip again into a vague 'someday'.

. . . If the people of Nazareth assumed privileges for themselves, that error is joined to a more serious one: resentment that Jesus has taken God's favour to others beyond Nazareth, especially Capaernaum, said to have had a heavy non-Jewish population. Jesus defends his ministry to outsiders by offering two Old Testament stories. Both Elijah (1 Kings 17:8-14) and Elisha (2 Kings 5:1-17), prophets in Israel, took God's favour to non-Jews. That these two stories were in their own scriptures and quite familiar, perhaps accounts in part for the intensity of their hostility. Anger and violence are the last defence of those who are made to face the truth of their own tradition, which they have long defended and embraced. Learning what we already know is often painfully difficult. All of us know what it is to be at war with ourselves, sometimes making casualties of those who are guilty of nothing but speaking the truth in love. For Luke, the tension that erupts here and will erupt again and again elsewhere is not between Jesus and Judaism or between synagogue and church; it is between Judaism and its own scriptures.

Fred B. Craddock
Luke: A Bible Commentary for Teaching and Preaching

Fourth Sunday of Epiphany
Ordinary Time 4

Luke 4:21-30 (RCL)

The prophet's life almost more than his words was predictive.

JESUS CHRIST
Wanted – for Sedition, Criminal Anarchy, Vagrancy and Conspiring to overthrow the Established Government. Dresses poorly. Said to be a carpenter by trade. Ill-nourished, has visionary ideas, associates with common working people, the unemployed and bums. Alien – believed to be a Jew. Alias: 'Prince of Peace', 'Son of Man', 'Light of the world', etc., etc. Professional Agitator, Red Beard, marks on hands and feet the result of injuries inflicted by an angry mob led by respectable citizens and legal authorities.

So runs the now well known 'warrant' which first appeared in a Christian underground newspaper in the United States.

Quoted by Hans Kung
On Being a Christian

His whole way was right, even though it became – had to become – the way of the cross. Here is a man of humble origin and insignificant family who seemed to be without education, possessions, office or title, called by no authority, authorised by no tradition, supported by no party. Yet through his very death his unparalleled claim was confirmed in an earth-shattering way and indeed finally justified. The innovator who set himself above law and temple, above Moses, kings, prophets, family, who relativised marriage and nation, appears now as the great fulfiller. The heretical teacher turns out to be the authorised teacher who shows people the right way. The false prophet is seen to be the true prophet. The blasphemer is now the saint of God. The seducer of the people will be the eschatological judge of the people. Thus he was definitively authenticated as God's advocate and as advocate of man.

Hans Kung
On Being a Christian

I seek thee,
    and sure as the dawn
    thou appearest as (perfect Light) to me.
Teachers of lies (have smoothed) thy people (with words),
    and (false prophets) have led them astray;
they perish without understanding
    for their works are in folly.

For I am despised by them
    and they have no esteem for me
    that thou mayest manifest thy might through me.
They have banished me from my land
    like a bird from its nest;
all my friends and brethren are driven far from me
    and hold me for a broken vessel.

But thou, O God,
    dost despise all Satan's designs;
it is thy purpose that shall be done
    and the design of thy heart
    that shall be established for ever.

G. Vermes
The Dead Sea Scrolls in English

In the New Testament (cf.1 Corinthians 12:14; Ephesians 4:11), prophets along with apostles and teachers held a spiritual office in the Christian community and till about the end of the second century they exercised their ministry within the Church. There is an account of a visit (Acts 11:27) made by prophets of the Church at Jerusalem to Antioch, on the occasion of which a prophet called Agabus made a prediction about a famine which, he said, was to be world-wide.

The function of the prophet in the early Church appears from the use of *propheteuein* (to prophesy) in the NT. This verb is employed in the sense of:

(1) to announce as a revelation made by God: Matthew 7:22 ('Many will say . . . "Lord, Lord, did we not prophesy by thy name?"'), Acts 19:6; 21:9; 1 Corinthians 11:4f; 13:9; 14:1, 3-5 (verse 3, 'He that prophesieth speaketh unto men, edification, and comfort, and consolation'), 24, 31, 39; Revelation 11:3;

(2) to reveal that of which the evidence has been hidden: Matthew 26:68 ('Prophesy unto us, thou Christ: who is he that struck thee?');

(3) to foretell the future: Matthew 11:13; 15:7; 1 Peter1:10.

The claim that Jesus fulfils the prophecies of the Old Testament is best established when taken as referring to the prophets' teachings and ideals rather than to predictions that may be extracted from their writings or from the OT in general. There is ample and legitimate ground for speaking of a preparation for Christ in the OT, and the account of Jesus' thought and life in the NT sufficiently confirms this without there being any need of doing violence to the character or exegesis of the OT such as the early and medieval Church was guilty of when it rested Jesus' claim as Fulfiller upon a fulfilment of predictions.

Alan Richardson
A Theological Word Book of the Bible

Real prophet

Remember what the prophets were. They were not merely predictors of the future. Nothing destroys the true conception of the prophets' office more than those popular books in which their mission is certified by curious coincidences. For example, if it is predicted that Babylon shall be a desolation, the haunt of wild beasts, etc., then some traveller has seen a lion standing on Birs Nimroud; or if the fisherman is to dry his nets on Tyre, simply expressing its destruction thereby, the commentator is not easy till he finds that a net has been actually seen drying on a rock. But this is to degrade the prophetic office to a level with Egyptian palmistry: to make the prophet like an astrologer, or a gypsy fortune-teller – one who can predict destinies and draw horoscopes. But in truth, the first office of the prophet was with the present. He read eternal principles beneath the present and the transitory, and in doing this of course he prophesied the future; for a principle true today is true for ever. But this was, so to speak, an accident of his office: not its essential feature. If for instance, he read in the voluptuousness of Babylon the secret of Babylon's decay, he also read by anticipation the doom of Corinth, London, of all cities in Babylon's state; or if

Jerusalem's fall was predicted, in it all such judgement comings were foreseen and the language is true of the fall of the world: as truly, or more so, than that of Jerusalem. A philosopher saying in the present tense the law by which comets move, predicts all possible cometary movements.

Now the prophet's life almost more than his words was predictive. The writer of [Hebrews] lays down a great principle respecting the prophet (Hebrews 2:11): 'Both he that sanctifieth and they who are sanctified are all of one.' It was the very condition of his inspiration that he should be one with the people. So far from making him superhuman, it made him more man. He felt with more exquisite sensitiveness all that belongs to man, else he could not have been a prophet. His insight into things was the result of that very weakness, sensitiveness, and susceptibility so tremblingly alive. He burned with their thoughts, and expressed them. He was obliged by the very sensitiveness of his humanity to have a more entire dependence and a more perfect sympathy than other men. The sanctifying prophet was one with those whom he sanctified.

He was more man, just because more divine – more a son of man, because more a son of God. He was peculiarly the suffering Israelite: his countenance marred more than the sons of men. Hence we are told the prophets searched 'what, or what manner of time, the Spirit of Christ which was in them did signify, when it testified beforehand the sufferings of Christ, and the glory that should follow' (1 Peter 1:11).

Observe, it was a spirit in them, their own lives witnessing mysteriously of what the Perfect Humanity must be suffering.

Thus especially Isaiah 53 was spoken originally of the Jewish nation: of the prophet as peculiarly the Israelite: and it is no wonder the eunuch asked Philip in perplexity, 'Of whom doth the prophet say this? of himself or some other man?' The truth is, he said it of himself, but prophetically of humanity: true of him, most true of the Highest Humanity.

F. W. Robertson
Sermons on Biblical Subjects, Volume 2

Fourth Sunday of Epiphany
Ordinary Time 4

Luke 2:22-40 (CWL)

*It is not so much
God who judges a
man; a man
judges himself;
and his judgement
is his reaction to
Jesus Christ.*

A dream realised

There was no Jew who did not regard his own nation as the chosen people. But the Jews saw quite clearly that by human means their nation could never attain to the supreme world greatness which they believed their destiny involved. By far the greater number of them believed that because the Jews were the chosen people they were bound some day to become masters of the world and lords of all the nations. To bring in that day some believed that some great, celestial champion would descend upon the earth; some believed that there would arise another king of David's line and that God himself would break directly into history by supernatural means. But in contrast to all that there were some few people who were known as 'the Quiet in the Land'. They had no dreams of violence and of power and of armies with banners; they believed in a life of constant prayer and quiet watchfulness until God should come. All their lives they waited quietly and patiently upon God. Simeon was like that; in prayer, in worship, in humble and faithful expectation he was waiting for the day when God would comfort his people. God had promised him through the Holy Spirit that his life would not end before he had seen God's own anointed king. In the baby Jesus he recognised that king and was glad. Now he was ready to depart in peace and his words have become the *Nunc Dimittis*, another of the great and precious hymns of the Church.

In verse 34 Simeon gives a kind of summary of the work and fate of Jesus.

(i) He will be the cause whereby *many will fall*. This is a strange and a hard saying but it is true. It is not so much God who judges a man; a man judges himself; and his judgement is his reaction to Jesus Christ. If, when he is confronted with that goodness and that loveliness, his heart runs out in answering love, he is within the kingdom. If, when so confronted he remains coldly unmoved or actively hostile, he is condemned. There is a great refusal just as there is a great acceptance.

(ii) He will be the cause whereby *many will rise*. Long ago Seneca said that what men needed above all was a hand let down to lift them up. It is the hand of Jesus which lifts a man out of the old life and into the new, out of sin into the goodness, out of the shame into the glory.

(iii) He will meet with *much opposition*. Towards Jesus Christ there can be no neutrality. We either surrender to him or are at war with him. And it is the tragedy of life that our pride often keeps us from making that surrender which leads to victory.

Fred B. Craddock
Preaching Through the Christian Year: 'C'

The text that provides a Gospel basis for the service of the presentation of Jesus is found only in Luke (2:22-40). In fact, Luke places between the nativity (2:1-20) and Jesus' beginning his public life at age 30 (3:23) three stories: the circumcision and naming when the child was eight days old (2:21); the presentation in the temple when he was about 40 days old (2:22-40; Leviticus 12:1-4); and the visit to the temple at age 12 (2:41-52). All this is to say that the Jesus who began his ministry at age 30 was thoroughly grounded and rooted in his tradition, that observance of the law and attendance to temple duties were very important, and that although he was a Galilean, neither he nor his disciples scorned Jerusalem after his ascension and from Jerusalem were to launch their mission (24:47-48). 'And [they] returned to Jerusalem with great joy; and they were continually in the temple blessing God' (24:52-53). It is no wonder that Jesus, the true Israelite, went to the synagogue on the Sabbath, 'as was his custom' (4:16). Jesus and some of the religious leaders disputed over the tradition, to be sure, but it was a tradition he knew and kept from childhood.

When one looks at the presentation account itself, it is evident that there is the story line (2:22-24, 39-40) into which two substories have been inserted: that of Simeon (verses 25-35) and that of Anna (verses 36-38). The principal story line seems to have as its basic purpose the demonstration that in the life of the Christ Child the law of Moses had been meticulously observed (verses 22, 23, 24, 27, 39). In the course of making that point, Luke has conflated two regulations: a mother was to be ceremonially purified after childbirth (Leviticus 12:1-4; in cases of poverty, Leviticus 12:6-8 was applied), and a firstborn male was to be dedicated to God (Exodus 13:2, 12-16). Of course, provision was made for parents to redeem their son from the Lord (Numbers 18:15-16) so they could keep him as their own. Luke says nothing about the redemption of Jesus; perhaps his silence serves to prepare the reader for the next story in which Jesus in the temple at age 12 said to his parents, 'Did you not know that I must be in my Father's house?' (verse 49). That story, along with verses 40 and 52, makes it evident that Luke is echoing the story of the boy Samuel, who was dedicated to God and who lived in the temple (1 Samuel 1-2).

In the persons of Simeon (verses 25-35) and Anna (verses 36-38) Luke tells how the Israel that is true, believing, hoping, devout, and temple-attending responded to Jesus. Simeon's acknowledgement of Jesus as 'the Lord's Messiah' was inspired by the Holy Spirit (verse 26), and Anna's was that of a true prophet who fasted and prayed continually (verses 36-37). Simeon longed for 'the consolation of Israel' (verse 25), a phrase referring to the messianic age. The *Nunc Dimittis* (verses 29-32) may have been a portion of a Christian hymn familiar to Luke and his readers. Simeon's words make it clear that Israel's consolation would not be a time of uninterrupted joy; hostility and death would be aroused by the appearance of the deliverer. Good news always has its enemies. Mary herself would pay a heavy price: 'and a sword will pierce your own soul too' (verse 35). Devout and obedient Israel, as portrayed in the old prophet Anna, also saw in Jesus 'the redemption of Jerusalem' (verse 38). Her thanks to God and her witness concerning Jesus provide a model of the Israel that accepted Jesus and saw in him the fulfilment of ancient hopes. Luke will write later of that portion of Israel that rejected Jesus and turned a deaf ear to the preaching of the early Church. But in Luke's theology, they are thereby rejecting their own tradition and their own prophets as it was interpreted to them by one who was a true Israelite, Jesus of Nazareth. He kept the law, held Jerusalem in great affection (13:34), and was faithful to the synagogue. Moreover, his teaching was in keeping with all that was written in Moses, the prophets, and the writings (24:44). No prophet is so powerful and so disturbing as the one who arises out of one's own tradition and presents to the people the claims of that tradition.

Fred B. Craddock
Preaching Through the Christian Year: 'C'

Fifth Sunday of Epiphany
Proper 1/Ordinary Time 5

Sunday between 3 and 9 February inclusive (if earlier than the Second Sunday before Lent)

Luke 5:1-11

If we want a miracle, we must take Jesus at his word when he bids us attempt the impossible.

The famous sheet of water in Galilee is called by three names – the Sea of Galilee, the Sea of Tiberias and the Lake of Gennesaret. It is thirteen miles long by eight miles wide. It lies in a dip in the earth's surface and is 680 feet below sea level. That fact gives it an almost tropical climate. Nowadays it is not very populous but in the days of Jesus in had nine townships clustered round its shores, none fewer than 15,000 people. Gennesaret is really the name of the lovely plain on the west side of the lake, a most fertile piece of land. The Jews loved to play with derivations, and they had three derivations for Gennesaret, all of which show how beautiful it was.

(i) From *kinnor*, which means a harp, either because 'its fruit is as sweet as the sound of a harp' or because 'the voice of its waves is pleasant as the voice of the harp.'

(ii) From *gan*, a garden, and *sar*, a prince – hence 'the prince of gardens.'

(iii) From *gan*, a garden, and *asher*, riches – hence 'the garden of riches.'

We are here confronted with a turning point in the career of Jesus. Last time we heard him preach he was in the synagogue; now he is at the lakeside. True, he will be back in the synagogue again; but the time is coming when the door of the synagogue will be shut to him and his church will be the lakeside and the open road, and his pulpit a boat. He would go anywhere where men would listen to him. 'Our societies,' said John Wesley, 'were formed from those who were wandering upon the dark mountains, that belonged to no Christian church; but were awakened by the preaching of the Methodists, who had pursued them through the wilderness of this world to the high-ways and the hedges – to the markets and the fairs – to the hills and the lanes of the cities, in the villages, in the barns, and the farmers' kitchens, etc. – and all this done in such a way, and to such an extent, as never had been done before since the Apostolic age.' 'I love a commodious room,' said Wesley, 'a soft cushion and a handsome pulpit, but field preaching saves souls.' When the synagogue was shut Jesus took to the open road.

There is in this story what we might call a list of the conditions of a miracle.

(i) There is the eye that sees. There is no need to think that Jesus created a shoal of fishes for the occasion. In the Sea of Galilee there were phenomenal shoals which covered the sea as if it was solid for much of an acre. Most likely Jesus' keen eye saw just such a shoal and his keen sight made it look like a miracle. We need the eye that really sees. Many people saw steam raise the lid of a kettle; only James Watt went on to think of a steam engine. Many people saw an apple fall; only Isaac Newton went on to think out the law of gravity. The earth is full of miracles for the eye that sees.

(ii) There is the spirit that will make an effort. If Jesus said it, tired as he was, Peter was prepared to try again. For most people the disaster of life is that they give up just one effort too soon.

(iii) There is the spirit which will attempt what seems hopeless. The night was past and that was the time for fishing. All circumstances were unfavourable, but Peter said, 'Let circumstances be what they may, if you say so, we will try again'. Too often we wait because the time is not opportune. If we wait for a perfect set of circumstances, we will never begin at all. If we want a miracle, we must take Jesus at his word when he bids us attempt the impossible.

William Barclay
The Daily Study Bible: The Gospel of Luke

On my very first visit to Israel as leader of a group of pilgrims, we arrived in Galilee with twelve 'pilgrims' in the late evening, so we had no idea of the scenery. It was a dark and moonless night.

After a light meal I made sure everyone was happy with their room and retired to my own. Wearily I dumped my bags on the floor and walked over to the window. Pulling back the heavy curtains I was taken aback at the romantic scene laid out before me. For there, before my eyes, was the Sea of Galilee, faintly discernible by starlight.

As I looked more closely I saw a large circle of lights bobbing up and down somewhere in the middle of the sea. It was breathtakingly beautiful to observe, and at first I was baffled as to what was actually happening. But suddenly it occurred to me what I was seeing: simply a small group of fishermen doing what they had done for thousands of years on Galilee. They had let down their nets for a catch, fishing for St Peter's fish, a large delicacy enjoyed locally at many a hotel.

Some days later we crossed over Galilee and, after visiting the Hermon range of mountains, ended up on a kibbutz on the eastern shore. There we all sat down to enjoy a whole St Peter's fish. It was an experience that made the story of Peter in today's Gospel really come alive for us all. And as I pondered the story I thought of some of the lessons in it for everyone who follows Christ.

I get the impression from my reading of the story that Peter thought he knew better then Jesus, who had asked him to lower the nets. I could imagine Peter saying to himself, 'Any fool knows we fish by night. You stick to carpentry and leave fishing matters to me.' However, after his obedience to Jesus in letting down the nets and the abundant catch, Peter feels his own unworthiness, and says, 'Depart from me, Lord, for I am a sinful man.' I noticed, though, that Jesus ignored the request, lifted Peter from his knees and commissioned him for his own service. It reminded me that at some point in our Christian discipleship we also must be where Peter was, on his knees in frank admission of who he was; and raised from his knees for practical service to the world. He was not allowed to wallow in his unworthiness. Neither are we. In all the tasks of discipleship, Jesus says, 'My grace is sufficient for you.' Peter later found how true those words were as did Paul, as do all who follow 'in the Way'.

Ron Dale, 1998

Sixth Sunday of Epiphany
Proper 2/Ordinary Time 6

Sunday between 10 and 16 February (if earlier than the Second Sunday before Lent)

Luke 6:17-26

There was a real joy in poverty, material poverty ... a dim recognition that if I sought to put God and his kingdom first, I would lack nothing.

Towards the end of the long, hot summer of 1959 I rode pillion on my friend's motor cycle as we cruised into my college car park in Derbyshire. I had been team leader of four students sent out by the college to preach and teach on village greens, in public houses, cinemas, village halls and churches, in fact so to do wherever people were to be found.

During that summer our route had taken us from Derbyshire into Surrey, returning via Lowestoft and Lincolnshire, covering over 750 miles and preaching nearly every day.

We had been sent out with enough food for one meal and a full tank of petrol for each of the three motor-bikes, but with no money. We were to be dependent upon the kindness of church people to provide all our food, accommodation and the venues to hold each service: and in the six weeks of the tour we had wanted for nothing. During that tour many people, both young and old, had been blessed in one way and another by God, and we had been privileged to witness it all.

Now the adventure was over and we were back in college for a couple of days before leaving to go our separate ways. Some of my friends went back to their old jobs, whilst others took up some form of full time Christian work. For myself I did not know what the future held. I stood in the college grounds with only enough money to travel home by train and a suitcase containing a few clothes and twelve books. All I possessed in the world was in the suitcase, and even the money for my train fare had arrived on the very day I was due to leave college. I was going home to my parents with no job and no prospects, no money, hardly any clothes and what appeared to be a bleak future.

The strange and mysterious truth was that in spite of all this, I was wonderfully happy and at peace with myself and the world. I was indeed poor, but I dimly perceived the truth of the beatitude of Jesus: 'Blessed are the poor.' As I look back over the years I do not think that I have known such a deep and abiding joy as I did then. I discovered that there was a real joy in poverty, material poverty, as well as the other kind of poverty of spirit: the recognition of a need of God and his kingdom through all the changes and chances of life. A dim recognition that if I sought to put God and his kingdom first, and to do his will rather than my own, I would lack nothing. So it has proved during the last forty years or so. Blessed be the God and Father of our Lord Jesus Christ who has made it so.

Ron Dale, 1998

It is not only the economically disadvantaged that fall under the rubric 'poor'. Cast a swift glance back into the Bible. Poor is the leper, ostracised from society, excluded from normal association with others, compelled often to live outside his town. Poor is the widow, who could not inherit from her husband, was an obvious victim for the exactions of a creditor, had no defender at law and so was often at the mercy of dishonest judges. Poor are the orphans with no parents to love them. Poor is the sinful woman who bathed Jesus' feet with her tears, the woman caught in the very act of adultery, to be stoned according to the law of Moses. Israel's poor were the afflicted, those of lower class oppressed by the powerful. The poor were all those on whose behalf the Lord castigated the chosen people through the prophets:

> Cease to do evil, learn to do good;
> seek justice, rescue the oppressed,
> defend the orphan, plead for the widow.
> (Isaiah 1:16-17)

Besides the obviously poor, I suggest that the word can be extended to embrace what has been called 'the predicament of the prosperous'. In a genuine sense, poor was wealthy toll collector Zacchaeus, a henchman of the Romans, a social outcast because of his job, no longer a 'true son of Abraham'. In our time, the poor include megabucks entertainer Michael Jackson; a Haiti president, Jean Aristide; a senator, Bob Packwood; a CBS president, Laurence Tisch; a presidential wife, Hillary Clinton; a D.C. mayor, Barry; a cardinal, Joseph Bernardin; a Supreme Court Justice, Sandra Day O'Connor; and so on and so forth. They carry on the biblical examples, the peculiar difficulties that confront the rich and the powerful as they struggle to enter the kingdom.

Not the prerogative of the preacher, therefore, to sympathise with the economically poor and the powerless while castigating the wealthy and 'the high and mighty', 'the bold and the beautiful'. All need our loving concern. All demand of the preacher the skilful approach Jesus took to differing needs: to Zacchaeus with his wealth as well as the widow with her mite; to the centurion with his sick boy as well as the robber crucified at his right hand; to Pilate washing his hands of him as well as the woman taken in adultery.

Walter J. Burghardt, SJ
Preaching the Just Word

Psalm 23 in a new dress

Fifteen years ago, a group of English and Dutch scholars and poets attempted a new translation of all the Psalms. Here is their version of Psalm 23.

My shepherd is the Lord;
I shall never want for anything.
He takes me to an oasis of green –
there I stretch out at the edge of the water, where I find rest.
I come to life again, then we go forward
along trusted roads – He leads the way.
For God is his name.
Although I must enter the darkness of death,
I am not anxious since you are with me –
in your keeping I dare to do it.
You invite me to sit at your table,
and all my enemies, with envious eyes,
have to look on while you wait upon me,
while you anoint me, my skin and my hair,
while you fill up my cup to the brim.
Happiness and mercy are coming to meet me everywhere,
every day of my life. And always I go back to the house of the Lord,
as long as I live.

I like the line: 'He takes me to an oasis of green . . . '
Having lived on the edge of the Libyan desert for 18 months, these words conjure up many pictures of desert life-lizards of all sizes and colours darting over the sand, or peer-

ing out from under rocks, scorpions charging about with their tails curled over ready to attack and the chameleon with its perfect camouflage, its revolving eyes and the expert way it shoots out its tongue to catch a fly for dinner.

I found the desert a place of rich variety and interest, but also a place where I sometimes had a raging thirst. At times, I'd have given anything for a long drink of cold, clear water. How I also longed to see some green grass instead of sand, sand and yet more sand. I yearned for an oasis. A place of shade and cool, clear water. If only I'd had then a deep thirst for God as well, it would have saved me much agony of spirit.

As another of the Psalms puts it: 'As the deer pants for water, so I long for you, O God. I thirst for God, the living God.' He will always slake our thirst for him, but are we thirsty, really thirsty, for him ?

Modern advertising tries to create a thirst for all kinds of drink and consumer goods, but how is a genuine thirst for God created? There's a pause for thought for you.

Ron Dale
Pause for Thought

Seventh Sunday of Epiphany
Proper 3/Ordinary Time 7

Sunday between 17 and 23 February (if earlier than the Second
Sunday before Lent)

Luke 6:27-38

*We must never
allow someone
else's character to
decide what we
shall do.*

At the end of the First World War our advancing British
forces were deep into Germany. We had come over three
hundred miles over mountain country, in the worst winter
weather, among people we had been told to hate – Germans,
men and women.

After days of bitter, muddy marching, we halted in a village, and the troops were billeted among the cottages. I wondered how they would treat their unwilling German hosts.
As we were spending a day resting, it gave me a chance to
visit some of the billets.

I called at a cottage where I knew there were two gunners. It was the home of an elderly German widow, the
whole house spotlessly clean and cared for. The bedroom
where my two gunners had been billeted was sparsely fur-
nished, but, again, spotlessly clean and comfortable.

I said to them, 'We had a poorish day yesterday, but you
must have had a good night's sleep last night. That bed
looks pretty cushy.'

They didn't say anything, so I went on, 'Why, what's the
matter? Isn't it as comfortable as it looks?'

Then one of them said, rather sheepishly, 'It was like this,
sir – we were so dirty, and that bed so clean – well, we just
slep' on the floor.'

T. Wingfield Heale
Crossing the Border

*Do good to those who hate you, bless those who curse
you, pray for those who abuse you.* (Luke 6:27-28)

What then is forgiveness if it is not the remission of punishment? In the story of Joseph and his brethren we have a very

good example of another common misunderstanding of the nature of forgiveness. There is very little doubt of the fact that Joseph, as a younger brother, behaved himself in such a way as to prove offensive to his older brothers. He was, besides being his father's favourite son, also a prig and a boaster. Finally, his brothers could not stand him any longer and got rid of him by selling him to some Midianite tradesmen. The story develops in such a way that later these same brothers had to come to Joseph seeking his help. When finally Joseph reveals himself to them, it is in a situation where they are at his mercy. They expect him to punish them for what they had done to him. But he forgives them and, as a token of his forgiveness, sends for his father and settles them all in a very fertile part of the land of Goshen. After many years, during which Jacob and his sons have enjoyed the kindness of Joseph, Jacob dies. Joseph and his brothers go to Canaan to bury their father.

Let us read what the record says at this point (Genesis 50:14): 'After he had buried his father, Joseph returned to Egypt with his brothers and all who had gone up with him to bury his father. When Joseph's brothers saw that their father was dead, they said, "It may be that Joseph will hate us and pay us back for all the evil we did to him". So they sent a message to Joseph, saying, "Your father gave this command before he died, 'Say to Joseph: "Forgive, I pray you, the transgression of your brothers and their sin, because they did evil to you."' And now, we pray you, forgive the transgression of the servants of the God of your father." It is said that Joseph wept when they spoke to him thus.'

In spite of the fact that Joseph's brothers enjoyed kindness at his hands, they did not feel forgiven. For years Joseph had looked after them, but somehow not only had the sense of guilt remained with them, but also fear that one day Joseph would pay them back. Why was this so?

Doing good for evil need not in itself be a token of forgiveness. It is quite possible to do good to those who have wronged us without forgiving them. One is almost tempted to say that in the injunction of Paul, 'If your enemy is hungry, feed him; if he is thirsty, give him to drink; for by so doing you will heap burning coals upon his head' (Romans 12:20), the good done is itself intended to be a way of paying back. Of course, Paul guards himself against this interpretation by adding, 'Do not be overcome by evil, but overcome evil with good'. The point, however, is that very rarely can an evil-doer be reformed by showering good upon him. When Jesus speaks of God as making his sun to shine on the good and the evil alike, and making his rain to fall on the just and unjust, he is intending to emphasise the way in which a person must always act out of his own nature rather than in response to what somebody else has done to him. When he acts in response to the action of another, he is allowing that other action to determine what he does. We must never allow somebody else's character to decide what we shall do. And, if evil finds lodgement in our character, the way to overcome it is by letting our own character assert itself in the doing of good.

D. T. Niles
The Power at Work Among Us

One day I was driving through a small village on the outskirts of Oldham when I saw a stocky young man with a big pack on his back trying to thumb a lift. So I stopped to enquire where he wanted to be.

It turned out that he was a Japanese university student hitch-hiking his way around the world. When he first eased himself into the passenger seat of my old Morris 1000, I had an overwhelming sensation of fear, caused, I think, by the fact that I had spent a lot of my youth watching war films. Films such as *Back to Bataan* and many others concerning the war against the Japanese. I had grown up with the idea that the Japanese were my enemies, never friends.

But I need not have worried. I had a most interesting conversation with the young student and looked upon the Japanese in a new light. They were, after all, human, just like me, and in need of a helping hand at times, just like me.

Ron Dale, 1998

Eighth Sunday of Epiphany
Second Sunday before Lent
Ordinary Time 8

Luke 6:39-49 (RCL)

A Christian!

I do not need to be rewarded for not stealing. I am a Christian.

The *Des Moines Tribune* (5 December 1968) reported an amazing event that occurred in South Africa. Two businessmen, Mr Rumbold, and his colleague, Mr Samuel, hung their coats over chairs while they had lunch in Luska, in the 'copper country.' Afterward, Mr Rumbold missed his wallet; it contained cash and coupons for gasoline.

Three days later, while driving back to Johannesburg, a middle-aged African, dressed in shorts, waved them down. 'Are you going to Johannesburg?' he asked. The travellers replied in the affirmative. Whereupon, the black man took a wallet from his pocket and said, 'Would you please try and find a Mr Rumbold there and give him this wallet? I found it in the street three days ago.' Rumbold was inarticulate. Showing the African his identification, he examined the wallet. Everything was intact. The poor, humble man refused a reward, saying, 'No, Sir. I do not need to be rewarded for not stealing. I am a Christian.'

G. Curtis Jones and Paul H. Jones
500 Illustrations: Stories from Life for Preaching & Teaching

John Hillaby was one of my favourite travel writers and for me, his *Journey Through Britain* is a small classic. The following extract is taken from another of his books called *Journey Home*, describing his walk from Ravenglass in Cumbria via the Lakes and Swaledale to a terminus in London.

The quotation describes how old ways of worship were destroyed and a new foundation for worship and life laid down.

Goodmanham was the high shrine of Northumbria when in AD 625 Edwin became king, ruling from the Humber river to the Firth of Forth, from the North Sea to the Isle of Man, and was overlord, the 'Bretwalda', of all the kingdoms of Britain except Kent. With Kent he made an alliance, cementing it by marrying Princess Ethelburga, who agreed to be his queen on condition that she, a Christian soul, might bring with her Paulinus, her priest, and that he would be free to practise and preach the religion of Christ.

For two years this young man of wisdom and ability could not make up his mind whether or not to adopt the religion of his queen. Three events led to a decision: first, an attempt by an envoy to stab him to death, foiled by a friend who rushed in and received the fatal blow; second, a victory in battle; and third, the birth of a daughter.

At the time of the spring full moon, Edwin called his counsellors to his hall at nearby Londesborough to deliberate the substance of this strange new religion that advocated love and forgiveness, not hatred and slaughter. Why, from such a position of strength, should they adopt it? He called on Paulinus to speak. The man who had been sent to England by Pope Gregory spoke simply: there is an eternal purpose in creation . . . Mankind has a special value in the sight of the Creator . . . Christ came into his own world . . . his crucifixion was a sacrifice . . . he is our reconciliation . . . the truth . . . our hope of resurrection like his . . . always present with his disciples . . .

Basic theological stuff, but it lacked the spark that achieved something close to a miracle. An aged priest, whose name we shall never know, stood up in the body of the hall to say that all Paulinus had said had answered his own need to know from whence he came, what his life was for, and what he might hope for after death. And then, in an inspired analogy which has been recounted again and again for thirteen centuries, he likened the earthly existence of man to the flight of a sparrow which, on the dark night of a winter storm, enters through a window of a banqueting hall, warms itself for a brief moment, and then flies out again, no man knows where.

It was Coifi, the high priest of the pagan cult of Northumbria, who made the decision. 'I have known long since,' he said, 'that there is nothing in this religion we have practised. The more I sought for truth in it, the less I found . . . *this* can give us life, salvation and eternal happiness. I advise that we now burn our useless sanctuary, and who better than myself to do it!' So saying, he borrowed a war stallion and a war axe, both of which were forbidden to him as a priest, galloped to the sanctuary, and flung the weapon into the holy place. Seeing that no ill befell him, the company, who thought he had gone mad, followed him, demolished the shrine, put fire to it, and burned it to the ground. 'This one-time place of idols,' says Bede, 'is called today Godmundingham, where the priest himself, inspired by the true God, polluted and destroyed those very altars he had once consecrated.'

Edwin, one hopes, gained his reward in heaven, for after seven years in a state of grace he was killed by Penda of Mercia, and Ethelburga and Paulinus, together with the children, fled to Kent.

John Hillaby
Journey Home

The Military Police sergeant major stood behind me and whispered in my right ear, 'Good turn out, Corp, get your hair cut'. I was furious. His eagle eyes had looked for faults in my badge, cap strap, battle dress, boots and gaiters. He had not been able to fault me on anything on his first inspection, so he had come back, looked me over again and ordered another hair cut. I had had one the day before. I was being got at. Usually on these daily inspections before our posting to North Africa, he said to me things like, 'Your stripes are a dirty, dingy, grey, get 'em white'; 'Your cap strap is indifferent', or 'Your boots need a shine, laddy'. There was always something wrong. Nobody escaped his criticism and he had a memory like an elephant. He never forgot the faults he found. So when I next paraded before him, he looked carefully to see if I had had my hair cut. Seeing I had, he immediately found fault with my cap badge. 'Get it cleaner, laddy, or I will have you put on a charge.' It was then I noticed that the sergeant major had not got a cap badge on that day, but I did not dare tell him. So he dismissed us, threatening us with all kinds of punishment if our turnout was not a big improvement on the following day. I walked angrily back to my barrack room. On the way I noticed somebody's cap badge lying on the barrack square. When I picked it up, I knew who it belonged to. It was the sergeant major's. Looking at it closely, I saw how brilliantly it shone. It was superbly polished and the sunshine made it sparkle like a diamond. I turned it over and got a shock, for the back was covered in a thick green mould and smelt. Whenever I think about that day now, some words of Jesus always come to me. 'How do you look at the speck of sawdust in your brother's eye and fail to notice the plank in your own!' I wondered what would have happened if I had said that to the sergeant major. By the way, how is your plank?

Ron Dale
Pause for Thought

Eighth Sunday of Epiphany
Second Sunday before Lent
Ordinary Time 8

Luke 8:22-25 (CWL)

Who can this be?

Hell is being defined by your circumstances and believing that definition.

Who are you? Remember that wonderfully intimidating scene in *Alice in Wonderland* – or is it in *Through the Looking-Glass*? I can never remember which occurs where – where the precocious and quite self-contained Alice, the soul of rationality, a sensible, well-put-together young girl, is confronted by the caterpillar on his toadstool and asked by this irrational, fantastic creature of wind, smoke, and myth, in tones of cool condescension, 'Who are you?'

The problem with the question put that way is that we suspect that the questioner already knows the answer and doesn't like it or doesn't believe it. The questioner knows that we are not who we think we are, or who we would like to be. We are impostors, and it is the job of the questioner to unmask us and reveal us for the frauds, fakes, and phoneys that we really are; and since all of us are possessed of doubts about our true selves, and all of us have problems with that part of ourselves that we believe to be real, if unpleasant, we all stand indicted by the question no matter what its motive, and we would prefer to be asked, quite frankly, 'How are you?' instead. At least we can deal with that question as it deserves to be dealt with.

Every two or three years at the midyear examination time, *The Crimson* reprints a series of examination horror stories, and one of their favourites, and mine, is of the student who sat for an exam and refused to stop writing when the proctor called time – a capital crime in the examination business. Finally, the proctor, losing all patience, demanded that the student come forward and present his blue book *now*. The student came forward, drew himself up to his full dignity, and said to the proctor, 'Do you know who I am?' The proctor, a democratic graduate-student type, offended by the implications of the question and its social assumptions, said, 'I mostly certainly do not, and I don't care who you are.' The student then replied with a grin, 'Good,' and threw his book into the large pile of examination books where its anonymity would protect him from censure and punishment.

Who are you? There is a tombstone in Vermont upon which is written 'John Brown: born a man, died a grocer'. You and I know lots of people who think that they are what they do.

One of the recurring nightmares or dilemmas for people who define themselves in this way, by what they do, is what happens when they no longer do what defines them. For them, the spectre of retirement or of being leveraged out is worse than the fear of death, for at least in death, presumably, you aren't around to worry about the way things used to be, you don't have to find something else to do, and more important, you don't have to watch someone else do what you once did.

Who are you? There is another form of response to that question. We know perfectly well who we are; the problem is, do others?

Who are you? Jesse Jackson has identified the greatest cause of social decay in America today, and it is not war, nor is it violence. Those are all symptoms and consequences, but they are not the root cause of the greatest social decay in our America today. The cause is a lack of self-worth, a lack of an identity worth respecting, a lack of self-respect and self-dignity, and that comes from not knowing who we really are.

You see the circumstances surrounding your life, the things by which others define you, and in which seemingly you have little say. You are a pregnant, unwed teenager in Chicago, a corporate executive about to be fired from a stock brokerage firm on Wall Street, a senior dreading graduation, an unemployed intellectual, a professor trapped in a passionless job or a hopeless marriage; you are fearful of too much work or of too little work. All of you, all of us, if we are defined by our circumstance alone, by those things so easily described and measured good, bad, or indifferent, then we are indeed trapped and there is no way out. We are who that person is, described by those horrid, dreadful, unavoidable circumstances.

That is what hell is. Not fire and brimstone and eternal torment, as the medievalists loved to paint it for us, but rather hell is being defined by your circumstances, and believing that definition. That is what hell is all about, and to that condition, the cause of low self-worth, of low self-esteem, of no identity beyond one's own set of particular circumstances, to thousands of teenagers across the country caught in that depressing self-definition, Jesse Jackson's mantra begins to make sense and open eyes, when he calls for them to repeat, 'I am somebody'. He urges them to continue, 'I affirm, I affirm that I am more than what others make me. I affirm that I am more than what others expect or do not expect of me. I affirm that I am more than the sum total of my circumstance and my history.' Or, as I would say it, I am not a child of my experience. I am a child of expectation.

That is the beginning of the work of redemption. That's the good news, that's the Gospel, that is the liberating intelligence for difficult times and depressed people. The redemptive answer to the hostile question is not to be found in experience, it is to be found in expectation. We are not, you and I, defined exclusively and determinably by where we have been, nor are we defined even by where we are, but rather by where we are going. To what do we aspire, what and where are our expectations to be found?

Who are you? The Christian answers that question with the phrase 'I am a follower of Jesus Christ'. I am in process, I am a pilgrim, I am on the journey, on the way, on the road. The purpose of my life is the purpose and praise of God: I live in expectation of great and good things. 'We who first hoped in Christ have been destined and appointed to live for the praise of his glory.'

Who are you? Surely I am what I do, in part, and I am where I come from, in part, and I am what others see and expect of me, in part. I am a part of all of that and all of that is a part of me. It is true for me, it is true for you, but the good news, the Gospel, is that there is more to it and therefore more to you and me than that. I am more than that. I am somebody of worth because I am made in the image of God who makes nothing bad. I come from somewhere! I am somebody because I come from somebody, and I am what I aspire to be; I am the child of expectations, which means, as a follower of Jesus Christ, a Christian. I aspire to a life in which all of the disparate, conflicting and confusing, competing parts and pieces nevertheless conduce to something that is greater than the sum of its parts.

If, then, I am made a person of worth because of the work of God before the beginning of time in God's creation of me, and if it is true that I am shaped by my expectations of a future worth living in because of Christ who has gone to prepare that future for me; if the past and the future are in order, what can possibly happen to me in the present, surrounded as I am on every hand by these signs of providence and these sign of promise?

Who are you? Let me suggest that you are:

Formed by God,
nourished by his love,
preserved by his mercy,

open to his promises,
expectant of his future;
you are the human expression of the Divine hope.
You are God's best and last chance in the world,
you are the means for hope and for love in the world.
Who are you?
That is who you are.
You are all of that, and more.
And for that, we praise God.

Peter J. Gomes
Sermons: Biblical Wisdom for Daily Living

Ninth Sunday of Epiphany

Luke 7:1-10

If only we had a faith like that, for us too the miracle would happen and life become new.

David L. McKenna, retired president of Asbury Theological Seminary, told the following story in a sermon:

Jewish people, it is said, have a story to answer every question that a child might ask. My favourite is the story that is told in answer to the child's question, 'Why did God choose to build his temple where he did?'

Two brothers in Jerusalem shared ownership of a mill for grinding grain. One brother was a bachelor, the other was married with three children. At the end of each day, they took the grain they had milled and divided it equally into separate sacks.

One night the bachelor brother thought, 'This is not right. I am alone and don't need much, but my brother has a wife and family. He deserves the larger share.' So, sneaking back to the mill each night, he took part of his share and poured it into his brother's sack.

The married brother also thought one night, 'This is not right. When I am old, I will have children to support me, but my brother will be all alone. He deserves the larger share.' So, sneaking back to the mill each night, he took part of his share and poured it into his brother's sack. They thought it a miracle to find their sacks refilled each morning.

One night, however, the brothers left home at the same time to sneak back to the mill, and by coincidence met on the streets with their sacks in hand. Instantly, they knew what was happening and fell into each other's arms weeping. God looked down upon the scene and said, 'Here is where love meets. Here I will build my temple.'

G. Curtis Jones and Paul H. Jones
500 Illustrations: Stories from Life for Preaching & Teaching

I once visited the old synagogue in Capernaum, under the guidance of Canon Ronald Brownrigg. His forty years of experience in the Holy Land made him a wonderful source of information. Telling us that the synagogue was one which Jesus would have known, Canon Brownrigg pointed out the two very different strata of building rock. One was a dark volcanic rock quarried locally and the other was a lighter rock imported for building purposes. The volcanic rock, we were told, went back to the time of Jesus so that when the synagogue had been re-built in the second century, it was quite obvious which bits went back to his time.

We sat on a small wall in the warm sunshine with the glorious bougainvillea in full flower a short distance away and listened to some readings from the New Testament, one of which was the lesson from Luke set for today, concerning the healing of the centurion's slave by Jesus.

After the reading, and after showing us the different 'board' games cut into the rock slab flooring of the Court of the Gentiles in the synagogue, we did a tour of the grounds, which contained all sorts of artefacts, such as a mill wheel for grinding corn and a press for oil.

Among all these artefacts there were some very interesting pieces of stone that, according to Canon Brownrigg, told us quite a lot about the centurion who had built the synagogue and paid for it out of his own pocket.

We saw, for example, a large piece of stone that had carved into it two scorpions head to head, looking as if they were locked in combat. This told us that the centurion was a member of the Tenth Legion, later stationed in York. There was also a carved piece of stone with a scallop shell on it, telling us that the centurion had the equivalent of the VC, so obviously a man of great courage. Canon Brownrigg told us that each of these stones would have formed part of the original synagogue and constituted a memorial to the centurion, underlining the words in Luke 7:5: 'He loves our nation and has built us a synagogue out of his own pocket.'

When I first saw and heard all of this I remember feeling deeply moved and the centurion became quite real. He certainly must have been a remarkable man, not only courageous and wealthy, but a man who recognised Jesus as having real power to heal and save. And Jesus himself was deeply impressed by the centurion, saying: 'I have never found faith like this anywhere, even in Israel.' The odd thing is that there is no record of what Jesus said or did to heal the slave. All the closing verse says is: 'Then those who had been sent by the centurion returned to the house and found the slave perfectly well' (Luke 7:10).

Ron Dale, August 1998

The central character is a Roman centurion; and he was no ordinary man.

(i) The mere fact that *he was a centurion* meant he was no ordinary man. A centurion was the equivalent of a regimental sergeant major; and the centurions were the backbone of the Roman army. Wherever they are spoken of in the New Testament they are spoken of well (compare Luke 23:47; Acts 10:22; 22:26; 23:17, 23, 24; 24:23; 27:43). Polybius, the historian, describes their qualifications. They must be not so much 'seekers after danger as men who can command, steady in action, and reliable; they ought not to be over-anxious to rush into the fight; but when hard pressed they must be ready to hold their ground and die at their posts.' The centurion must have been a man amongst men or he would never have held the post which was his.

(ii) *He had a completely unusual attitude to his slave.* He loved this slave and would go to any trouble to save him. In Roman law a slave was defined as a living tool; he had no rights; a master could ill-treat him and even kill him if he chose. A Roman writer on estate management recommends the farmer to examine his implements every year and to throw out those which are old and broken, and to do the same with his slaves. Normally when a slave was past his work he was thrown out to die. The attitude of this centurion to his slave was quite unusual.

(iii) *He was clearly a deeply religious man.* A man needs to be more than superficially interested before he will go to the length of building a synagogue. It is true that the Romans encouraged religion from the cynical motive that it kept people in order. They regarded it as the opiate of the people. Augustus recommended the building of synagogues for that very reason. As Gibbon said in a famous sentence: 'The various modes of religion which prevailed in the Roman world were all considered by the people as equally true; by the philosopher as equally false; *and by the magistrate as equally useful.*' But this centurion was no administrative cynic; he was a sincerely religious man.

(iv) *He had an extremely unusual attitude to the Jews.* If the Jews despised the Gentiles, the Gentiles hated the Jews. Anti-semitism is not a new thing. The Romans called the Jews a filthy race; they spoke of Judaism as a barbarous superstition; they spoke of the Jewish hatred of mankind; they accused the Jews of worshipping an ass's head and annually sacrificing a Gentile stranger to their God. True, many of the Gentiles, weary of the many gods and loose morals of paganism, had accepted the Jewish doctrine of the one God and the austere Jewish ethic. But the whole atmosphere of this story implies a close bond of friendship between this centurion and the Jews.

(v) *He was a humble man.* He knew quite well that a strict Jew was forbidden by the law to enter the house of a Gentile (Acts 10:28); just as he was forbidden to allow a Gentile into his house or have any communication with him. He would not even come to Jesus himself. He persuaded his Jewish friends to approach him. This man who was accustomed to command had an amazing humility in the presence of true greatness.

(vi) *He was a man of faith.* His faith is based on the soundest argument. He argued from the here and now to the there and then. He argued from his own experience to God. If his authority produced the results it did, how much more must that of Jesus? He came with that perfect confidence which looks up and says, 'Lord, I *know* you can do this'. If only we had a faith like that, for us too the miracle would happen and life become new.

William Barclay
The Daily Study Bible: The Gospel of Luke

This story opens a section in Luke (7:1-8:3) sometimes called 'the little insertion' because it consists of material (six units) inserted at this point into the framework of Mark. Some of the content is found also in Matthew but not in Mark. Luke will at 8:4 return to the Markan structure which in general provided the frame for Luke's Gospel.

Luke begins this section with a literary transition (the Sermon on the Plain is ended) and a geographical move (Jesus goes to Capernaum). Matthew and John agree on the location for this healing. In fact, Matthew and Luke tell the story with more than sixty identical words.

The centurion is a Gentile, perhaps in service to Herod Antipas, tetrarch of Galilee, or to Pontius Pilate, procurator of Judea, headquartered at Caesarea. He represents the believing Gentile living within Jewish territory. Luke's practice of relating parallel events from the life of Jesus and the life of the Church is evident here. Remarkably similar to 7:1-10 is Acts 10. The Acts account begins, 'At Caesarea there was a man named Cornelius, a centurion of what was known as the Italian Cohort, a devout man who feared God with all his household, gave alms liberally to the people, and prayed constantly to God' (Acts 10:1-2). What is important about these parallels is that 7:1-10 both foreshadows the mission to the Gentiles which is unfolded in Acts and provides an authoritative precedent for that mission in the ministry of Jesus himself.

The centurion is a man of admirable qualities. That his slave is gravely ill is a concern to him and that Jesus can heal him is held in firm faith (verses 3, 7, 10). According to leaders of the Jewish community, the centurion is worthy, he loves the Jewish people, and he built a synagogue for them (verses 3-5). According to friends, presumably Gentile, the centurion feels himself unworthy of Jesus' presence in his home (verses 6-7a). In addition, he believed there was power in Jesus' word. After all, as a military officer, he knew the power of a command given and received (verses 7b-8). Jesus praises the man's faith as unmatched in Israel, and the slave is healed.

The centurion himself never came in contact with Jesus; that fact is important to the story in at least two ways. First, the centurion anticipates all those believers yet to come who have not seen Jesus but who have believed his word as having the power of his presence (verse 7; John 20:29). Such faith is not disadvantaged as though it were second-hand or belief at a distance, a consideration of major importance to those of us who believe in Jesus Christ but who are of another time and another place. The word of Christ, effective and present to faith in all times and places, creates and sustains the Church. The Church could not otherwise survive, having a past but no present, finding small comfort in a book of fond memories of what Jesus once said and what he once did.

Second, and more immediate to Luke's purpose, is the fact that the centurion had his contact with Jesus through two sets of intermediaries, some Jewish, some Gentile. The officer himself is probably a proselyte-at-the-gate, a person who accepted Judaism's faith but who had not submitted to the rites whereby a Gentile became a Jew. The two sets of delegates dramatise his situation as a bridge between two worlds, Jew and Gentile, believing in the God who is the God of both and trusting that the word of Jesus had the power to move past any barriers between the two. The time would come when missionaries would take that word into the Gentile world (Acts 1:8); Simon Peter himself would, reluctantly and with the prodding of the Spirit, enter into a centurion's house, preach, baptise, and break bread with

Gentiles (Acts 10). But that story is yet to unfold; Luke is moving the reader in that direction. The healing of the centurion's slave not only anticipates that story but begins it; in fact, it authorises it by the healing word of Christ.

Fred B. Craddock
Luke

Last Sunday of Epiphany
Sunday next before Lent
Transfiguration Sunday

Luke 9:28-36 (37-43)

It is a vision beyond this world that all of us ultimately need.

Earlier in this chapter of Luke's Gospel, King Herod hears about the marvellous deeds of Jesus. Rumours have reached him that some people believe Jesus to be John the Baptist risen from the dead and that others think Jesus is the promised return of Elijah. In consternation, Herod asks, 'John I beheaded; but who is this about whom I hear such things?' (Luke 9:9). The question 'Who is this?' runs throughout the Gospel, of course, but it is especially important in this section of Luke.

One answer to Herod's question comes in the form of Peter's confession in Luke 9:20: '[You are] the Messiah of God.' To identify Jesus as God's 'Messiah' however, is to offer more questions than answers, for the word connoted many things to many different groups within early Judaism. Jesus' immediate response (Luke 9:21-22) indicates that the meaning of Messiahship may be more complicated than either the disciples or Luke's readers have yet anticipated.

The transfiguration account provides yet another way of answering Herod's question. By means of this elusive event, Luke identifies Jesus in terms of Israel's past (Moses and Elijah), foreshadows his upcoming death on the cross, and anticipates his resurrected glory. Luke also uses this story to teach about the nature of discipleship.

First, the transfiguration identifies Jesus with Moses and Elijah. The disciples recognise these two crucial figures from Israel's past, confirming that they are heavenly beings, not conformed to earthly limitations. That they talk with Jesus might suggest a kind of peer relationship among the three figures, a conclusion that seems confirmed by Peter's proposal. However the heavenly voice speaks only of Jesus, and only when the other two have disappeared from the scene. It is Jesus alone who is 'my Son, my Chosen'. If Jesus stands in the line of Moses and Elijah, he is nevertheless far superior to that line.

Second, the transfiguration foreshadows Jesus' death on the cross. When Moses and Elijah talk with Jesus, they discuss his *exodus*, which the NRSV translates as 'departure' and which literally means exodus and figuratively refers to death or departure . . .

If the transfiguration anticipates the death of Jesus, it also hints that death will not be the final word in this story. The dominant motif of this account, after all, is one of glory, a glory that most appropriately anticipates the resurrected Jesus. Several elements in the passage draw attention to Jesus' glory. The change in his appearance recalls Daniel's description of the Ancient One (Daniel 7:9) and signals divine favour (Ecclestiastes 9:8). The glory of Jesus is visible to Peter and the other disciples, even when he stands alongside Moses and Elijah, and even though they are themselves overwhelmed with sleep (verse 32)! The cloud, the arrival and movement of which Luke depicts in some detail, is associated elsewhere with the very presence of God (see, for example Exodus 16:10; 19:9; 1 Kings 8:10-11; Psalm 18:11). That these features of the story anticipate Jesus' resurrection is clear when we recall that, at Jesus' ascension, it is a cloud that removes him from the sight of the disciples (Acts 1:9).

As fascinating as the transfiguration itself are the responses of Peter and John and James. Initially, Luke explains that they were 'weighed down with sleep', a problem that will overtake them again at the time of Jesus' arrest (Luke 22:45). This odd little detail may serve to emphasise the utterly astonishing nature of the event, in that it serves to wake them from such a sleep. Another possibility is that their grogginess explains the inappropriateness of Peter's suggestion in Luke 9:33.

The proposal of Peter, that dwellings be erected to honour each of the three men, Luke immediately interprets as something of a *faux pas* ('not knowing what he said', verse 33). Despite his own identification of Jesus as Messiah, Peter still does not understand *either* the vast superiority of Jesus to even these giants of Israel *or* the impossibility of locating any of them in a building (compare Acts 7:47-49). The final response of the three is that of *awe* (Luke 9:43) and *silence* (verse 36). That seems to be the only possible response to what they have witnessed. Their silence acknowledges the mystery of this event and the magnitude of its implications. Their silence also signals their obedience to Jesus' earlier warning that they should not tell anyone Jesus' identity (Luke 9:21). Their silence also reflects their own lack of readiness for the task of witnessing that will later be theirs (Acts 1:8); it is not yet time for the disciples to speak.

The silence of the disciples does not mean that they fully comprehend what they have seen and heard, as is clear from the stories that immediately follow. They are unable to cast out a demon from a severely afflicted boy (Luke 9:37-42); they do not understand Jesus' comments about his upcoming death (Luke 9:43-45); worse yet, they quarrel over which of them is greatest (Luke 9:46-48). They still must learn to listen to the Chosen One (Luke 9:35) but that hearing has its rightful beginning in their awed silence.

Beverly R. Gaventa
Texts for Preaching: A Lectionary Commentary Based on the NRSV – Year C

Dare I suggest we most of us come to this festival, 'summoned by bells' this morning, to this act of worship, here in Holy Trinity where the Cluniac monks once worshipped, to be renewed in vision; to 'lift up our eyes unto the hills' – perhaps through the beauty of the country that surrounds us; perhaps also through what Rose Macaulay called 'the pleasure of ruins'; perhaps simply through being again for a while with 'golden friends'.

We are right sometimes consciously to withdraw awhile from the battle of life, to seek some transfiguring time before we return again to the fray: as the disciples of Jesus withdrew with him, one day – as your Lady Chapel window records – and ascending, apart, their local Wenlock Edge – Mount Hermon or Mount Tabor – he was transfigured. A festival like this can provide such a transfiguring time.

But, even while we're here, I think it right for us to bear in mind those in our society for whom such withdrawal is simply not possible.

There is an increasing custom in our society of blaming the victim, scapegoating those who are already marginalised and excluded; identifying them as the problem; responsible for holding back society from a more prosperous future. But in Christian scripture and history, those outside the mainstream of society have often been called by God to be the source and promise of its salvation.

The renewal of our vision comes in many different ways. In homeless people the Christian Church tries to recognise and minister to the person of the suffering Christ, outside the boundaries of what is most often considered a so-called 'normal' life for the mass of the population. Perhaps that's why those who work with the homeless so often come to feel it is *they* who are being ministered to. The homeless strip us of all illusions about ourselves and our society. They earth us in reality and minister *to* us.

Yes, the renewal of our vision comes in many and various ways. And we are right to take time out for such a festival as this, so long as we do not totally turn our backs on the world in need. But, of course, in the end, it is a vision beyond this world that all of us ultimately need. Houseman's vision ended in darkness in 'thine eternal shade'. I believe that faith – and thankfulness for what we have received and experienced in this life – can do better than that.

Parry, who gave us his incomparable setting of Blake's *Jerusalem*, also set to sublime music the vision of Henry Vaughan – *The Silurist*, which it is apt to quote, I think, in the setting of the Silurian limestone of Wenlock, and is as apt to end what I have to say to you this morning:

My soul, there is a country
far beyond the stars,
where stands a winged sentry
all skilful in the wars:

There above noise and danger,
sweet Peace sits crowned with smiles,
and One born in a manger
commands the beauteous files.

He is thy gracious friend,
and – O my soul awake! –
did in pure love descend,
to die here for thy sake.

If thou canst get but thither,
there grows the flower of peace,
the Rose that cannot wither,
thy fortress and thy ease.

Leave then thy foolish ranges,
for none can thee secure
but one who never changes,
thy God, thy life, thy cure.

Eric James
A Time to Speak

First Sunday in Lent

Luke 4:1-13

Spiritual poverty means a mind and heart which so trusts in God as its rock, refuge and strength that nothing in creation can deflect from God.

In his 'Two Standards' meditation, Ignatius gives an image of evil, picturing Lucifer sitting on a smoky throne in the plain of Babylon and surrounded by little demons whom he sends throughout the world 'so that no Province, no place, no state of life, no individual is overlooked'.

The little demons are instructed to ensnare all human beings in three stages: to teach them to covet riches, so leading them on to love the honours of this world until they are trapped in the prison of their pride.

Riches, in themselves, are not evil, nor are honours, position in society and status. In themselves these things are good and can be used for the praise, reverence and service of God, but riches are for sharing, not for hoarding, and honour and power are for the greater service of others, not to enhance a false sense of self-importance. Riches and honour can become our idols, our Mammon, so that our lives revolve around our bank balance, whether its abundance or deficit, or around the esteem, or lack of it, in which we imagine we are held.

As individuals, as a Church, and as a nation we need to ponder the truth in this representation of Satan's Standard and why he is called 'the enemy of our human nature'. The riches of the earth are a blessing. Destructiveness enters when they become an idol, so that we value ourselves and other people not for their intrinsic worth, but for their market value. We are all worthy of honour, far more worthy than we think. It is not riches and honour which are wrong, but the way we use them. We fail to honour one another because we do not cherish one another for what we are in ourselves, images of God, but we value people for the wealth they possess, the power they can exercise. Consequently, those who have neither riches nor honour are devalued, considered worthless and, unless they have great inner strength, come to look on themselves as worthless. There is a high suicide rate among the unemployed of Britain today. The rich pride themselves on their wealth and the powerful take delight in their status, which is to devalue their own real worth. As individuals and as a nation we can become so enamoured of our riches and our prestige that we cling to them as life itself, will go to any lengths to secure them, even to mass murder and the risk of annihilation. The spirit of evil is rightly called 'the father of lies' and 'the enemy of our human nature'.

'Mammon' and riches mean not only money and material possessions, but stand for any idol in our lives, any created thing which becomes the focus of our praise, reverence and service. Mammon can be an ideology or any 'ism' which we allow to possess us. Mammon can be patriotism, 'my country right or wrong', or it can be the way in which we practise religion, when our dedication becomes dedication to particular structures or formulations of the Christian message, and their preservation in the form familiar to us becomes more important than the worship and service of God, the God of mystery and of love, before whom all human structures must be provisional. 'The Sabbath is made for man, not man for the Sabbath', as Jesus said to the Pharisees.

In the 'Two Standards' meditation, in contrast to Satan on his smoky throne, Ignatius pictures Christ standing in a plain near Jerusalem with his friends around him, 'his appearance beautiful and attractive'. Unless we see Christ and his teaching as attractive, as the answer to our deepest desires, we shall never follow him wholeheartedly. It is only in the strength of our attachment to him that we shall become detached, indifferent to riches and honour.

As Satan is pictured sending the little demons all over the world, Ignatius pictures Christ sending his friends to all human beings, 'no matter what their state or condition', a phrase reminiscent of the wedding feast parable in which the king sends the servants to the hedgerows and byways to invite everyone they can find, good and bad alike. They are to help all people by attracting them first to the highest spiritual poverty, and even to actual poverty, if that is what God is asking of them, and secondly to accept and even to desire the insults and contempt of the world, because this will lead them to humility, the source of all other virtues.

At a first reading, Christ's programme of poverty, insults and contempt leading to humility, sounds most unattractive. Spiritual poverty means a mind and heart which so trusts in God as its rock, refuge and strength that nothing in creation can deflect from God. Spiritual poverty is a phrase which describes one aspect of Christ's relationship to the Father, namely that he is so anchored and rooted in the life of his Father that nothing could possess him, neither his desire to have ('Turn these stones into bread') nor his desire to count and be important ('Leap down from the pinnacle of the Temple'), nor the desire to have power ('Take over the kingdoms of the world'). St Paul expresses his own poverty of spirit in these words to the Philippians, 'I know how to be poor and I know how to be rich too. I have been through my initiation, and now I am ready for anything anywhere: full stomach or empty stomach, poverty or plenty. There is nothing I cannot master with the help of the one who gives me strength' (4:12-13).

Spiritual poverty is the opposite of diffidence, timidity, self-depreciation, crawling servility. It is the possession of all things in Christ, while being possessed by none, the ability to enjoy and delight in God's creation without being trapped by it; it is the discovery of our true identity, that we live in, through and with Christ in the life of the Father. Spiritual poverty is spiritual freedom.

'Blessed are the poor in spirit, theirs is the kingdom of heaven' (Matthew 5:3). This, the first of the beatitudes, is a summary of the whole of Christ's Sermon on the Mount, the essence of his teaching.

Actual poverty, if understood as material deprivation imposed on people against their will, is not a good, but an evil, and therefore to be opposed and overcome. The riches of this world are for the benefit of all human beings. The material deprivation of half the world is not because there is not enough food and resources, but because of their unjust distribution. A Christian who is not striving to be spiritually poor has ceased to be a Christian. It is of the nature of spiritual poverty, because it is the attitude which allows God's goodness, generosity and compassion to act in us, to combat material deprivation and oppose all that contributes to it, whether it be our own individual selfishness and greed, or our corporate selfishness and greed expressed in our political and economic system.

Gerard Hughes
God of Surprises

Second Sunday in Lent

Luke 13:31-35

With repentance comes forgiveness – an offer to the world, beginning with Jerusalem.

Proclaiming the prophetic message

Every sermon preached from the prophetic literature needs to be formed with the prophet's central call for love and trust in mind. Prophetic preaching deals with the hearts of the covenant people, and its goal is to awaken that faith in the congregation that will enable them to trust their Lord in all circumstances and to obey him with willing and grateful hearts. Prophetic preaching consists not in exhortation alone, but in that proclamation of God's gracious acts toward his covenant people that inspires them to respond to his love in reciprocal love, acted out in obedience.

Israel's failure to respond with such love and obedience is her sin, according to the prophets. Sin, in their writings, is not Israel's breaking of ethical and ritual rules or the violation of moral and religious norms, but the failure to love and trust her Lord. In every realm of her life, Israel rejects an intimate and faithful relationship with her God. In the light of all that the Lord has done for his people, that is almost incomprehensible.

> Have I been a wilderness to Israel, or a land of thick darkness? Why then do my people say, 'We are free, we will come no more to thee'?
> Can a maiden forget her ornaments, or a bride her attire? Yet my people have forgotten me days without number.
> (Jeremiah 2:31-32)

As in Genesis 3 and throughout the Bible, sin in the prophet's view is real but finally inexplicable. Given all that God has done in Jesus Christ in the history of the Christian Church, why should we forget him days without number? The prophets recount Israel's past with God in order to reawaken her faith in her Lord, and we modern preachers tell 'the old, old story' in order that faith may come by hearing (Romans 10:17).

There is no denial in the Bible of the reality and power of sin, and those modern sects and success preachers who would proclaim '"Peace, peace", when there is no peace' with God (Jeremiah 6:14; 8:11) have nothing in common with the prophets. The latter know the awful, binding power of sin as it affects their people. Sin lames all power of self-assessment, so that Israel does not even see the evil she is doing (Jeremiah 8:6-7), and part of the purpose of the prophets is to enable Israel to see, in order that she may repent, in order that she may turn around and walk her daily way in the opposite direction.

The prophets also find to their dismay, however, that sin holds their people captive and that Israel has no power within herself to repent and correct her ways (Hosea 5:4; Jeremiah 13:23). She is slave to sin and helpless to heed the call to repent (cf. Isaiah 6:9-10; Romans 6:17-22). Israel is therefore one with all the peoples and nations, joining with them in a common rebellion against the rule of the Lord over human life.

It is obvious therefore why moralistic preaching of itself cannot heal a people's life or effect their return to God. Sin, 'is written with a pen of iron; with a point of diamond it is engraved on the tablet' of our hearts (Jeremiah 17:1), and there is nothing we can do to expunge the writing. To be told by a preacher to turn from evil and do the good by our own power is to be assigned an impossible task. Sin is one slave master from which persons cannot escape on their own.

Sinful rejection of the Lordship of God also bears with it consequences, however. God will not put up with rebellion against his rule or overlook rejection of his love (cf. Jeremiah 7:16-20). He is not mocked (Galatians 6:7), and he will not countenance wrong (Habakkuk 1:13). He declares to Israel:

> What is in your mind shall never happen – the thought, 'Let us be like the nations' . . . 'As I live', says the Lord God, 'surely with a mighty hand and an outstretched arm, and with wrath poured out, I will be king over you.'
> (Ezekiel 20:32-33)

God will be king over Israel, over his Church, over his world – if not in love, then in wrath. The result is that the pre-exilic prophets announce God's warfare against his covenant people. An unrepentant people can no longer be forgiven their sins. Sin must finally be done to death (cf. Amos 7:1; 8:1-2). In the Lord's own fearful words:

> My heritage has become to me like a lion in the forest, she has lifted up her voice against me; therefore I hate her.
> (Jeremiah 12:8)

The divine hatred of sin can get rid of it only by destroying it. So we read the awful repetition in Ezekiel 7:5-7:

> Disaster after disaster! Behold, it comes. An end has come, the end has come; it has awakened against you. Behold it comes. Your doom has come to you, O inhabitant of the land; the time has come.

Perhaps we modern preachers have never made such a message clear to our congregations – that God is not mocked and that we too therefore daily suffer under the wrath of a sovereign Lord. The breakdown of our communities, our darkness, pain, and strife, our warfare, our hatreds, our destruction, and our death are not just the automatic effects of our blind wrongdoings but are in fact God actively giving us up to our sins, returning them upon our own heads, as the Old Testament puts it, or subjecting us to the fire of his very real judgements. Our people do not believe that God does anything any more (cf. the same attitude in Zephaniah 1:12), and so they do not believe there is actual, active judgement from God when we reject his fellowship. We are very much like the people in Jeremiah's time (Jeremiah 7:8-11). We believe we can break the commandments and go and stand before God in his house, which is called by his name, and say, 'We are delivered!' – only to go on doing all these abominations. We have turned the place of worship into a 'den of robbers' (cf. Mark 11:17), where we think to hide and be safe from the consequences of our sins. We have little of the prophetic sense of God's active work of judgement, of God's purification and discipline and crucifixion of his people. Surely part of the task of prophetic preaching is to announce that 'strange deed' and 'alien work' of God's judgement (Isaiah 28:21) – strange because we believe ourselves exempt and 'alien' because God's nature is love that always desires that we live and not die (Ezekiel 18:32).

Elizabeth Achtemeier
Preaching from the Old Testament

Luke 13:31-35 is especially appropriate for the Lenten Season in that the text looks toward Jerusalem and the passion of Jesus. And if Lent be understood as a pilgrimage to Good Friday and Easter, this passage is doubly appropriate, for it falls within Luke's lengthy 'journey narrative' (9:51-19:27). This large section begins with a declaration: 'he set his face to go to Jerusalem' (9:51). That controlling image of Jesus had been repeated as recently as 13:22: 'Jesus went through one town and village after another . . . as he made his way to Jerusalem.' Luke is fond of the journey format not only for presenting Jesus' ministry in the Gospel and Paul's in Acts, but also for characterising the Christians as pilgrims, those of 'the Way' (Acts 9:2; 19:9, 23; 22:4; 24:14, 22). When the travel narrative is understood as Luke's way of giving a frame to a number of sayings and events in Jesus' life, then the extremely difficult task of reconstructing a chronology for the journey to Jerusalem ceases to be of primary importance . . .

Perhaps most striking here is the favourable picture of the Pharisees, especially for those of us who had been given the impression that the Pharisees were always and everywhere the villains in the story of Jesus. Herod Antipas, son of Herod the Great, was tetrarch of Galilee (Luke 3:1) during Jesus' ministry. He had beheaded John the Baptist and now was perplexed about Jesus, especially because there was a rumour that Jesus was John raised from the dead (Luke 9: 7-9). Apparently Herod now wants to cure his perplexity by killing Jesus also (13:32). Jesus is neither intimidated nor deterred in his ministry, for he lives and works under the divine necessity: 'I must be on my way' (verse 33). This means that even though death for Jesus is near ('the third day' is surely intended here to refer to what is impending and not to the exact time frame), he will continue to exorcise demons and heal the sick, he will bring his ministry to its consummation (verse 32), and he will die in Jerusalem (verse 33). This reaffirms the divine imperative with which this entire section began (9:51). That the Pharisees, in an act of friendship, would warn Jesus about Herod should not surprise the reader of Luke. Whereas Mark 3:6 states that Pharisees and Herodians joined in the design to kill Jesus, Luke's parallel to that omits the Herodians and offers the more moderate description of the Pharisees discussing 'what they might do to Jesus' (6:11). In Luke, many Pharisees seem open to Jesus (7:36; 11:37; 14:1), even though they do differ strongly with him on certain interpretations of the law. A Pharisee, Gamaliel, was a moderating voice in the Jewish council when dealing with the followers of Jesus (Acts 5:34), and some of the early Christians were, according to Luke, Pharisees (15:5), including, by his own admission, Paul (23:6). But even so, Luke wants us to understand that both friends (Pharisees) and foes (Herod) could not alter Jesus' sure obedience to the will of God.

Very likely it is the attention on Jerusalem that prompts Luke to place here the lament over the city (verses 34-35). Jerusalem is central in Luke's narrative, not only about Jesus but also about the early Church. Luke mentions Jerusalem ninety times; in the remainder of the New Testament, it is mentioned only forty-nine times. But the fact that verse 33 ends with the word 'Jerusalem' is hardly sufficient reason for Luke to locate here a passage that seems so clearly out of place. 'How often have I desired to gather your children' (verse 34) implies a Judean ministry that has yet to occur. Matthew places the saying near the close of Jesus' ministry in Jerusalem (23:37-39), a natural setting for it. Hence, when Jesus says in Matthew, 'You will not see me again until' (verse 39), the reference is to the final crisis. In Luke, however, Jesus is on his way to the city, therefore, when he says, 'You will not see me until', the reference is to his arrival at Jerusalem when the people shout, 'Blessed is the king who comes in the name of the Lord!' (19:38), almost the exact words of 13:35.

By locating this apostrophe to Jerusalem earlier, Luke is saying that there is yet time to repent, yet time to receive the Christ, yet time to avoid the final catastrophe. With repentance comes forgiveness – an offer to the world, beginning with Jerusalem (24:47).

Fred B. Craddock
Preaching Through the Christian Year: 'C'

> *'You serpents, you brood of vipers,*
> *how are you to escape being sentenced to hell?'*
> (Matthew 23:33)

The chapter in Matthew's Gospel from which this saying is quoted presents a series of woes pronounced against the scribes and Pharisees – or perhaps we should say laments uttered over them. The series may be regarded as an expansion of

Mark 12:38-40, where the people who listened to Jesus as he taught in the temple precincts in Jerusalem during Holy Week were warned against 'the scribes, who like to go about in long robes, and to have salutations in the market places and the best seats in the synagogues and the places of honour at feasts, who devour widows' houses and for a pretence make long prayers. They will receive the greater condemnation.'

The scribes were the recognised exponents of the law. Most of them – certainly most of those who appear in the Gospels – belonged to the party of the Pharisees. The Pharisees traced their spiritual lineage back to the pious groups which, in the days of the Maccabees, resisted all temptations to assimilate their faith and practice to paganising ways, and suffered martyrdom rather than betray their religious heritage. In the first century AD they are reckoned to have numbered about 6,000. They banded themselves together in fellowships or brotherhoods, encouraging one another in the defence and practice of the law. The law included not only the written precepts of the Old Testament but the interpretation and application of those precepts – what Mark describes as 'the tradition of the elders' (Mark 7:3). They were greatly concerned about ceremonial purity. This concern forbade them to have social contact with Gentiles, or even with fellow Jews who were not so particular about the laws of purity as they themselves were. They attached high importance to the tithing of crops (that is, paying ten per cent of the proceeds of harvest into the temple treasury) – not only of grain, wine and olive oil but of garden herbs. They would not willingly eat food, whether in their own houses or in other people's, unless they could be sure that the tithe had been paid on it.

From their viewpoint, they could not help looking on Jesus as dangerously lax, whether in the sovereign freedom with which he disposed of the Sabbath law and the food laws or in his readiness to consort with the most questionable persons and actually sit down to a meal with them. It was inevitable that he and they should clash; their conflict, indeed, illustrates the saying about the second-best being the worst enemy of the best.

The Pharisaic way of life lent itself to imitation by people who had no worthier motive than the gaining of a popular reputation for piety. The rabbinical traditions illustrate this fact: seven types of Pharisee are enumerated, and only one of these, the Pharisee who is one for the love of God, receives unqualified commendation. The New Testament picture of the Pharisees is generally an unfavourable one, but more so in the Gospels than in Acts. In Acts they are depicted as not unfriendly to the observant Jewish Christians of Jerusalem: the two groups had this in common (by contrast with the Sadducees), that they believed in the resurrection of the dead.

The gathering together of the woes or laments regarding the Pharisees in Matthew 23 probably reflects the situation in which this Gospel was written, later in the first century, when the Pharisees and the Jewish Christians were engaged in polemical controversy with one another. That provided an opportunity to collect from all quarters criticisms which Jesus had voiced against the Pharisees, and to weave them together into a continuous speech, with its refrain (as commonly translated) 'Woe to you, scribes and Pharisees, hypocrites!'

Pharisees as such were not hypocrites, and Jesus did not say that they were; he was not the one to bear false witness against his neighbour. 'Hypocrite' in New Testament usage means 'play-actor'; it denotes the sort of person who plays a part which is simply assumed for the occasion and does not express his real self. The 'hypocrites' in this repeated denunciation, then, are those who play at being scribes and Pharisees, who 'preach but do not practise' (Matthew 23:3) who assume the actions and words characteristic of scribes and Pharisees without being motivated by true love of God. The genuine Pharisee might disapprove of much that Jesus said and did, but if he was a genuine Pharisee, he was no play-actor. So we might render the recurring refrain of Matthew 23 as 'Alas for you, hypocritical scribes and Pharisees!' – alas for you, because you are incurring a fearful judgement on yourselves.

But what about the 'brood of vipers'? This expression was used by John the Baptist as he saw the crowds coming to listen to his proclamation of judgement and his call to repentance: 'You brood of vipers! Who warned you to flee from the wrath to come?' (Luke 3:7). He compared them to snakes making their way as quickly as possible out of the range of an oncoming grass fire. In Matthew 3:7 John directs these words to Pharisees and Sadducees among his hearers. Jesus' use of the same figure may convey a warning that those who pay no heed to impending doom cannot escape it – cannot escape 'the judgement of Gehenna' (to render it literally). And if it is asked how they had incurred this judgement without being aware of it, the answer suggested by Matthew's context would be that by their unreality they were hindering, not helping, others in following the way of righteousness. (In Matthew 12:34 those who charged Jesus with casting out demons by the power of Beelzebub are similarly addressed as 'You brood of vipers!')

Finally, Matthew himself apparently indicates that this hard saying, with its context, should be understood as lamentation rather than unmitigated denunciation. For at the end of the discourse, after the statement that the martyr-blood of all generations would be required from that generation, Matthew places the lament over Jerusalem ('O Jerusalem, Jerusalem . . .') which Luke introduces at an earlier point in Jesus' ministry. It is easy to see why Luke introduces it where he does: Jesus has been warned in Galilee that Herod Antipas wants to kill him, and he replies that that cannot be, since Jerusalem is the proper place for a prophet to be put to death (Luke 13:31-33). Then comes 'O Jerusalem, Jerusalem, killing the prophets . . .' (verses 34-35). Actually, the lament would be *chronologically* appropriate if it were uttered at the end of Jesus' last visit to Jerusalem before the final one, for it ends with the words: 'You will not see me until you say, "Blessed is he who comes in the name of the Lord"' (Luke 13:35; Matthew 23:39). This may simply mean, 'You will not see me until festival time'. But Luke and Matthew place the lament in contexts where it is *topically* appropriate; Matthew in particular, by placing it where he does (Matthew 23:37-39), communicates something of the sorrow with which Jesus found it necessary to speak as he did about those who should have been trustworthy guides but in fact were leading their followers to disaster.

F. F. Bruce
The Hard Sayings of Jesus

Third Sunday in Lent

Luke 13:1-9

Repeatedly, Jesus reminded people that they would be judged according to the opportunities they had.

The world is a violent place. The Biblical comment that 'the earth was filled with violence' (Genesis 6:11) is as true now as when it was written. Religions and their thinkers and spokespersons (theologians) have always faced the challenge of offering a reason for it, and the question of 'theodicy' (how can a loving God permit suffering?) has engaged them. Of course, there may be no reason for it, no explanation. Violence may need no exegete to give it meaning. It has been argued that it is simply a given, a fact of life which needs no explanation, since none can be satisfactorily given for it. This is one possible answer to the problem of suffering. But it may not satisfy everyone. For some reason, people – whether religious or not – have always tried to give a rationale for pain. Christian theism, for example, has always tried to answer the problem of suffering (which is a consequence of violence), classically at least since the time of Augustine. And whether or not it is a concern of thinkers and theologians, in the experience of individuals and communities, and in popular religion, it is one of the great issues for which people look for an answer. In antiquity, the classical religions into whose world Christianity was born were very concerned with suffering. Ramsay Macmullen has said that the primary purpose of ancient religions was to heal, i.e. to relieve suffering (Macmullen 1967 and 1981). Thus, at a practical level, the cults of the Roman world dealt with the pains of life, bringing their remedies and cures. The competitiveness and conflicts in this regard are well seen, for instance, in Luke's account of the growth of the Church in the New Testament book of Acts (Acts 19:11-16). Of this world, Macmullen comments: 'It was a real melting pot' (1981, Introduction).

But as well as the suffering caused by disease and other similar causes, religions also often seek to offer explanations for suffering caused by human actions. Indeed, the two are sometimes linked, for example in the connection made between sin (human actions which produce unpleasant consequences) and suffering. Any direct connection between these two things is often discussed and then rejected in the biblical tradition. For example, in the book of Job, his suffering is shown to be caused by something other than his personal actions, despite the received wisdom of his friends to the contrary. Parts of the Christian gospel tradition likewise (such as Luke 13:1-5; John 9:1-3) serve to break the link between human action and pain as a consequence. Yet the picture is not simple, for a link between personal morality and suffering or divine judgement does surface in other biblical traditions, such as the Deuteronomic law (Deuteronomy 28:15-29:1) and some of the Jesus tradition (e.g. Matthew 9:2, 5) The consequence connection is not a simple one.

Clive Marsh and Gaye Ortiz
Explorations in Theology and Film

The question why

Just over four years ago I was caught in a very frightening thunderstorm. I was paddling an aluminium canoe down the Little Miami River in Ohio at the time and felt like a drowned rat when I reached my destination.

But that Little Miami River is one I'm fond of because Tecumseh, the last and greatest of all the Shawnee warrior chiefs, grew up by it.

One day he and his brother had a painful discussion about God. Tecumseh said, 'If God loves us and we love and respect him, why then does he permit the white man to hunt us down? Why does he let them destroy our forests and our crops? . . . Our homes and our families? Why?'

Many thousands of miles away in Africa warriors of the Masai tribe still ask the same kind of question.

Why, in the midst of all these good things, are there so many bad things? Look at all the trouble people cause one another. They argue and fight and hate. What kind of world is this? Is it just a place where people are played with, teased and crushed with sorrow; given many glimpses of happiness only to have it taken away?

And what of God? What is he really like?

Tecumseh the Shawnee chief, the Masai warriors, you and me, have one thing in common. We all desire a gracious, loving God to trust and worship.

Jesus died to show that we have one.

Ron Dale
Never on Sunday

The Gospel of the other chance and the threat of the last chance

Here is a parable at one and the same time lit by grace and close packed with warnings.

(i) The fig tree occupied *a specially favoured position*. It was not unusual to see fig trees, thorn trees and apple trees in vineyards. The soil was so shallow and poor that trees were grown wherever there was soil to grow them; but the fig tree had a more than average chance; and it had not proved worthy of it. Repeatedly, directly and by implication, Jesus reminded people that they would be judged according to the opportunities they had. C. E. M. Joad once said, 'We have the powers of gods and we use them like irresponsible school-boys'. Never was a generation entrusted with so much as ours and, therefore, never was a generation so answerable to God.

(ii) The parable teaches that *uselessness invites disaster*. It has been claimed that the whole process of evolution in this world is to produce useful things, and that what is useful will go on from strength to strength, while what is useless will be eliminated. The most searching question we can be asked is, 'Of what use were you in this world?'

(iii) Further, the parable teaches that n*othing which only takes out can survive.* The fig tree was drawing strength and sustenance from the soil; and in return was producing nothing. That was precisely its sin. In the last analysis, there are two kinds of people in this world – those who take out more than they put in, and those who put in more than they take out.

In one sense we are all in debt to life. We came into it at the peril of someone else's life; and we would never have survived without the care of those who loved us. We have inherited a Christian civilisation and a freedom which we did not create. There is laid on us the duty of handing things on better than we found them.

'Die when I may,' said Abraham Lincoln, 'I want it said of me that I plucked a weed and planted a flower wherever I thought a flower would grow.' Once a student was being shown bacteria under the microscope. He could actually see one generation of these microscopic living things being born and dying and another being born to take its place. He saw, as he had never seen before, how one generation succeeds another. 'After what I have seen,' he said, 'I pledge myself never to be a weak link.'

If we take that pledge we will fulfil the obligation of putting into life at least as much as we take out.

(iv) The parable tells us of *the Gospel of the second chance*. A fig tree normally takes three years to reach maturity. If it is not fruiting by that time it is not likely to fruit at all. But this fig tree was given another chance.

It is always Jesus' way to give a person chance after chance. Peter and Mark and Paul would all gladly have witnessed to that. God is infinitely kind to the one who falls and rises again.

(v) But the parable also makes it quite clear that *there is a final chance*. If we refuse chance after chance, if God's appeal and challenge come again and again in vain, the day finally comes, not when God has shut us out, but when we by deliberate choice have shut ourselves out. God save us from that!

William Barclay
The Daily Study Bible: The Gospel of Luke

Fourth Sunday in Lent

Luke 15:1-3, 11b-32

*The Father's
love knows no
limitations.*

'There was a man who had two sons.' Even in these days of rampant biblical illiteracy, many in the congregation will recognise the so-called 'Parable of the Prodigal Son' immediately from its opening sentence. The astonishing theological implications, the penetrating psychological insights, and centuries of representations and retellings make this among the most familiar of biblical passages. That very familiarity may prompt preachers to turn to other readings or to seek to wrench some new insight from the parable, but this parable can stand on its own. Simply to tell it once more is to preach the Gospel afresh.

. . . The younger son initiates the action in the parable. For reasons that remain unstated, he asks that his father give him the property that he stands to inherit on the father's death. Attempts to clarify the legal details of this situation are not terribly successful, given our limited knowledge of first century Palestinian practice. Clearly the younger son could expect to receive a fraction of what the elder son would receive.

Heedless of the advice of Sirach 33:19-23, the father accedes to the son's request. The son then leaves for a 'distant country' and squanders his inheritance. Because of assumptions often made of his behaviour, it is worth noticing that Jesus says only that the son was engaged in 'dissolute *(asotos)* living', which simply refers to inappropriate or undisciplined habits. Later on, the *elder* son accuses him of spending the father's money 'with prostitutes' (verse 30), but that charge should be read with some suspicion, since the elder son is scarcely a neutral observer of his brother's habits! What concerns Jesus is that the young man runs out of money and finds himself in a position utterly abhorrent to Jews, that of tending pigs.

Verse 17 marks the turning point in the younger brother's story: 'He came to himself.' The Greek expression has connotations very like those in contemporary English. What prompts the recognition is irrelevant, for what is important is that the son recognises his situation. As a hired hand in his father's household, he would be better off than at present.

The younger son's recognition of his situation stems from a perception of his own plight. It is crucial to see, however, that the father's recognition stems, not from the son's recognition (or from his repentance), but from the sheer joy of seeing his 'lost' son once more. The father, essentially absent from the story since verse 12, suddenly becomes the primary actor; he sees, he is filled with compassion, he embraces, he kisses. Before the son can complete his own confession of recognition, he calls for the best clothing and the best food and initiates a magnificent celebration. Both father and son are found.

Contemporary readers enjoy this moment in the parable, for we identify with the relief of the son and the joy of the father. What that enjoyment overlooks is that the father has acted with an exuberance that would merit scorn from his neighbours. The wise and dignified patriarch ought not to run to meet anyone. Certainly he ought to enquire about this son's behaviour, to ascertain his intent, to hear his confession before extending forgiveness. At the very least, the neighbours will mutter about cheap grace.

The older son does more than mutter, of course. For him there is no recognition scene. He does not run to meet his brother or even assent to his father's generosity. Instead, this 'loyal' son gives voice to the complaint of all 'good' children everywhere. He has worked, not as a hired hand, but as a slave. Never has he received even a goat for celebrating with his friends. But the 'bad' child has been rewarded simply for coming home when no other option was left to him anyway.

How to respond to the older son, who has indeed done everything right and never been rewarded for his goodness? Two options come to mind. The father might agree with the son's assessment and offer him his own fatted calf and grand celebration, humouring him into acceptance. Or the father might defend himself and scold the son for his selfishness, enjoining him to put aside such legalistic measurements.

Perhaps the most poignant moment of the father in the story is in relation to this good, loyal older son. When the son refuses to enter the celebration, the father takes the initiative to find him and plead with him (verse 28). When the son makes his case, the father does not disagree or belittle. He restates his own recognition but with these words of introduction: 'Son, you are always with me, and all that is mine is yours' (verse 31). The generosity lavished on the son who was lost outside the household is now extended also to the son who is lost within the household. The father's love knows no limitations.

Beverly R. Gaventa
Texts for Preaching: A Lectionary Commentary Based on the NRSV – Year C

The fact that Jesus' favourite form of instruction is the parable adds a further layer of density. For if these are stories told by Jesus, it is also true that they have the same sort of realism as the Gospels themselves. They do not tell us about magic and wonders, as do the apocryphal gospels, but about fathers and sons, masters and servants, poor men and rich. A few, it is true, are purely schematic, but the great ones, like the Gospels themselves, require not decipherment, but a response such as one would accord to Hamlet or Lear.

Let us look at what happens when we read a parable like that of the Prodigal Son. It may indeed be the case, as scholars have argued, that a certain tradition of reading it in purely ethical terms has caused us to overlook its allegorical and eschatological thrust. It may well be that the elder son is meant to stand for the Jews, the younger for the Christian Church. But what will first strike the reader is how well the parable conforms to the ethos of the rest of Luke's Gospel. His narrative everywhere strives to reconcile conflicting positions rather than, like Mark, to drive a wedge between them. Here he is not simply showing the elder son as cursed and the younger as blessed, but attempting to bring out the self-destructiveness of envy:

> And he said unto him, 'Son, thou art ever with me, and all that I have is thine. It was meet that we should make merry, and be glad; for this thy brother was dead, and is alive again, and was lost, and is found.' (Luke 15:31-32)

We may start to read this with the firm notion that the elder son 'stands for' this or that, but once we enter the narrative we have to abandon our preconceptions and surrender ourselves to it. This means that we have to experience what the father and *both* sons are going through. Though the elder son gets no chance to reply (perhaps *because*, as with the end of the book of Jonah, he gets no chance to reply), we are left with a sense of him struggling to come to terms with what has just happened. And whether we want to or not, we too enter his struggle. John Drury is absolutely right to see echoes of Joseph and his brothers here, and just as we saw that the problem with Judah was to come to terms with the fact that parental love is never distributed fairly, so it is here. The story makes something happen inside us; we are forced to shift our ground, to acknowledge feelings we too have had but perhaps never admitted, even to ourselves. The parable works upon us like this because it does not try to deny these feelings but rather to bring them out into the open and turn them into something positive rather than destructive and self-destructive. It is like all the great narratives, easy to read while teaching a hard lesson.

Bernard Harrison* has generalised from this insight to good effect: 'The parabolic narrative is . . . set askew to these underlying structures of social practices and their corresponding systems of concepts, so that the mind can find no resting place in the story; cannot find, in terms of the underlying scheme of practices and associated concepts, a clear point and structure in the story.'

That is, where our parable is concerned, 'the father's behaviour makes nonsense of common considerations of fairness and justice in the management of family affairs.' The parables, Harrison argues, force the mind to reach beyond accepted social and ethical structures 'to something which transcends these structures and constitutes a kind of judgement upon them'. Yet if we try to discover a general scheme from which to operate, try, that is, to generalise the ethical lessons of the parables, by saying, for example, that the dignity of the person has to come before any considerations of fairness, we find ourselves once more in a manifestly false position.

For suppose I wish to make this idea of the 'dignity of the person' into the basis of my relationships with other people: what exactly, in practical terms, am I to do?

'Am I, for example' (Harrison continues), 'with my strength of character, my moral vision and my remarkable powers of love transcending all commonplace moral relationships, to take charge of my weaker fellow men in the manner of Dostoevsky's Grand Inquisitor? Or more prosaically should I, if I have servants, treat them 'as one of the family', taking an interest in their lives, helping them in trouble and so on?'

The parable gives no help. And of course we all know how spiritual guidance can become spiritual tyranny and helping those in inferior social positions a hypocritical paternalism. So how can we know the difference? In other words, what is it the parables are teaching, and how are they doing it? Harrison's answer is to invoke the later Wittgenstein:

'Wittgenstein says that we show that we have understood the principle of a series by continuing the series. What we have in the parables . . . is precisely a series of narratives bound to one another by a single principle . . . How can we

*Parable and Transcendence, Bernard Harrison

show our understanding but by continuing, in other narratives or in our own lives, the series of which we have been given, as it were, the first few integers?'

In other words we cannot stand back as uninvolved spectators and simply work out the allegorical or ethical implications. Reading narratives of this kind means learning how to continue the series (or discovering that we do not know how to continue it). This is something every reader of the Bible grasps immediately and intuitively, but errors tend to creep in when we try to conceptualise our intuitions. There is, moreover, so much anxiety attached to the reading of religious documents that the natural processes of reading are interfered with by external notions of what it is one should be looking for far more than with other writings.

The parables bring us back to the question of authority. Kierkegaard, trying to rescue Christianity from a vague Romantic ethic, argued that it is not so much *what* is said in the New Testament that is important as the authority of the speaker. If I said you were to love your neighbour you could ignore me, is the form of his argument, but because it is Jesus who says it we have to obey. One can sympathise with Kierkegaard's project while disagreeing with this kind of argument . . . What the parables show us is that authority resides in the mode of telling. We read, or listen, because we have come to trust the teller. And, reading or listening, we are then constrained to carry on the series.

Gabriel Josipovici
The Book of God

Fifth Sunday in Lent

John 12:1-8

In relation to Jesus Christ, the words and actions of others have meanings and effects far beyond what may have been intended at the time.

No one notices that Mary has gone until she comes back, holding a slender clay jar in her hands. Without a word she kneels at Jesus' feet and breaks the neck of the jar, so that the smell of spikenard fills the room – a sharp scent somewhere between mint and ginseng. As everyone in the room watches her, she does four remarkable things in a row.

First she loosens her hair in a room full of men, which a respectable woman never does. Then she pours balm on Jesus' feet, which is also not done. The head, maybe, but not the feet. Then she touches him, a single woman caressing the feet of a rabbi – also not done, not even among friends – and then she wipes the salve off again with her hair. It is totally inexplicable, the bizarre end to an all-round bizarre act. Only in John's account does the woman have a name – Mary – and a relationship with Jesus. She is not a stranger, not a sinner, but his long-time friend – which makes her act all the more peculiar. He knows she loves him. He loves her too. So why this public demonstration, this odd pantomime in front of all their friends? It is extravagant. It is excessive. She has gone overboard as Judas is quick to note.

'Why was this ointment not sold for three hundred denarii and the money given to the poor?' That is what he wants to know. 'A day labourer and his family could live a year on that much money and here she has blown it all on your feet, for God's sake.' It reminds me of those wine auctions you read about in the newspaper sometimes – fabulously old bottles of Chateau Lafitte Rothschild discovered in some castle cellar, sold for thousands, even millions of dollars. These treasures are not to be drunk, however. They are to be bought and admired, maybe sold again. Heaven forbid that anyone should uncork one and pour it out, not even for the Last Supper.

'Leave her alone,' Jesus says, brushing all objections aside. 'She bought it that she might keep it for the day of my burial. You always have the poor with you, but you do not always have me.' Now that is about as odd a thing to say as anything Mary did. Here is the champion of the poor, who makes a regular practice of putting their needs ahead of his own, suddenly pulling rank. Leave her alone. Leave me alone. You will have the poor to look after till the end of time. Just this once, let her look after me, because my time is running out.

Barbara Brown Taylor
Bread of Angels

All four Gospels record this event (Matthew 26:6-13; Mark 14:3-9; Luke 7:36-39) but with important differences. Matthew and Mark place the story in Bethany, in the home of Simon the leper, where 'a woman' anoints Jesus' head. Anointing the head was, in the biblical tradition, the ceremony for the coronation of a king. Luke locates the act in Galilee in the home of Simon the Pharisee, where a sinful woman anoints Jesus' feet with tears and with ointment. Luke, like John, knows of Jesus' visits to the home of Martha and Mary, but Luke 10:38-42 and John 12:1-11 are otherwise quite different. For this message, we give our attention solely to the text before us. What would John have us hear?

First, in this Gospel the anointing at Bethany is a passion story, that is, it focuses on the death of Jesus. In this regard John is like Matthew and Mark but unlike Luke, whose anointing story is early, unrelated to Jesus' death, and is told to dramatise the nature of forgiveness. John not only locates the anointing within the passion narrative but weaves into the brief account all the dark foreboding of death. The scene is Bethany, where there waits an empty and available tomb (11:38-44); at the table is Lazarus to whom Jesus gave life, an act that will now cost Jesus his (11:4; 12:9-11); the time is Passover (12:1), which in this Gospel is death time; into this pleasant circle of friends comes Judas, the dark intruder, who, in the time and place of this Gospel, was viewed as betrayer and as thief (12:46); and finally there is Mary's act, an anointing for Jesus' burial. The approaching death of Jesus is clearly the governing theme of the story.

Second, this evangelist repeats a conviction common to the entire Gospel: in relation to Jesus Christ, the words and acts of others have meanings and effects far beyond what may have been intended at the time. Caiaphas, the High Priest, unwittingly prophesied that Jesus' death would save the world (11:49-52); the Pharisees unwittingly acknowledged that the whole world was going to Jesus (12:19). So here, Mary performs an act of hospitality, friendship, and gratitude for a brother restored; but in that act she unwittingly prepares Jesus for burial. However, this is a message not only in John, but in the entire Bible: God uses our acts beyond our intent or capacity. Abraham was hospitable to strangers and entertained angels unawares; two disciples from Emmaus invited a fellow traveller to rest and eat, and a supper became a sacrament; Paul wrote letters to the Churches, and a New Testament canon had its beginnings. We never know; our task is to speak and act in a way appropriate to faith's response to the occasion and to leave the conclusions to God.

Third, Mary's act will bless and plague every minister who has to counsel and evaluate similar acts of devotion and gratitude. Three hundred poinsettias announce Christmas; five hundred lilies embellish Easter; and then there are the memorial chimes, the memorial silver communion ware, and the memorial window. 'A gift in gratitude', says the donor; 'a sinful waste', says not only Judas but everyone who has looked into hollow eyes and heard the cries of a hungry child. Sound sense and Christian duty know the need is for potatoes, not perfume, and yet checking the shopping list even of the poor reveals that among flour, beans, and pork there will be candy and cologne. The appropriate word is not easily found or easily spoken.

Fred B. Craddock
Preaching Through the Christian Year: 'C'

Palm/Passion Sunday

Luke 22:14-23:56 or Luke 23:1-49

Whatever happens to us, we have a companion who has been there before us.

I once had the privilege of visiting a holy place in Jerusalem which not all tourists see – the Russian Orthodox part of the Garden of Gethsemane. It was an experience I shall never forget. Led by our guide, Canon Ronald Brownrigg, who was dressed in a long white cloak, we arrived by moonlight, seeing the great onion domes gleaming peacefully in the pale light of moon and stars.

We were asked to split up, either into twos and threes, or to be alone with our own thoughts in the Garden. I chose to be alone, sitting under an old, gnarled olive tree. I observed the figure of Ronald Brownrigg, a ghostly white in the moonlight, on his knees and praying hard. He struck me forcibly as a kind of Christ figure asking his Heavenly Father that the cup of suffering, the cross, might pass him by; nevertheless, not as he would choose, but as God would.

As I looked around at my fellow pilgrims scattered amongst the olive trees of Gethsemane I noticed that some appeared to be asleep due to the lateness of the hour and all the travelling they had done. My gaze came full circle, back to Canon Brownrigg still offering his prayers, and he reminded me of Jesus who, in the end, had to suffer and bear terrible pain all alone. There was no one to fully understand and share his saving work; and some words of an old hymn came to mind:

> 'There was no other good enough
> to pay the price of sin;
> he only could unlock the gate
> of heaven, and let us in.'

As I meditated on all of this and how all the disciples ran away at his arrest and crucifixion, the lonely figure in white, kneeling apart under the olive trees, was a most moving sight.

Ron Dale, 1998

We have, in the course of the Gospels, come to take it for granted that Jesus is someone essentially like ourselves: someone who can be kind but also gets angry; who has inexhaustible reserves of self-confidence yet can suddenly lose heart; someone who, like Joseph, knows he is right, and yet, like Joseph in the pit, can suddenly fear for his life. There are two moments in particular where Jesus' sense of failure and despair becomes, paradoxically, the index both of his own success and that of the evangelists. The first is the moment in the Garden of Gethsemane, when he 'began to be sore amazed, and to be very heavy' (Mark 14:33; cf. Matthew 26:36-46, Luke 22:39-46). The second is on the cross, when Jesus, rather than discoursing at length about his power, as he does in the apocryphal gospels, calls out in agony to God, asking why he has forsaken him, and then cries 'with a loud voice, and gave up the ghost' (Mark 15:37; cf. Matthew 27:50; Luke 23:46; John 19:30). Neither of these moments is conceivable in the apocryphal gospels. External reality and internal desire clash here, as they so often do in the Hebrew Bible, and it is the dream and desires that have to give way. At such moments, as with Phalti and David, we experience what it means to be a human being in this world of ours. Sensing how alone they are in their sorrow which no words can convey, we find we are at one with them.

Gabriel Josipovici
The Book of God

In his book *Messengers of God*, Holocaust survivor Elie Wiesel talks about the difference between Judaism and Christianity by comparing the two mountains that rise high in each one. For Judaism, it is Mount Moriah, where Abraham bound his son Isaac, his only son Isaac, whom he loved, and laid him on a bed of kindling wood. For Christianity, the mountain is Golgotha, where according to tradition, another father bound another only son to a deadly piece of wood. The difference between the two religions, Wiesel says, is that in the Jewish story the father does *not* kill the son, but in the Christian story he does, founding a religion that has gone on to use death as a means of glorifying God through centuries of inquisitions and holy wars. 'For the Jew, ' Wiesel says, 'all truth must spring from life, never from death.'

Whether you agree with him or not, he has a point. It is very difficult to reconcile a God of love with a God who wills a child's death, for whatever reason. How do you relate to a parent like that? I will tell you how: cautiously, if not fearfully. If God would do that to Jesus, whom God loved, what in the world might happen to those of us who have nothing at all to recommend us? And even if we had, wouldn't that be bad news too? Isn't the deep down message of the cross that if you are really good, like Jesus, you will die?

The earliest surviving picture of the crucifixion is a carved ivory tablet from northern Italy, made sometime between AD 420 and 430. It shows five figures, all short and stocky, their faces all but rubbed away by time. From right to left, they appear to be a Roman soldier, Christ on the cross, John the beloved disciple, Mary the mother of God, and right behind her, his limp hand brushing her elbow, Judas hanging from a tree, with his blood money scattered on the ground beneath his feet. He is clearly the villain in the scene, who has received his just reward, but in later crucifixion scenes it is more difficult to tell who is at fault . . .

In one classic arrangement, Jesus' friends are placed on his right side – his mother is there, and the beloved disciple, along with the converted centurion and the thief who repented. His enemies are placed on his left – the soldiers, the chief priests, the unrepentant thief. But none of them actually killed Jesus, unless you count the unlucky one whose job it was to hammer the nails. It is hard to say exactly who did. Was it Judas, who sold privileged information to the chief priests so that they knew where to arrest Jesus? Or was it Annas, who turned Jesus over to Caiaphas the high priest? Or was it Caiaphas, who turned Jesus over to Pilate because Jewish law forbade him to put Jesus to death himself? Or was it the mob, who chose to pardon Barabbas instead of Jesus, or was it Pilate, who gave in to public pressure and handed Jesus over to be crucified? Or was it the soldiers themselves, who carried out the death sentence and then squabbled over Jesus' clothes?

Pick one. Pick any one of them and you have still not solved the crime, which is as complicated as any murder mystery ever written. It is as hard as deciding who is to blame for any crime reported in the morning paper. Sure, the close-faced man in the mug shot is the one who did it, but who else is to blame? How about the mother or father who abused him before he could walk, or the teacher who graduated him when he could not write his name, or the bootlegger who sold him grain alcohol when he was twelve, or the pusher who introduced him to crack, or the judge who sent him to jail instead of to treatment, or the parole officer who misplaced his file?

Ask questions like these and it begins to sound as if the whole fallen creation is to blame, as if the real enemy – past, present and future – is everything in this world that is set against God. Like Judas and the mob, the enemy within us wants to deal with our disappointments by betraying those who have let us down. Like Annas and Caiaphas, the enemy in us wants to deal with our fear by condemning those who threaten us. Like Pilate, the enemy in us wants to deal with public pressure by throwing up our hands; and like the soldiers, the enemy within us wants to deal with the call to personal responsibility by just following orders. Whose will put Jesus on the cross? Was it God's? Or was it our own?

. . . Whose will put Jesus on the cross? God knows. But there is a direct possibility that it was Jesus' own magnificent will, by which he offered himself to us and offers himself to us still – a gift, a pardon, a release, a sacrifice, a meal – not to satisfy some cosmic bookkeeper in the sky but to leave no doubt about his feelings for us. By upending the cup that was handed to him, he made sure that wherever we go in this life and whatever happens to us, we have a companion who has been there before us, who has done ferocious battle with all the powers of darkness that try to separate us from God and from one another and *who has won*. Amen.

Barbara Brown Taylor
God in Pain: Teaching Sermons on Suffering

Easter Day

John 20:1-18 or Luke 24:1-12

The afterlife begins to make most sense 'after life' – when someone we love is dead on the premises.

To suggest in the early going of grief that the dead body is 'just' anything rings as tinny in its attempt to minimalise as it would if we were to say it was just a 'bad hair' day when the girl went bald from her chemotherapy. Or that our hope for heaven on her behalf was based on the belief that Christ raised his 'just a body' from the dead. What if, rather than crucifixion, he'd opted for suffering lowly self-esteem for the remission of sins? What if, rather than 'just a shell', he'd raised his personality, say, or the Idea of Himself? Do you think they'd have changed the calendar for that? Done the Crusades? Burned witches? Easter was a body and bloody thing, no symbols, no euphemisms, no half measures. If he'd raised anything less, of course, as Paul points out, the deacon and several others of us would be out of business or back to Saturday Sabbaths, a sensible diet and no more Christmases.

The bodies of the newly dead are not debris or remnant, nor are they entirely icon or essence. They are, rather, changelings, incubates, hatchlings of a new reality that bear our names and dates, our image and likenesses, as surely in the eyes and ears of our children and grandchildren as did word of our birth in the ears of our parents and their parents. It is wise to treat such new things tenderly, carefully, with honour.

And there are elements of the reverend clergy who have come to the enlightenment that, better than baptisms or marriages, funerals press the noses of the faithful against the windows of their faith. Vision and insight are often coincidental with demise. Death is the moment when the chips are down. That moment of truth that we die makes relevant the claims of our prophets and apostles. Faith is not required to sing in the choir, or bake cakes or building drives; to usher or deacon or elder or priest. Faith is for the time of our dying and the time of the dying of the ones we love. Those parsons and pastors who are most successful – those who have learned to 'minister' – are those who allow their faithful flocks to grieve like humans while believing like Jews or Christians or Muslims or Buddhists or variants of these compatible themes. They affirm the need to weep and dance, to blaspheme and embrace the tenets of our faiths, to upbraid our gods and to thank them.

Uncles find nickels behind our ears. Magic pulls rabbits out of hats. Any good talker can preach pie in the sky or break out the warm fuzzies when the time is right. But only by faith do the dead arise and walk among us or speak to us in our soul's dark nights.

So rabbi and preacher, pubbah and high priest do well to understand the deadly pretext of their vocation. But for our mortality, there'd be no need for churches, mosques, temples or synagogues. Those clerics who regard funerals as so much fuss and bother, a waste of time better spent in prayer, a waste of money better spent on stained glass or bell towers, should not wonder for whom the bell tolls. They may have heard the call but they've missed the point. The afterlife begins to make most sense *after life* – when someone we love is dead on the premises. The bon vivant, a-bob in his hot tub, needs heaven like another belly button. Faith is for the heart-broken, the embittered, the doubting and the dead. And funerals are the venues at which such folks gather. And some among the clergy have learned to like it. Thus they present themselves at funerals with a good cheer and an unambiguous sympathy that would seem like duplicity in anyone other than a person of faith. And I count among the great blessings of my calling that I have known men and women of such bold faith, such powerful witness, that they stand upright between the dead and the living and say, 'Behold I tell you a mystery . . .'

Thomas Lynch
The Undertaking

But the story sounded like a fairy tale.
(Luke 24:11, *Living Bible* translation)

Like the world of dreams or the world of memory, the world of the fairy tale is one of the worlds where most of us at one time or another lived, whether we read fairy tales as children or read them still or not, because *Cinderella* and the *Sleeping Beauty* are part of the air we breathe, and my inclination is to approach their world not as some kind of archaeologist, try-ing to excavate and analyse, but simply as a tourist guide, trying only to describe some of the principal sights to be seen.

To start with, the stories that do not tell us just about the world of the fairy tale in and of itself but tell us something about where it is located and how to reach it, most, if not all of them, seem to agree that it is not as far away as we might think and under the right circumstances not really all that hard to get to. The house where the children are playing hide-and-seek is an ordinary house just as the tent where Abraham and Sarah laughed until the tears ran down their cheeks was an ordinary tent. The young man Anodos woke up in his bedroom just as he'd awakened there hundreds of times beforehand; there was nothing particularly unusual about the time and place where Alice curled up beside the fire with her cat, Dinah, anymore than there was anything particularly unusual about Alice herself living in Victorian London, or about Dorothy Gale living in turn-of-the-century Kansas or about the cyclone that came twisting across the prairie as cyclones had come before and come still. The fairy-tale world that they all stepped into was very different from the world they normally lived in and very different, too, from the ordinary world of who they were inside themselves, their inner worlds, but the point seems to be that they did not have to go a great distance to enter it, any more than you have to go a great distance to enter the world of dreams – you just have to go to sleep – or the world of memory – you just have to cast your mind's eye backward and let it float up out of the past.

It might be more accurate to say that the world of the fairy tale found them, and found them in the midst of their everyday lives in the everyday world. It is as if the world of the fairy tale impinges on the ordinary world the way the dimension of depth impinges on the two-dimensional surface of a plane, so that there is no point on the plane – a Victorian sitting-room or a Kansas farm – that can't become an entrance to it. You enter the extraordinary by way of the ordinary. Something you have seen a thousand times you suddenly see as if for the first time like the looking glass over the mantle or the curtains of the bed. Furthermore, even the fairy tales that do not describe the actual passing from one world to the other as such, tell about people who, though they come in more exotic guise than most of us – poor woodchoppers and fair maidens – are people more or less like ourselves who suddenly, usually without warning, find themselves on the dim frontier. A bankrupt merchant picks a rose for his beautiful daughter and suddenly hears the terrible voice of a beast at his side. A brother and a sister lost in the wood come unexpectedly upon a house made of gingerbread. Cinderella, who lives in a loneliness and a despair all too familiar, is visited by an old woman who changes a pumpkin into a golden coach. In each case, a strange world opens up, and when they enter it things happen, that in the inner world of who they are and the outer world of where they ordinarily live their lives, couldn't possibly happen.

And what is it like, this world itself, once they have entered it? Maybe the first thing to say is that it is a world of darkness and danger and ambiguity. Almost the first thing that Lucy's brother Edmund sees when he too steps through the wardrobe into Narnia is a sleigh being pulled through the deep snow by reindeer and seated in the sleigh, wrapped in furs, a queen with a face as white as death who holds the whole land under her icy sway. There are fierce dragons that guard the treasure and wicked fairies who show up at royal christenings. To take the wrong turning of the path is to risk being lost in the forest forever, and an awful price has to be paid for choosing the wrong casket or the wrong door. It is a world of dark and dangerous quest where the suitors compete for the hand of the king's daughter with death to the losers, or the young prince searches for the princess who has slept for a hundred years, or the scarecrow, the tin man and the lion travel many a mile in search of the wizard who will make them whole, and all of them encounter on their way great perils that are all the more perilous because they are seldom seen for what they are. That is another mark of the fairy-tale world. The beautiful queen is really a witch in disguise, and to open the lid of the golden casket is to be doomed. Not only does evil come disguised in the world of the fairy tale but often good does too. Who could guess that the little grey man asking for bread is a great magician who holds in his hands the power of life and death?

. . . Beasts talk and flowers come alive and lobsters quadrille in the world of the fairy tale, and nothing is apt to be what it seems. And if this is true of the creatures that the hero meets on his quest, it is also true of the hero himself who at any moment may be changed into a beast or a stone or a king or have his heart turned to ice. Maybe above all they are tales of transformation, where all creatures are revealed in the end as what they truly are – the ugly duckling becomes a great white swan, the frog is revealed to be a prince, and the beautiful but wicked queen is unmasked at last in all her ugliness. They are tales of transformation where the ones who live happily ever after, as by no means everybody does in fairy tales, are transformed into what they have it in them at their best to be. The Beast falls sick for love of Beauty and lies dying in his garden when she abandons him until she returns out of compassion and says that for all his ugliness she loves him and will marry him, and no sooner has she kissed him on his glistening snout than he himself becomes beautiful with royal blood in his veins. The scarecrow gets his brain from the great and terrible Oz, the lion his courage, the tin man his heart. For better or worse, in the world of the fairy tale transformations are completed, and one thinks of the angel in the Book of Revelation who gives to each a white stone with a new name written on it which is the true and hidden name that he was named with even from the foundations of the world.

It is a world of magic and mystery, of deep darkness and flickering starlight. It is a world where terrible things happen and wonderful things too. It is a world where goodness is pitted against evil, love against hate, order against chaos, in a great struggle where often it is hard to be sure who belongs to which side because appearances are endlessly deceptive.

Yet for all its confusion and wildness, it is a world where the battle goes ultimately to the good, who live happily ever after, and where in the long run everybody, good and evil alike, becomes known by his true name.

Frederick Buechner
Telling the Truth: The Gospel as Tragedy, Comedy & Fairy Tale

117

Second Sunday of Easter

John 20:19-31

The only truths which have an absolute value in reality are those which the eyes of flesh cannot see and hands of flesh and blood can never handle.

My grandfather who was a lawyer once said, 'Let us observe truth, but only when truth is made manifest unto us.'

When Jesus called me, I heeded him, for his command was more potent than my will; yet I kept my counsel.

When he spoke and the others were swayed, I listened immovable. Yet I loved him.

Three years ago he left us, a scattered company to sing his name, and be his witnesses unto the nations.

At that time I was called Thomas the Doubter. The shadow of my grandfather was still upon me, and always I would have truth made manifest.

I would even put my hand in my own wound to feel the blood ere I would believe in my pain.

Now a man who loves with his heart yet holds a doubt in his mind, is but a slave in a galley who sleeps at his oar and dreams of his freedom, till the lash of the master wakes him.

I myself was that slave, and I dreamed of freedom, but the sleep of my grandfather was upon me. My flesh needed the whip of my own day.

Even in the presence of the Nazarene I had closed my eyes to see my hands chained to the oar.

Doubt is a pain too lonely to know that faith is his twin brother.

Doubt is a foundling unhappy and astray, and though his own mother who gave him birth should find him and enfold him, he would withdraw in caution and fear.

For Doubt will not know truth till his wounds are healed and restored.

I doubted Jesus until he made himself manifest to me, and thrust my own hand into his very wounds.

Then indeed I believed, and after that I was rid of my yesterday and the yesterdays of my forefathers.

The dead in me buried their dead; and the living shall live for the Anointed King, even for him who was the Son of Man.

Yesterday they told me that I must go and utter his name among the Persians and the Hindus.

I shall go. And from this day to my last day, at dawn and at eventide, I shall see my Lord rising in majesty and I shall hear him speak.

Kahlil Gibran, *Jesus the Son of Man*

Thomas, after the scandal of the crucifixion, was not at all disposed to believe a hearsay report of the resurrection. He had seen his first beliefs too roughly disabused to put any faith now in his equally deceived companions. And he answered to those who joyfully brought him the news, 'Except I shall see in his hands the print of the nails, and thrust my hand into his side, I will not believe'.

He had said at first, 'Except I shall see'. But he corrected himself at once; even his eyes could deceive him, and many men were cheated by visions. And his thoughts went on to a material test, to the coarse, brutal proof of fact – to put his finger there where the nails had been, to put his hand, his whole hand, where the lance had penetrated. To do as a blind man does who sometimes is less mistaken than men who see.

He rejected faith which is the higher vision of the soul. He even refused to have faith in the sight of his eyes, the most divine of our bodily senses. He put his faith only in his hands, flesh handling flesh. This double denial left him in the dark, groping like a blind man, until the Light made Man, through a supreme loving concession, gave him back light for his eyes and for his heart.

But this answer of Thomas has made him one of the most famous men in the world: for it is Christ's eternal characteristic to immortalise even those men who affronted him. All those afraid to touch spiritual concepts for fear of breaking them, all cheap sceptics, all the misers in academic chairs, all tepid half-wits stuffed with prejudices, all the faint-hearted, the sophists, the cynics, the beggars and the retort-cleaners of science; in short, all rush-lights jealous of the sun, all geese hissing at the flight of soaring falcons, have chosen for their protector and patron Thomas called Didymus. They know nothing of him except this: he does not believe in what he cannot touch. This answer seems to them the sum total of perfect good sense. Let anybody who wishes claim that he sees in the darkness, hears in the silence, speaks in solitude, lives in death; the followers of Thomas can get no such idea into their thick, dense heads. So-called 'reality' is their stronghold, and they will not budge from it. They prefer to fill their lives with gold which satisfies no hunger, with land in which they will occupy so small a cavity, with glory so fleeting a whisper in the silence of eternity, with flesh which is to become worm-eaten corruption, and with those noisy, magic discoveries which after enslaving men hurry them towards the formidable discovery of death. These and other things like them are 'real things', beloved by the devotees of Thomas. But perhaps if they had ever had the idea of reading what happened after that answer made by Thomas, they would have their doubts even of him who doubted the resurrection.

A week later, the disciples were in the same house as on the first occasion and Thomas was with them. He had hoped all that week that he also might be permitted to see the risen Master, and sometimes he had trembled, thinking that his answer might be the reason for Christ's absence; but suddenly there came a voice at the door, 'Peace be unto you'.

Jesus entered, his eyes seeking out Thomas: he came for Thomas, for him alone, because Christ's love for him was greater than any affront. And he called him by name and came up to him so that he could see him clearly, face to face: 'Reach hither thy finger, and behold my hands; and reach hither thy hand, and thrust it into my side: and be not faithless, but believing.'

But Thomas did not obey him. He dared not put his finger in the nail print nor his hand in the wound. He only said to him: 'My Lord and my God.'

With these words which seemed an ordinary greeting, Thomas admitted his defeat, fairer than any victory; and from that moment he was wholly Christ's. Up to that time he had revered him as a man more perfect than others, now he recognised him as God, as his God.

Then Jesus, who could not forget Thomas' doubt, answered, 'Thomas, because thou hast seen me, thou hast believed: blessed are they that have not seen, and yet have believed'.

This is the last of the Beatitudes and the greatest: blessed are they that have not seen and yet have believed, for in spite of the theories of the dissectors of corpses, the only truths which have an absolute value in reality are those which the eyes of the flesh cannot see and hands of flesh and blood can never handle. These truths come from on high and reach the soul directly: the man whose soul is locked shut cannot receive them, and will see them only on the day in which his body, with its five limited doorways, is like a shabby worn-out garment left upon a bed, in the interval before men hide it underground like a noisome afterbirth.

Thomas is one of the saints and yet he was not one of those blest by that Beatitude. An old legend relates that up to the day of his death his hand was red with blood, a legend true with all the truth of a terrible symbolical meaning, if we understand from it that incredulity can be a form of murder. The world is full of such assassins who have begun by assassinating their own souls.

Giovanni Papini
Life of Christ

Third Sunday of Easter

John 21:1-19

The first breakfast

On the whole, human beings are not so good at endings. We are much better at beginnings, when everything is new and exciting and full of possibilities. We like to hold babies better than we like to visit nursing homes. We like daybreak better than midnight. We like saying hello better than we like saying goodbye, but it is not as if we get to choose. We have plenty of both in our lives – beginnings and endings – roughly one of each for everything that really matters to us at all. So it is hard to blame John for lingering over his ending for a while. He wanted to make sure he had said it all. He wanted to make sure he had given us everything we would need to make it through the long nights we might have to wait before our next daybreak came. He did not know how long it would be for us, but he knew how long it had been for some of the disciples, so he decided to tell us a story about them that might help us out.

It happened sometime after the first Easter, no one knows when exactly, but long enough for the disciples to have left Jerusalem and made the long trek back to Galilee. It was home for them. It was the place where everything had begun for them, which made it the natural place for them to return once it seemed that everything had come to an end. There were seven of them, John says, which means that they were already coming apart at the seams, some of them going one direction while the others went another. These seven decide to go fishing, and that makes a lot of sense. Fishing is a good excuse for thinking, after all, for just sitting quietly and letting silence do its healing work. It is a good thing to do when you want to do nothing, nothing but sit and watch your cork drift, knowing that your line is down there somewhere in the deep waters, just like you are, waiting to catch something that will make it all worth while.

But fishing has added meaning for these seven, because it is their occupation – or was, before Jesus showed up. They do not fish for pleasure; they fish for a living. They do not fish with lines and hooks, they fish with big, heavy nets that smell of seaweed and dried fish scales, hauling them out of the bottom of the boat with hands that are calloused from

121

years and years of casting and knotting and straining against the ropes. So when they decide to go fishing, it is not a decision to daydream but a decision to return to their former way of life, to go back to the only thing they know how to do without him.

He is gone, after all. They have not seen him since Jerusalem, and while that was a powerful time none of them will ever forget, it is time to get on with life. Memory is one thing, but the future is another. His life on earth may have ended, but theirs have not, and they have to do something about getting food on their tables and roofs over their heads. He is gone, and it is time for them to start looking after themselves again.

So they go fishing, each of them sunk in his own thoughts as he climbs into the old familiar boat again, one of them reaching out to steady the prow while the others step inside and take their old familiar places, swamped with *déjà vu*. They have all been here before, but when? A hundred years ago or just yesterday? Maybe it was all a dream too good to be true, the way he walked up to them and spoke to them like someone they had known all their lives so that there was no doubt what they would do when he called out to them to follow.

They should have known better than to have believed it, to have staked their lives on something that could come to such a quick and bloody end. They should have known that it would all boil down to business as usual, back to the grind, all their wild, joyful expectation reduced to grim resignation as they go back to their nets. Only it does not work. They fish all night long without catching a single thing. Time after time their nets come up empty, a perfect match for their hearts. So now what? All they can do is sit in the dark and watch the sky change colour as the sun rises behind the hills. That is when they hear him. They cannot see him but they can hear him, someone, calling out to them across the water, guessing the truth – that they have no fish – and suggesting they try the other side of the boat. So they do, and the water begins to boil, all at once so dense with fish that some of them are pushed right out of the water, their shiny fins glinting in the morning light. It is *déjà vu* again: the boats, the nets, the stranger calling out to them. It is not the end after all, or else the end has led them back to the beginning again.

'It is the Lord!' says the beloved disciple, also guessing the truth, and what has been a dismal midnight scene becomes pure daybreak pandemonium. Peter throws himself into the water, leaving the others with all the hard work.

They scramble for their oars, catching him just as he reaches the beach, and what all of them arrive to find is a charcoal fire with fish on it, and bread, and Jesus, their beloved cook.

'Come,' he says to his wet, happy disciples, 'and have breakfast.' If you have ever eaten breakfast on a beach, then your imagination is already working overtime: copper coloured coals glowing in the sand, heat rising in the cold morning, wood smoke curling through your hair, fish sizzling over the low flames, the sound of the sea shushing behind you. It is a dream, all right, only a dream too good *not* to be true. He is not serving supper this time. That was the last meal of their old life together. This is the first meal of their new life together – a resurrection breakfast, prepared by the only one who knows the recipe.

I do not know why so many of Jesus' post-resurrection appearances have something to do with food, but they do. It happens twice in Luke – first on the road to Emmaus, where Jesus is made known to two of his disciples in the breaking of the bread, and then later, when he appears to them all and eats a piece of broiled fish in their presence. Then there is this meal, which is so reminiscent of that other meal by the Sea of Galilee, where he took five loaves and two fishes and fed everyone in sight.

Maybe it is because eating is so necessary for life, and so is he. Or maybe it is because sharing food is what makes us human. Most other species forage alone, so that feeding is a solitary business, but human beings seem to love eating together. Even when we are stuck alone with a frozen dinner, most of us will open a magazine or turn on the television just for company. It is, at any rate, one of the clues to his presence. There is always the chance, when we are eating together, that we will discover the risen Lord in our midst.

. . . 'It is the Lord.' That is what the beloved disciple said. How did he know? How does any of us know? By staying on the lookout, I suppose. By watching the shore, and the sky, and each other's faces. By listening really hard. By living in great expectation and refusing to believe that our nets will stay empty or our nights will last forever. For those with ears to hear, there is a voice that can turn all our dead ends into new beginnings.

'Come', that voice says, 'and have breakfast.'

Barbara Brown Taylor
Gospel Medicine

Fourth Sunday of Easter

John 10:22-30

Discourse and controversy at the Feast of Dedication

Stick with the flock. It is where the shepherd can be found, which makes it your best bet not only for survival but also for joy.

It was the Feast of Dedication. It is quite usual for this evangelist suddenly to insert a note of place and time in to the middle of a discourse (e.g. 6:59-61). The note may be regarded as an historical attachment of the raw material out of which the chapter is constructed. It attracted him because it contained certain features that lent themselves to symbolism. The Feast of Dedication took place in the month of Kislev (November-December). It was originally instituted to commemorate the purification of the temple from the pollutions of Antiochus Epiphanes (1 Maccabees 4:36, 39). The Feast is closely connected in Jewish thought with the Feast of Tabernacles. The ceremonial of both feasts was distinguished by the use of lights (2 Maccabees 10:6). The evangelist has already made use of the lights to introduce the saying, 'I am the Light of the World' (8:12; 9:5). Here he makes use of another feature of the ceremonial of the Feast of Dedication. The altar was rededicated. Here Jesus dedicates himself to death (verse 36). It was winter and Jesus was walking in the temple in Solomon's porch. The Jews therefore came round about him (verses 23f.). The scene is regarded as a symbolic picture of Jewish hostility, manifesting itself in the temple, the very centre of Jewish religion. The pressing round him of the Jews is not mere eagerness to hear his answer to their question (verse 24), but the manifestation of their hostile intentions. It was indeed winter, a display of cold and implacable enmity. Yet, in spite of all these men may do, the Shepherd's own sheep are safe, he and they are both in the Father's hand (verse 29). 'I and the Father are one' (verse 30), literally 'one thing'. The unity is a unity of invincible divine purpose, which is to be shared by the flock, the Church of God.

R. H. Strachan
The Fourth Gospel

The Voice of the Shepherd

One of my favourite names for Jesus is the Good Shepherd – the Lord who lays down his life for the sheep, who knows his sheep by name and who leads them beside the still waters. All of this makes for good sermons, except that somehow or another the preacher must deal with the congregation's likeness to sheep, which does not always sit well, since most of us think of sheep as slobbering, untidy *dumb* animals who exist only to be shaved or slaughtered.

Imagine my delight, then, when I discovered last Tuesday that someone I know actually grew up on a sheep farm in the Midwest, and that according to him sheep are not dumb at all. It is the cattle ranchers who are responsible for spreading that ugly rumour, and all because sheep do not behave like cows. According to my friend, cows are herded from the rear by hooting cowboys with cracking whips, but that will not work with sheep at all. Stand behind them making loud noises and all they will do is run around behind you, because they prefer to be led. You *push* cows, my friend said, but you lead sheep, and they will not go anywhere that someone else does not go first – namely, their shepherd – who goes ahead of them to show them that everything is alright.

Sheep tend to grow fond of their shepherds, my friend went on to say. It never ceased to amaze him, growing up, that he could walk right through a sleeping flock without disturbing a single one of them, while a stranger could not step foot in the fold without causing pandemonium. Sheep seem to consider their shepherds part of the family, and the relationship that grows up between the two is quite exclusive. They develop a language of their own that outsiders are not privy to. A good shepherd learns to distinguish a bleat of pain from one of pleasure, while the sheep learn that a cluck of the tongue means food, or a two-note song means that it is time to go home.

In Palestine today, it is still possible to witness a scene that Jesus almost certainly saw two thousand years ago, that of Bedouin shepherds bringing their flocks home from the various pastures they have grazed during the day. Often those flocks will end up at the same watering hole around dusk, so that they get all mixed up together – eight or nine small flocks turning into a convention of thirsty sheep. Their shepherds do not worry about the mix-up, however. When it is time to go home, each one issues his or her own distinctive call – a special trill or whistle, or a particular tune on a particular reed pipe – and that shepherd's sheep withdraw from the crowd to follow their shepherd home. They know whom they belong to; they know their shepherd's voice, and it is the only one they will follow.

'You do not believe, because you do not belong to my sheep,' Jesus says, but *listen* to what he says. He does not say we are in or out of the flock depending on our ability to believe, but the exact opposite, in fact. He says that our ability to believe depends on whether we are in or out of the flock, and there is every reason to believe that we are in, my woolly friends, if only because we are sitting right here with the flock this morning.

If that is the case, then chances are that the way true believers believe is the way most of us believe: valiantly on some days and pitifully on others, with faith enough to move mountains on some occasions and not enough to get out of bed on others. Since we believe in what we cannot know for sure, our belief tends to have a certain lightness to it, and openness to ambiguity and a willingness not to be sure about everything. Our belief is less like certainty than trust or hope. We are betting our lives on something we cannot prove, and it is hard to be very smug about that. Most of the time the best we can do is to live 'as if' it were all true and when we do, it all becomes truer somehow.

Be patient with yourself, and while you are at it, be patient with the rest of us too. You cannot follow a shepherd all by yourself, after all. You are stuck with this flock or some flock, and everyone knows that sheep are, well, sheep. They panic easily and refuse to be pushed. They make most of their decisions based on their appetites and they tend to get into head-butting contests for no reason at all.

But stick with the flock. It is where the shepherd can be found, which makes it your best bet not only for survival but also for joy.

Barbara Brown Taylor
The Preaching Life

Fifth Sunday of Easter

John 13:31-35

Jesus now becomes the distinctive definition of love.

France, 1861. A young silk breeder has to travel overland to distant Japan, out of bounds to foreigners, to smuggle out healthy silkworms, when an epidemic has wiped out the European hatcheries. He sets eyes on his Japanese host's concubine and is at once in love, with never a word spoken (from the cover of *Silk*). Hervé Joncour receives a beautiful and tender love letter and leaves his wife to go searching for the concubine. Before doing so however, he and his wife take a holiday in Nice. This is how it is described:

At the end of June Hervé Joncour left with his wife for Nice. They took a small villa by the seashore. This had been Hélène's wish, convinced as she was that the tranquillity of an out-of-the-way retreat might succeed in alleviating the depression that seemed to have taken hold of her husband. She had nonetheless been shrewd enough to make it pass for a whim of his own, thus according to the man she loved the satisfaction of seeing his whim humoured.

They enjoyed three weeks of modest, unassailable contentment. On the days when the heat was sufficiently moderate they would hire a trap and take pleasure in discovering the villages hidden up in the hills, from where the sea looked like a backdrop of coloured paper. Occasionally they would venture into town for a concert or social event. One evening they accepted an invitation from an Italian baron who was celebrating his sixtieth birthday with a formal dinner at the Hotel Suisse. They had reached the dessert when Hervé Joncour happened to look across to Hélène. She was seated on the other side of the table, next to a charming English gentleman who, curiously, sported in the buttonhole of his tailcoat a little garland of tiny blue flowers. Hervé Joncour observed him lean towards Hélène and whisper something in her ear. Hélène burst out laughing, the prettiest of laughs, and as she did so she leaned slightly towards the English gentleman, brushing his shoulder with her hair, in a gesture completely devoid of embarrassment, but suggesting rather a disconcerting meticulousness. Hervé Joncour looked down at his plate. He could not but notice that his hand, which tightly grasped a silver dessert spoon, was indubitably shaking.

Later in the smoking-room Hervé Joncour, staggering on

account of the excessive alcohol he had drunk, approached a man who was sitting alone at the table staring in front of him with a rather absent look on his face. He leant towards him and slowly remarked: 'I have something most important to tell you, monsieur. We're all disgusting. We're all marvellous, and we're all disgusting.' The man was from Dresden. He dealt in calves and understood little French. He burst into uproarious laughter, nodding repeatedly: it looked as if he would never stop.

Hervé Joncour continued their stay on the Riviera into the beginning of September. They left the little villa with regret because amid those walls *their call to love each other had lain lightly upon them.* (Compiler's italics.)

Alessandro Baricco
Silk

It may seem a bit strange to be directed during the Easter season to texts that are set in the last few moments of Jesus' life. One would think them more appropriate for Lent than for Easter. In John's Gospel, however, Jesus' farewell conversations with his disciples immediately before the crucifixion regularly speak of his 'departure', a term that includes his death, resurrection and return to the Father. The language is typical of John's Gospel, where the incarnation is depicted as a journey from the Father to the world and back to the Father (for example 13:1). Thus today's selection (John 13:31-35) is particularly apt for the season between Easter and Pentecost.

First, we must observe the context. The verses preceding the assigned lesson recount Jesus' prediction of Judas' betrayal, concluding with his departure from the group and the poignant observation, 'And it was night.' The verses following the lesson relate Jesus' prediction about Peter's denials. Between these two dark and foreboding brackets comes the declaration of Jesus' glorification (13:31).

The irony should not be lost. At the darkest moment in the narrative, when the anticipation of human failure seems certain because colleagues are conspiring to undermine their leader, the announcement is made of Jesus' glorification. His moment of exaltation, honour, and praise is set against the backdrop of betrayal and denials.

But the prominent 'now' of 13:31 has a double reference.

On the one hand, Jesus' glorification comes at a time of incredible disloyalty and faithlessness. On the other hand, it is the right moment, the moment of fulfilment, the time for returning to the Father (13:1). Nothing has been left undone or incomplete; as Jesus' last words from the cross will put it, 'It is finished' (19:30). The betrayal and denials do not deter or thwart the divine intention.

. . . The anticipated actions of Judas, Peter, the religious authorities, Caiaphas, Pilate, and the soldiers only serve as a foil for the *real* action, namely, the reciprocal disclosure of the identity of Son and Father.

Then there is an appropriate word for the disciples who are faced with the impossibility of following Jesus at his departure: 'I give you a new commandment, that you love one another' (13:34). The pain of separation is addressed with a reminder about their mutual relationships in the community of faith. But if the commandment is a reminder (see Leviticus 19:18) then why is it called 'new'? What distinguishes it from the many other places in the Bible where people are told to love one another?

Two features about the commandment make it 'new.' (1) A new and unparalleled model for love has been given the disciples: 'Just as I have loved you, you also should love one another.' Jesus, who had loved his own in the world and was returning to the Father, 'loved them to the end' (John 13:1), or, as it might be translated, 'loved them to the uttermost' (see 15:13). In Jesus the disciples have a concrete, living expression of what love is. Love can no longer be trivialised or reduced to an emotion or debated over as if it were a philosophical virtue under scrutiny. Jesus now becomes the distinctive definition of love. (2) Jesus' love for the disciples not only provides a new paradigm; it also inaugurates a new era. The Johannine eschatology is tilted heavily in a 'realised' rather than a futuristic direction. While one can speak of continuity with the past and hope for the future, the present moment is the decisive one. Jesus' coming opens up a radically new and different situation, in which the life of the age to come (eternal life) is no longer only to be awaited as a future possibility (for example 17:3). As the writer of 1 John put it, 'I am writing you a new commandment that is true in him and in you, because the darkness is passing away and the true light is already shining' (1 John 2:8).

At the centre of the new era is the community established by Jesus, the intimate (though at times unfaithful) family, whom he affectionately addresses as 'little children' (John 13:33). What holds the family together and makes it stand out above all the rest is the love members have for one another – dramatic, persistent love like the love Jesus has for them.

It troubles interpreters sometimes that the command Jesus left is not a command to love the world or to love one's enemies, but to love one another. In other places the Johannine narrative expresses the divine concern for the world (3:16) and directs the disciples to engage it (20:21), but here Jesus' concern is for the community itself. He makes love the distinguishing mark of the Church, that characteristic of its life by which even outsiders can discern its authenticity.

Needless to say, this text lays a heavy challenge before the contemporary Church to evidence in the world a unique quality of life and action. Lest that becomes too burdensome a challenge, the Church needs also to be reminded that it is itself the object of unconditional love ('Just as I have loved you . . .').

Charles B. Cousar
Texts for Preaching: A Lectionary Commentary Based on the NRSV – Year C

Sixth Sunday of Easter

John 14:23-29 or John 5:1-9

I am the Way, my son, Via Crucis, Via Pacis meet and are one.

We must reflect further upon the Spirit as the spirit of freedom. Again, it is no coincidence that the Christian tradition has explored the notion of freedom (expressed more recently, and with different nuances, as 'liberation') in terms of the work of God as Spirit. . . . The spirit in Christian theology has symbolised release and free expression in individual experience and in corporate worship, building upon insights which reverberate through the Bible (e.g. 1 Samuel 19:19-24; John 8:31-36, 14:25-7, 15:26; 1 Corinthians 12; 2 Corinthians 3:17). This has frequently led to the opposite of what the Apostle Paul was struggling to emphasise to the Corinthian Church. Instead of the unity which was needed as the expression of oneness in Christ, the strangeness of the Spirit's effects upon believers often seemed to cause disunity. Nevertheless, such an emphasis is crucial within an understanding of the Spirit as the Spirit of God. The strange Spirit which is God at work freeing people from what restricts and oppresses them will not be bound by human institutions, not even the Church, necessary though such institutions may be . . . God questions the rationality of human enterprise and the desire for order and control through the work of the Spirit in human affairs. Shirley (Valentine) can only experience her own release through the costly (and irrational) risk-taking of her flight to Greece and the challenge to the institutional structure of her own marriage through her brief encounter with Costas. Whether the specifics of her actions can be said to be 'the will of God' is open to question. But the work of the Spirit, as the spirit of freedom, nevertheless presses her to break out of her present situation, as a direct result of her prayer and quest for relationship. On this understanding, the Spirit as the spirit of freedom is none other than the redemptive Spirit of Christ, who rescues (saves) people from what constrains and crushes them . . . This theme of liberation/redemption . . . is often a dominant theme in films (*One Flew over the Cuckoo's Nest*, *The Shawshank Redemption*) and frequently dealt with more darkly. In approaching *Shirley Valentine* from a pneumatological perspective, however, and drawing attention to the link between spiritual presence and liberation, we are also suggesting where explorations of other films, whose focus is redemption/liberation, might usefully lead.

(Excerpt from a discussion on the film *Shirley Valentine* from
a theological perspective.)
Clive Marsh and Gaye Ortiz
Explorations in Theology and Film

My peace I leave with you

Thy peace! Thou pale, despised Christ!
What peace is there in thee,
nailed to the cross that crowns the world,
in agony?

No peace of home was thine; no rest
when thy day's work was done.
When darkness called the world to sleep
and veiled the sun,

no children gathered round thy knee,
no hand soothed care away:
thou hadst not where to lay thy head
at close of day.

What peace was thine?
Misunderstood, rejected by thine own,
pacing thy grim Gethsemane,
outcast and lone.

What peace hast thou to give the world?
There is enough of pain;
always upon my window beats
the sound of rain.

The source of sorrow is not dried,
nor stays the stream of tears,
but winds on weeping to the sea,
all down the years.

For millions come to Golgotha
to suffer and to die,
forsaken in their hour of need,
and asking, Why?

Man's Via Crucis never ends,
earth's Calvaries increase,
the world is full of spears and nails,
but where is peace?

Take up thy cross and follow me
I am the Way, my son,
Via Crucis, Via Pacis
meet and are one.

G. A. Studdert Kennedy
The Unutterable Beauty

There is no wrong day to relieve human misery.

The preacher who chooses to use the alternate text will want
to fix in mind that this is a Johannine story with all the traits
of a healing account in that Gospel. John 5:1-9 records a sign
act followed by a discourse on the issue aroused by that act
(verses 10-18). The invalid is like others we meet in this
Gospel (Jesus' mother, Nicodemus, the Samaritan woman,
Martha and Mary, the Twelve), in that expectation of something from Jesus is at one level (aid in entering the pool),
whereas Jesus responds in a way different from and greater
than the expectation. Also as a sign act the story is designed
to reveal truth about God, in this instance regarding Sabbath
activity (verses 9b-18). And because it is a sign act, all the initiative is with Jesus; the attention is upon him and not on the
invalid or his situation. One will want to avoid, therefore,
finding the causes for the healing in the circumstances. Calling the man a hypochondriac is a modern psychological
imposition on the story. Neither do we know the invalid's
character. And this is certainly not a 'Your faith has made
you well' story; the man did not even know who healed him
(verse 13), and when he learned it was Jesus, he testified
against him as a Sabbath breaker (verse 15).

The story is about Jesus revealing a God who continues
to act for human good, even on the Sabbath. There is no
wrong day to relieve human misery (verse 17). In this case
Jesus acts to heal a man who is a threefold victim. He is a victim of paralysis. He is a victim of a cruel tradition that offers
healing only to the first one in the pool. And who would that

be? Not the severely crippled but someone able to move quickly, perhaps suffering from chapped lips or a hangnail. And he is a victim of a kind of religion that honours its rules over human need.

When Jesus acts favourably towards one in whom no reasons for the favour can be found, we call it grace, radical grace.

Fred B. Craddock
Preaching Through the Christian Year: 'C'

Seventh Sunday of Easter

John 17:20-26

We believe in the purpose of God to unite in Christ everything, spiritual and secular.

Verses 20-26 represent a branching out from the disciples of John's acquaintance to those who would come to believe through their evangelising efforts. John cannot possibly have Jesus pray for all who believe in him, 'each in his own way', as the modern phrase has it. Such latitude would be incomprehensible to John. He looks for unity of belief in Jesus' words as he sees it. A variety of christologies he both knows and deplores. A variety of Churches he could have no part or lot with. John's only prayer is for unity in God and Christ as he conceives it, namely, in terms of right faith.

The prayer is prayed with increasing confidence by Christians to include all who believe in Jesus on any terms, indeed, anyone anywhere in the world. There was a time when it was prayed *against* other believers in what may have been a more authentically Johannine spirit. But now that it is realised how unfaithful to Jesus all believers are, John 17 is being prayed in a newer, humbler tone.

Do preachers regularly invite their congregants to anything like the high standard of John 17, which actually is 13-16 summed up? Whether they do or not, they should. It may not be done in a sectarian spirit, as if the preacher has 'seen' and 'known' the Father through Jesus quite as the evangelist has and hence has a unique possession of the truth. This possession of eternal life should be preached, but in a state of awe that the evangelist and his company did so know God, and in hope that preacher and hearer may do the same.

It was a remarkable time in the history of one infant Church, the Johannine, when a vision of the world as it might be and the history of one actual community came together. The congruence of the world believed in and the world lived in may already have passed by the time the Gospel was written. Its author wants believers to live in hope until the parousia, but knows that the only way to make any sense out of that strange concept of the final coming is to live it *now*: in an 'everlasting life' of entertaining the Spirit as a guest, not unlike the 'ongoing now' (*nunc fluens*) of the philosophers. Go with the flow, says the evangelist. All the way to heaven is heaven because Jesus said, 'I am the way'.

The lengthy discourse of 13:31-17:26 could be the purist gnostic speculation if it were not for John's gift for keeping one foot firmly planted in history. A Church that forgets either Johannine realism or Johannine other-worldliness will find itself off the way, into the mire on the right or left of the path.

It is literally worth one's life to be a member of a Church like the Johannine Church.

Gerard Sloyan
'John'

One world

We believe in one world,
full of riches meant for everyone to enjoy.
We believe in one race,
the family of humankind,
learning to live together by the way of self-sacrifice.
We believe in one life,
exciting and positive,
which enjoys all beauty, integrity and science,
uses the discipline of work to enrich society,
harmonises with the life of Jesus
and develops into total happiness.

We believe in one morality: love,
the holiness of sharing the sorrows and joys of others,
of bringing people together as true friends,
of working to get rid of the causes of poverty, injustice,
    ignorance and fear;
Love: the test of all our thoughts and motives.
Love: which is God forgiving us, accepting us,
    and making us confident under the Holy Spirit's control.

We believe in Jesus, and the Bible's evidence about him,
whose life, death and resurrection prove God's permanent
    love for the world,
who combines in himself life, love, truth, humanity,
    reality and God,
saving, guiding, reforming and uniting all people
    who follow the way.

We believe in the purpose of God
to unite in Christ everything, spiritual and secular,
to bring about constructive revolution in society,
    individuals and nations
and to establish world government
    under his loving direction.

Subir Biswas

Pentecost

John 14:8-17 (25-27)

The Spirit is no other than God himself . . . God's personal closeness to human beings.

There is no mechanical solution to true spirituality or the Christian life. Anything that has the mark of the mechanical upon it is a mistake. It is not possible to say, 'Read so many chapters of the Bible every day, and you will have this much sanctification'. It is not possible to say, 'Pray so long every day, and you will have a certain amount of sanctification'. It is not possible to add the two together and to say, 'You will have this big a piece of sanctification . . .' The Christian life, true spirituality, can never have a mechanical solution. The real solution is being cast up into the moment-by-moment communion, personal communion, with God himself; and letting Christ's truth flow through me through the agency of the Holy Spirit.

Francis Schaeffer
True Spirituality

Creativity and spirituality are intimately related. One cannot do without the other. Traditional society has required certain of its members to behave spiritually without becoming at the same time creative . . . Liberation is a deeply spiritual matter. Basically, it is the inter-relatedness between spirituality and creativity that poses a radical challenge to the institution called the Church.

A Church with true spirituality is a creative Church. It is creative not only in matters strictly religious but must be creative also in all areas and dimensions of human life. A truly creative spirituality is one that enables us to realise and experience the divine presence in all that we do, not only in religious worship, but also in all realms of our activities. It breaks down the barrier between the sacred and the profane, the religious and the nonreligious, the holy and the secular. To encounter other human beings in the rough and tumble of this world, to experience life in the midst of death, and to perceive meaning in the face of meaninglessness – this is spirituality.

Choan-Seng Song
Third Eye Theology

Unholy and Holy Spirit

We cannot overlook the fact that any talk of the Holy Spirit is so unintelligible to many today that it cannot even be regarded as controversial. But there can also be no doubt that the blame for this situation may be laid to a large extent on the way in which the concept of the Holy Spirit has been misused in modern times both by the official Church and by pious individuals.

When holders of high office in the Church did not know how to justify their own claim to infallibility, they pointed to the Holy Spirit. When theologians did not know how to justify a particular doctrine, a dogma or a biblical term, they appealed to the Holy Spirit. When mild or wild fanatics did not know how to justify their subjectivist whims, they invoked the Holy Spirit. The Holy Spirit was called in to justify absolute power of teaching and ruling, to justify statements of faith without convincing content, to justify pious fanaticism and false security in faith. The Holy Spirit was made a substitute for cogency, authorisation, plausibility, intrinsic credibility, objective discussion. It was not so in the early Church or even in the medieval. This simplification of the role of the Holy Spirit is a typically modern development, emerging on the one hand from Reformation fanaticism and on the other hand from the defensive attitude of the great Churches, seeking to immunise themselves from rational criticism.

But we may look at the matter in another way. In primitive Christendom how was the fact to be expressed that God, that Jesus Christ, is truly close to the believer, to the community of faith: wholly real, present, effective? To this the writings of the New Testament give a unanimous response, but without regard to power claims for Church, theology and piety: God, Jesus Christ are *close in the Spirit* to the believer, to the community of faith; present in the Spirit, present through the Spirit and indeed as Spirit. It is not then through our memory, but through the spiritual reality, presence, efficacy of God, of Jesus Christ himself. What is the meaning of 'Spirit' here?

Perceptible and yet not perceptible, invisible and yet powerful, real like the energy-charged air, the wind, the storm, as important for life as the air we breathe: this is how people in ancient times frequently imagined the 'Spirit' and God's invisible working. According to the beginning of the creation account, 'spirit' (Hebrew, *ruah*; Greek, *pneuma*) is the 'roaring', the 'tempest' of God over the waters. 'Spirit' here does not mean in the idealistic sense a capacity for knowledge or a psychological power, still less an immaterial, intellectual or ethical principle, and certainly not spiritual or mental reality in the modern sense as opposed to sensible, corporeal reality or to nature. 'Spirit' as understood in the Bible means the force or power proceeding from God, which is opposed to 'flesh', to created, perishable reality: that invisible force of God and power of God which is effective creatively or destructively, for life or judgement, in creation and in history, in Israel and in the Church. It comes upon human beings powerfully or gently, stirring up individuals or even groups to ecstasy, often effective in extraordinary phenomena, in great men and women, in Moses and the 'judges' of Israel, in warriors and singers, kings, prophets and prophetesses.

But the age of the great prophets was long past in Israel. In early Judaism at the time of Jesus, according to rabbinical teaching, the Spirit had ceased to be active with the last prophetical writers. The Spirit was expected again only for the end-time and then, according to the famous prophecy of Joel 3, he would be 'poured out' not only over individuals but over the whole people. Is it surprising that the primitive Christian communities, who had seen Jesus as the great Spirit-bearer (at his baptism?), regarded this prophetic experience as having been fulfilled in the fact of their existence? The descent of the Spirit was therefore seen as the signal for the beginning of the end-time and indeed – as it was written in Joel – not only for the privileged few, but also for the non-privileged: not only for the sons, but also for the daughters; not only for the old, but also for the young; not only for the masters, but also for the menservants and the maids.

This Spirit then is not – as the word itself might well suggest – the spirit of man, his knowing and willing living self. He is the Spirit of God, who as Holy Spirit is sharply distinguished from the unholy spirit of man and his world. It is true that he has dynamistic and animistic features which are scarcely clearly separable: he appears sometimes as impersonal force (*dynamis*), sometimes as personal being (*anima*). But in the New Testament he is certainly not any sort of magical, substance-like, mysterious supernatural aura of a dynamistic character or even a magical being of animistic character. The Spirit is no other than God *himself*: God close to humankind and the world, as comprehending but not comprehensible, self-bestowing but not controllable, life-giving but also directive power and force. He is then not a third party, not a thing between God and humankind, but God's personal closeness to human beings. Most misunderstandings of the Holy Spirit arise from setting him apart from God mythologically and making him independent. In this respect the Council of Constantinople itself in 381, to which we owe the extension of the Nicene Creed to include the Holy Spirit, expressly emphasises the fact that the Spirit is of one nature with the Father and the Son.

Primitive Christendom's view of the Holy Spirit however is not uniform in its details. The operation of the Holy Spirit appears in a very different light particularly in the Lucan Acts of the Apostles and in Paul.

Luke is very interested in the operation of the Spirit, particularly in its extraordinary forms and, as we saw, places an interval of time between Easter and a Christian Pentecost with the reception of the Spirit (is the 'driving wind' of the Spirit meant to recall God's 'tempest' before all creation?). In the Acts of the Apostles the Spirit appears frequently as the natural consequence of becoming a believer and receiving baptism. But at the same time he appears also as the source of the extraordinary charismatic force which is ascribed in special cases to the Spirit of God, as a special gift for certain supplementary activities. It is the Spirit who gives a mandate, capability, power, authorisation, continuity in the Church, and the imposition of hands is the sign of this.

The Holy Spirit is God's Spirit. He is God himself, as gracious power and force, gaining dominion over the mind and heart of man, in fact the whole man, becoming inwardly present to man and giving effective testimony of himself to man's spirit.

As God's Spirit he is also the Spirit of Jesus Christ exalted to God: through him Jesus is the living Lord, the model for the Church and the individual Christian. No hierarchy, no theology, no fanaticism, seeking to invoke the 'Spirit' without regard to Jesus, to his word, his behaviour and his fate, can in fact lay claim to the Spirit of Jesus Christ. The spirits therefore are to be tested and discerned in the light of this Jesus Christ.

As Spirit of God and of Jesus Christ, for *humanity* he is never identified with humanity's own possibilities, but is *force, power and gift of God.* He is not an unholy spirit of humankind, spirit of the age, spirit of the Church, spirit of office, spirit of fanaticism, but is and remains always the Holy Spirit of God, who moves where and when he wills and does not permit himself to be used to justify absolute power of teaching and ruling, to justify unsubstantiated theology, pious fanaticism and false security of faith.

It is the person who truly submits in faith to the message

and thus to God and his Christ who receives the Holy Spirit. He does not operate in a magical, automatic way, but allows a free consent. So far as baptism is sign and sacrament of faith, baptism and reception of the Spirit go together. For baptism is an expression of readiness wholly and entirely to submit to the name of Jesus, in fulfilment of the will of God for the well-being of our fellow men.

As Christians we believe in the Holy Spirit (*'credo in Spiritum Sanctum'*) who is in the holy Church, but not *in* the Church. The Church is not God. We ourselves, the believers, are the Church. In the strict sense we believe, not in ourselves, but in God, who in his Spirit makes possible the community of believers. In the light of the sanctifying Spirit we believe *the* holy Church (*'credo sanctam Ecclesiam'*).

Hans Kung
On Being a Christian

Trinity Sunday

John 16:12-15

Introducing men to the Trinity

> *Baptise men everywhere in the name of the Father
> and the Son and the Holy Spirit.*
> (Matthew 28:19 NEB)

Here is a young man, a Communist, well-informed, ardent, disciplined, one of the most promising of his group, being instructed how he is to conduct himself in the industry where he has just been signed on for employment. 'I want you, wherever you go, and among whatever people you find yourself, to seize every opportunity to introduce them to the Marxist interpretation of life. It is what you believe and what you are confident will be for their benefit if they believe it too.'

We begin with this illustration in order to deal with the word 'baptise' in the text, because if we do not deal with it, it is likely to cause a deaf ear to be turned in its direction. Baptism is a 'churchy' word, an ecclesiastical word. But suppose the analogy be accepted, then here is the young Christ, well-informed, ardent and disciplined, addressing himself to his disciples gathered round him. 'I want you, wherever you go, and among whatever people you find yourselves to seize every opportunity to introduce them to belief in the Father, the Son and Holy Spirit. It is what you believe in yourselves and what you are confident will be for their benefit if they believe it too.'

And we are astonished! What difference can such a belief possibly make to people if they are introduced to it? What good can it possibly do to a bus driver, a refrigerator salesman, a dressmaker, or the manager of a laundry, to be introduced to the Father, the Son and the Holy Spirit? 'All the difference in the world', will be the honest answer of those who have experienced it for themselves. It alters a person's complete outlook on life, providing a purpose almost wholly lacking before. But not immediately. Do not let us deceive ourselves. It is no easy stance to come to the point of making. There are formidable difficulties to be overcome.

1. *God the Father*. Take first the belief in God the Father. Is the Divine Fatherhood in any way obvious? That is to say, does God's care of people stand out a mile? Because that is what fatherhood means in this connotation. What man would

143

come to this conclusion if he were born on the pavements in Calcutta, and saw no prospect of living or of dying anywhere better than the pavements of Calcutta! Nor is there need to travel to Calcutta to encounter this problem. Children are born in every country of the world deformed, crooked and diseased, with no hope of a full life. If anyone has not encountered the sharp point of this aspect of human existence they should read Archie Hill's *Love Within Closed Walls*. It concerns a spastic child who lived till he was 27 and then developed cancer. For all the long twenty-seven years he was unable to hear, speak, turn his head or perform his natural functions without help – almost a thing. Where does God come in all this? Or for that matter in a world in which there is the tsetse fly, the hookworm, bacteria and rabies? Whatever then we may say about belief in God the Father, it certainly is not trite, sickly or sentimental. Indeed, the first words of the Apostles' Creed are almost a broadside on experience. 'I believe in God the Father Almighty, maker of heaven and earth.' Well might we ask how any observant person could have got themselves to the place of writing this down. Take up the newspaper any day, there is no edition without the report of some calamity somewhere. And the situation is not as one little girl posed the question at one of the BBC's popular 'Any Questions' sessions – 'Why do not the newspapers report happy events?' The truth is, the ugly ones are more newsworthy, because they actually exist. 'O God', we feel the urge to cry out, if we are sensitive at all to others' pain, 'Why did you make a world like this?'

But at the end of the day when we have quietened down from our resentment, shouting and rebellion, we know in our bones that if we do not hold to the belief in God as Father against all odds – yes, even in the face of that man who found it in his heart to catch a young woman's back in the sights of his rifle just outside Belfast and pull the trigger, while she was pregnant and just out walking with her father – if we do not believe in 'God the Father Almighty, maker of heaven and earth', we are lost, we have no anchor at all, everything is futile, or in the sentiments of Jean Paul Sartre, 'life is absurd'.

Therefore we introduce people to belief in God the Father because without it the blackness is impenetrable. This belief provides a light by which to go on hoping, and while there is hope there is life.

2. *Jesus Christ his only Son our Lord*. Secondly, we introduce people to belief in the Son, that is, Jesus Christ. This belief is sharp and clear. It implies that what we know of the

character and purpose of God is spread out before us as if it were on a table. Jesus was a man. He breathed as we breathe. His heart beat at a rate a cardiograph would register. His blood belonged to a distinctive blood group. He had to eat, drink, wash, clean his teeth, brush his hair and perform bodily functions. And the measure of our shock when we so describe him is the index of how hesitant we are to recognise him as a man. But such he was. The Apostles' Creed affirms that he suffered, died and was buried, as a man. That is to say he went though the range of experiences common to man, boyhood, youth, manhood. And then pain in the most cruel form of execution invented. All that life is spread out as it were on a table for us to examine. Why? Because in that life, in that death and in that resurrection, what God is and what God does is exhibited.

There is of course an exhibition of God in nature, in poetry, in music, and science too, but it is fragmentary. The face of Jesus Christ is where we must look to see God as he really is, a God who not only creates but cares, and not only makes but remakes. This is why we introduce men and women everywhere to 'the Son', so that they shall come to know what is the heart of the Father. Like Father, like Son, like Son, like Father, or in the words of a striking text, 'No one has ever seen God; but God's only Son, he who is nearest to the Father's heart, he has made him known' (John 1:18 NEB).

3. *The Holy Spirit*. Thirdly, we introduce men everywhere to the Holy Spirit. Suppose we refrained from this. Suppose we stopped short at the Father and the Son. What difference would this abbreviation make? It would lead to fossilisation of the Gospel! If we did not include the Holy Spirit, we should have to say, 'Yes, maybe God created the world and sustains it. Yes, Jesus was the finest type of manhood known, pity we did not live in Palestine two thousand years ago, we might have encountered him ourselves.' But because we believe in the Holy Spirit we know that God operates in the lives of people now, lifting them up and often transforming their potentialities with unexpected results.

Here, for example, are three young men and two young women in a college at Oxford, all five of them from non-church-going homes whose lives have been so altered by responding to the Christian Gospel that they have nothing to do with the promiscuity, rebellion and experimentation with drugs so common in their age group, but who are discovering instead ways of serving the community. Because of the Holy Spirit, Christianity is not a museum exhibit, but a contemporary dynamic force actually changing the direction of people's lives with constructive results in place of drift. We introduce people therefore to the Father, the Son and the Holy Spirit, the one whom the Nicene Creed describes as 'the Lord and Giver of Life'.

And now we must come back to that word 'baptise' in our text. 'Baptise men everywhere in the name of the Father and the Son and the Holy Spirit'. We substituted the word 'introduce' for 'baptise' as a means of gaining a hearing. But we cannot be satisfied with the substitute. We cannot let it stand. Those who are introduced to the faith and come to commit themselves to it mark their entry with a rite. It is carried out with water and the name of the Trinity. This is baptism, a sacrament, and a sacrament is not merely an indicator, it is a means of grace, an instrument by which strength comes from God to the one who receives it. So we not only introduce men everywhere to the name of the Father, the Son and the Holy Spirit, we baptise them into the name, so that by this sacrament they receive not only a new status but a new energy from that entry and from that status.

Here then we encounter the foundation on which the Church is built and so long as it is true to that foundation it will not fail. Indeed Christ added his own promise to his conviction, 'Go forth,' he said, . . . 'make disciples . . . baptise . . . teach . . . And be assured, I am with you always, to the end of time.'

D. W. Cleverley Ford
New Preaching from the New Testament

Human parents know their children. We know when they're ill. We know when they're hurting. We know when they're troubled. We know when they're hiding something. We know when they're afraid. We know when we've reached them and we know when we haven't. We know when their spirits are changing and are reflecting growth. We know when we must intercede because they have got into water too deep for them or when they have strayed from their course. How much more does our heavenly Father, who made us in his own image and blew into us the breath of life, who put every blink into our eyelids, every beat in our hearts, the flow into our blood, who made every cell in our bodies, and coloured every strand of hair upon our heads, know all about us.

Our heavenly Father, our divine Parent, knows when we're not well. He knows when we're hurting. He knows when we're lying and pretending to be something that we're not. He not only knows when we're hiding something, but he knows what we're hiding. He knows when we're afraid, and when our confidence is shaken. He knows when we're becoming stronger, and when we're getting weaker. He knows when he must intercede because we're in over our heads in sin, sorrow, sickness, or trouble. In other words our heavenly Father knows just how much we can bear.

We know that he knows because somehow from somewhere we receive the strength to bear what we must. We may not know just how we're going to make it but our heavenly Father does. He has power, from when he lit the sun and ten thousand other stars, to give us. He has love left over from Calvary to give us. He has anointing left over from the Day of Pentecost to bestow upon us.

William D. Watley
Are You the One?

I answered, 'I don't quite grasp how it is possible to be absolutely sure of living in God's Spirit. How can it be proved? . . .'

Then Father Seraphim gripped me firmly by the shoulders and said: 'My friend, both of us, at this moment, are in the Holy Spirit, you and I. Why won't you look at me?'

'I can't look at you Father, because the light flashing from your eyes and face is brighter than the sun and I'm dazzled!'

'Don't be afraid, friend of God, you yourself are shining just like I am; you too are now in the fullness of the grace of the Holy Spirit, otherwise you wouldn't be able to see me as you do.'

Then I looked at the Staretz and was panic-stricken. Picture, in the sun's orb, in the most dazzling brightness of its noon-day shining, the face of a man who is talking to you. You see his lips moving, the expression in his eyes, you hear his voice, you feel his arms round your shoulders, and yet you see neither his arms, nor his body, nor his face, you lose all sense of yourself, you can only see the blinding light which spreads everywhere, lighting up the layer of snow covering the glade, and igniting the flakes that are falling on us both like white powder.

147

'What do you feel?' asked Father Seraphim.

'An amazing well-being!' I replied. 'I feel a great calm in my soul, a peace which no words can express . . . A strange, unknown delight . . . An amazing happiness . . . I'm amazingly warm . . . There's no scent in all the world like this one!'

'I know,' said Father Seraphim, smiling . . . 'This is as it should be, for divine grace comes to live in our hearts, within us. Didn't the Lord say: "The Kingdom of God is within you"? (Luke 17:21). This kingdom is just the grace of the Holy Spirit, living in us, warming us, enlightening us, filling the air with his scent, delighting us with his fragrance and rejoicing our hearts with an ineffable gladness.'

Nicholas Motovilov
in *Valentine Zander St Seraphim of Sarov*
trans. Sr Gabriel Anne

Proper 4/Ordinary Time 9

Sunday between 29 May and 4 June inclusive (if after Trinity Sunday)

Luke 7:1-10

If only we had a faith like that, for us too the miracle would happen and life become new.

The central character is a Roman centurion; and he was no ordinary man.

(i) The mere fact that *he was a centurion* meant that he was no ordinary man. A centurion was the equivalent of a regimental sergeant-major; and the centurions were the backbone of the Roman army. Wherever they are spoken of in the New Testament they are spoken of well (compare Luke 23:47; Acts 10:22; 22:26; 23:17, 23, 24; 24:23; 27:43). Polybius, the historian, describes their qualifications. They must be not so much 'seekers after danger as men who can command, steady in action, and reliable; they ought not to be over-anxious to rush into the fight; but when hard-pressed they must be ready to hold their ground and die at their posts.' The centurion must have been a man amongst men or he would never have held the post that was his.

(ii) *He had a completely unusual attitude to his slave.* He loved this slave and would go to any trouble to save him. In Roman law a slave was defined as a living tool: he had no rights; a master could ill-treat him and even kill him if he chose. A Roman writer on estate management recommends the farmer to examine his implements every year and to throw out those which were old and broken, and to do the same with his slaves. Normally when a slave was past his work he was thrown out to die. The attitude of this centurion to his slave was quite unusual.

(iii) *He was clearly a deeply religious man.* A man needs to be more than superficially interested before he will go to the length of building a synagogue. It is true that the Romans encouraged religion from the cynical motive that it kept people in order. They regarded it as the opiate of the people. Augustus recommended the building of synagogues for that very reason. As Gibbon said in a famous sentence: 'The various modes of religion which prevailed in the Roman world were all considered by the people as equally true; by the philosopher as equally false; and by the magistrate as equally useful.' But this centurion was no administrative cynic; he was a sincerely religious man.

149

(iv) *He had an extremely unusual attitude to the Jews.* If the Jews despised the Gentiles, the Gentiles hated the Jews. Anti-Semitism is not a new thing. The Romans called the Jews a filthy race; they spoke of Judaism as a barbarous superstition; they spoke of the Jewish hatred of mankind; they accused the Jews of worshipping an ass's head and annually sacrificing a Gentile stranger to their God. True, many of the Gentiles, weary of the many gods and loose morals of paganism, had accepted the Jewish doctrine of the one God and the austere Jewish ethic. But the whole atmosphere of this story implies a close bond of friendship between this centurion and the Jews.

(v) *He was a humble man.* He knew quite well that a strict Jew was forbidden by the law to enter the house of a Gentile (Acts 10:28); just as he was forbidden to allow a Gentile into his house or have any communication with him. He would not even come to Jesus himself. He persuaded his Jewish friends to approach him. This man who was accustomed to command had an amazing humility in the presence of true greatness.

(vi) *He was a man of faith.* His faith is based on the soundest argument. He argued from the here and now to the there and then. He argued from his own experience to God. If his authority produced the results it did, how much more must that of Jesus? He came with that perfect confidence which looks up and says 'Lord, *I know* you can do this'. If only we had a faith like that, for us too the miracle would happen and life become new.

William Barclay
The Daily Study Bible: The Gospel of Luke

Proper 5/Ordinary Time 10

Sunday between 5 and 11 June inclusive (if after Trinity Sunday)

Luke 7:11-17

*It's that sort of
light sprung
Lazarus.
Unstoppable.*

Christ Harrows* Hell

'Hold still,'
Truth said: 'I hear some spirit
speaking to the guards of hell,
and see him too, telling them
unbar the gates.' 'Lift your heads,
you gates'
and from the heart
of light
a loud voice spoke.
'Open
these gates, Lucifer,
Prince of this land: the King of glory,
a crown upon his head,
comes.'

Satan groaned and said to his hell's angels,
'It's that sort of light sprung Lazarus.
Unstoppable. This'll be big, big
trouble, I mean all sorts of bother
for the lot of us. If this bigshot
gets in he'll fetch the lot out, take them
wherever that Lazarus got to
and truss me up quick as you like.
Those old Jesus freaks and the weathermen
round here have been going on about
this for years. Move yourself, Greaser Boy,
get all those crowbars your grand-dad used
to hit your mum with. I'll put a stop
to this one. I'll put his little light
out. Before he blinds us with neon
get all the gates closed. Get the locks on,
lads, stuff every chink in the house.

*Harrow in Middle English means 'rob'.

151

Don't let pieces of light in! Windows,
fanlights, the lot. Moonshot, whip out, get
the boys together, Horse and his lot
and stash the loot. Any of them come
near the walls, boiling brimstone, that's it!
Tip it on top of them, frizzle them
up like chips. Get those three-speed crossbows
and Ye Olde Englishe cannon and spray
it round a bit – blind his mounted foot
with tintacks. Put Muhammad on that
crazy catapult, lobbing millstones.
We'll stab them with sickles, clobber them
with those spiky iron balls on string.'
'Don't panic,' said Lucifer, 'I know
this guy and his shining light. Way back
in my murky past. Can't kill him off.
Dirty tricks don't work. Just keeps coming.
Still he'd better watch out, so help me.'

Again
the light said unlock:
Said Lucifer, 'Who
goes there?'

A huge voice replied, 'The Lord
of power, of strength, that made
all things. Dukes of this dark place
undo these gates so Christ come
in, the son of heaven's King.'
With that word, hell split apart,
burst its devil's bars; no man
nor guard could stop the gates swing
wide. The old religious men,
prophets, people who had walked
in darkness, 'Behold the Lamb
Of God', with Saint John sang now.
But Lucifer could not look
at it, the light blinding him.
And along that light all those
our Lord loved came streaming out.

William Langland
The Vision of Piers Ploughman
translated from the Middle English by Ronald Tamplin

In the mid-eighties I visited the Arab-Christian village of Nain as spiritual leader of a group of fifty pilgrims. We had come to Nain for one reason only: to see how the people of Nain commemorated the story of Jesus raising the poor widow's son from the dead.

On leaving the coach on a beautiful sunny day, a crowd of women and children soon gathered and followed us as we made our way to the church. The lady caretaker opened the doors and graciously, with a certain amount of hesitant shyness, showed us the interior which had a huge mural on the wall picturing Luke's Gospel story of the widow's son being raised from the dead.

It reminded us all that whenever possible a church has been built and maintained on important Gospel sites to ensure the story is always remembered and, as in Nain, by a living worshipping people.

As the leader I made a monetary gift, as generous as I possibly could, to help the congregation maintain its worship and witness.

On the way back to the coach a crowd of small boys followed us, smiling and shouting. Before re-embarking I stood at the doors of the coach, wondering what gift I could give these poor young lads. As I was thinking quickly over what to give, I suddenly remembered some BBC Radio Devon retractable ball-point pens, colourfully decorated, that I had been given by the station as small gifts. So opening my bag I found about a dozen and began to give them to eager hands that clamoured for them. After all the excitement of that, we drove on to the next holy place, and as we drove along I thought to myself that a ball-point pen was not much of a gift. But I comforted myself as I remembered the happy smiles of all the recipient children. In a lovely way they had received with joy the gifts given, and there was a new hope and sense of life in all of the children I saw. But of course nothing in comparison with the gift of life Jesus gave to the widow of Nain's son as he raised him from the dead.

Ron Dale, 1998

Proper 6/Ordinary Time 11

Sunday between 12 and 18 June inclusive (if after Trinity)

Luke 7:36-8:3

A sense of need will open the door to the forgiveness of God, because God is love, and love's greatest glory is to be needed.

This story is so vivid that it makes one believe that Luke may well have been an artist.

(i) The scene is the courtyard of the house of Simon the Pharisee. The houses of well-to-do people were built round an open courtyard in the form of a hollow square. Often in the courtyard there would be a garden and a fountain; and there, in the warm weather, meals were eaten. It was the custom that when a rabbi was at a meal in such a house, all kinds of people came in – they were quite free to do so – to listen to the pearls of wisdom which fell from his lips. That explains the presence of the woman.

When a guest entered such a house three things were always done. The host placed his hand on the guest's shoulder and gave him the kiss of peace. That was a mark of respect that was never omitted in the case of a distinguished rabbi. The roads were only dust tracks, and shoes were merely soles held in place by straps across the foot. So always cool water was poured over the guest's feet to cleanse and comfort them. Either a piece of sweet-smelling incense was burned or a drop of attar of roses was placed on the guest's head. These things good manners demanded, and in this case not one of them was done.

In the east the guests did not sit, but reclined at table. They lay on low couches, resting on the left elbow, leaving the right arm free, with the feet stretched out behind; and during the meal the sandals were taken off. That explains how the woman was standing beside Jesus' feet.

(ii) Simon was a Pharisee, one of the separated ones. Why should such a man invite Jesus to his house at all? There are three possible reasons. (a) It is just possible that he was an admirer and a sympathiser, for not all the Pharisees were Jesus' enemies (compare Luke 13:31). But the whole atmosphere of discourtesy makes that unlikely. (b) It could be that Simon had invited Jesus with the deliberate intention of enticing him into some word or action which might have been made the basis of a charge against him. Simon may have been an *agent provocateur*. Again it is not likely, because in verse 40 Simon gives Jesus the title, Rabbi. (c) Most likely,

154

Simon was a collector of celebrities; and with a half-patronising contempt he had invited this startling young Galilean to have a meal with him. That would best explain the strange combination of a certain respect with the omission of the usual courtesies. Simon was a man who tried to patronise Jesus.

(iii) The woman was a bad woman, and a notoriously bad woman, a prostitute. No doubt she had listened to Jesus speaking from the edge of the crowd and had glimpsed in him the hand which could lift her from the mire of her ways. Round her neck she wore, like all Jewish women, a little phial of concentrated perfume; they were called alabasters and they were very costly. She wished to pour it on his feet, for it was all she had to offer. But as she saw him the tears came and fell upon his feet. For a Jewish woman to appear with hair unbound was an act of the gravest immodesty. On her wedding day a girl bound up her hair and never would she appear with it unbound again. The fact that this woman loosed her long hair in public showed how she had forgotten everyone except Jesus.

The story demonstrates a contrast between two attitudes of mind and heart.

(i) Simon was conscious of no need and therefore felt no love, and so received no forgiveness. Simon's impression of himself was that he was a good man in the sight of men and of God.

(ii) The woman was conscious of nothing else but a clamant need, and therefore was overwhelmed with love for him who could supply it, and so received forgiveness.

The one thing that shuts a person off from God is self-sufficiency. And the strange thing is that the better a man is the more he feels his sin. Paul could speak of sinners 'of whom I am foremost' (1 Timothy 1:5). Francis of Assisi could say, 'There is nowhere a more wretched and a more miserable sinner than I'. It is true to say that the greatest of sins is to be conscious of no sin; but a sense of need will open the door to the forgiveness of God, because God is love, and love's greatest glory is to be needed.

William Barclay
The Daily Study Bible: The Gospel of Luke

One of the deepest needs of the human heart is the need to be appreciated. Every human being wants to be valued. Every human being craves to be accepted, accepted for what he is . . . When I am not accepted, then something in me is broken . . . Acceptance means that the people with whom I live give me a feeling of self-respect, a feeling that I am worthwhile. They are happy that I am who I am. Acceptance means that I am welcome to be myself. Acceptance means that though there is need for growth, I am not forced. I do not have to be the person I am not. Neither am I locked in, by my past or present. Rather I am given room to unfold, to outgrow the mistakes of the past. In a way we can say that acceptance is an unveiling. Every one of us is born with many potentialities. But unless they are drawn out by the warm touch of another's acceptance, they will remain dormant. Acceptance liberates everything that is in me. Only when I am loved in that deep sense of complete acceptance can I become myself. The love, the acceptance of other persons, makes me the unique person that I am meant to be. When a person is appreciated for what he *does* he is not unique; someone else can do the same work perhaps better than the other. But when a person is loved for what he *is*, then he becomes a unique and irreplaceable personality. So indeed, I need that acceptance in order to be myself. When I am not accepted, I am a nobody. I cannot come to fulfilment. An accepted person is a happy person because he is opened up, because he can grow.

To accept a person does not mean that I deny his defects, that I gloss over them or try to explain them away. Neither does acceptance mean to say that everything the person does is beautiful and fine. Just the opposite is true. When I deny the defects of the person, then I certainly do not accept him. I have not touched the depth of that person. Only when I accept a person can I truly face his defects . . .

I am accepted by God *as I am* – as I am – and not as I should be. He loves me with my ideals and disappointments, my sacrifices and my joys, my successes and my failures. God is himself the deepest ground of my being. It is one thing to know I am accepted and quite another thing to realise it. It is not enough to have just once touched the love of God. There is more required to build one's life on God's love. It takes a long time to believe that I am accepted by God as I am.

Peter G. van Breeman, SJ
As Bread that is Broken

156

Proper 7/Ordinary Time 12

Sunday between 19 and 25 June (if after Trinity Sunday)

Luke 8:26-39

God did it. God can do everything.

Shim

Middle forties. A ruddy, open-air kind of man. Sturdy and muscular. Slow-speaking, like a man used to long silences or solitude. Steady, grey eyes. Big, capable hands.

You are surprised to hear that I've never been across the lake, across the Sea of Galilee. Well, let me tell you that there are many people here in Gerasa who haven't even been out of the town gates. Why should they? How much you travel depends a lot upon what you do for a living, I think. A cousin of mine, who sells cloth, is always going across the lake – or round the top of it, into Galilee.

Well, I look after pigs. A pigman, a swineherd. I've one or two of my own, but mainly I look after other people's. I've always done it. I know every inch of the country round here that's good for pigs. But not far afield, not far away. Pigs don't go far afield. And the buying and selling, the cattle market, is here in Gerasa.

It's a quiet place, Gerasa. Nothing much happens here, although your mentioning Jesus of Galilee brings back to me a remarkable day, remarkable. I don't often recall it, except with strangers. Most people here in the town remember it as clearly as I do. And, of course, it is some time ago now. About ten or eleven years. Jesus has been gone, how long is it, eight, nine years?

Well, Jesus came here, to Gerasa, just once. And once was enough, believe me. I nearly lost my job because of Jesus – although I must admit that I saw remarkable things because of him, too. I know that since he died he has become very well known, but he wasn't then. He'd only just started, and news travels slowly round here. At that time, too, the two sides of the lake were separate provinces. We were Philip, Galilee was Antipas. If you count Decapolis, the ten towns, *three* provinces. Many changes since. They're all gone, Antipas, Philip, Pilate, too. And we are part of Syria. I don't change; I go on looking after pigs.

Yes, just once, Jesus came. By boat. He landed just south

of the town, where the low cliffs are. I was up on the top with the pigs. I saw this fishing boat with about six people in it and it looked as if they were intending to land at the bottom of the graveyard slope. Well, I left the pigs and started to make my way down there to tell them not to, for it was dangerous, because of the madman.

He's lived in the graveyard, in among the tombs and graves, for years, the madman. He was mainly the reason they closed it. People were afraid to go there. He was a tall, skinny man, filthy dirty, naked. His hair and beard were matted and crusted with blood, for he was always falling down and cutting his head on the stones. His eyes were ghastly, wide-staring open and sort of terrified. And he screamed from morning till night. Terrible noise.

I used to leave food for him. For weeks on end there would be only the two of us on that bit of shore, me up on the cliffs and him down among the tombs. I was used to him. If he came too near, I'd throw a stone and he would scream and run away and hide. I don't think he would have hurt me but I wasn't taking any chances. There's been a time when the authorities used to catch him and chain him up, but then he'd go berserk, like a wild, trapped animal, and seem to have the strength of ten, and he'd break his chains and fetters and cover himself with cuts and bruises and blood. Pitiful.

So eventually they left him alone, poor soul. Left him to rot. A pigman's life is not much, but, when I used to see him, I used to count my blessings and collect food for him. He became known as 'Shim's Friend'. People used to say to me, 'Shim, how's your friend?' and have a laugh. I didn't mind, if they put some food in the basket for my 'friend'.

But my 'friend' was mad, and full of demons and terror, and strong enough for ten, strong enough to kill anyone. So, when I saw the men in the boat, I started round the edge of the cliff, shouting. They didn't hear, and beached the boat. The madman was nowhere to be seen, so I decided to risk it and I ran down the slope through the graves towards the boat.

Jesus, although I didn't know it was him then, had landed and was walking up the beach. He waved his hand to me. I was about fifty yards away. Then, suddenly, half-way between us, the madman got to his feet from a clump of dwarf bushes. And began to scream. He had his back to me so I went on, picking up a big rock in case of trouble.

I heard Jesus say something, like a sharp order, a command, and the madman's screaming took shape, became words, although I couldn't make them out. He seemed to be asking permission; there was fear in it. Then he was silent. Everything was silent. It was weird. The madman went to Jesus and sat down near him, looking up at him. There was no sound.

Then, suddenly, from the top of the low cliffs, the screaming began again, tenfold. It frightened the life out of me. It was the pigs. I started up the slope to them. I thought maybe some wild dogs had got in among them. The screaming got louder and louder. As I reached the top, I was aware of a new noise. A great splashing and thudding. I stopped and looked round. Below me the graveyard sloped down to the sea. To either side, the cliffs. And from the edge of the cliffs the pigs were jumping, screaming, into the sea! Many, many more than my herd, hundreds more! Among them, pigmen from miles inland, shouting in despair and rage. It went on and on, and suddenly stopped. No more pigs. Silence. Down below, Jesus, with the naked madman sitting in front of him.

Well, the other pigmen and I rushed off to our farmers. We feared for our jobs. And what could we tell them? Only the truth – which sounded as though we were mad, or drunk! That some strangers had landed and done some magic and filled the pigs with mad demons which made them all jump into the sea or smash themselves on the rocks below the cliffs! The word went round like a fire and half the town turned out, rushing back to the cliffs and down through the graveyard.

When we got back, the madman at first was not to be seen. Then I realised that the man nearest to Jesus was my 'friend'. Jesus and the fishermen had washed him and found some clothes for him, and there he sat, as calm and sane as I am. As I realised it and recognised my 'friend', so, it seemed, did everybody else. It was somehow more frightening than the pigs. The town elders stepped forward and asked Jesus to go away and not come back, as his magic was powerful – and very costly, for some two thousand pigs were missing. Most of the elders were our big farmers, and I could see their point.

Jesus didn't argue. He and his friends turned and prepared to push their boat off. The madman went after them, imploring Jesus to take him also, but Jesus said no. Then, when the madman began to cry with gratitude, Jesus stopped him. 'God did it,' he said. 'God can do everything. Go and tell everyone what God has done for you.' And he and his friends sailed away.

Then there was an odd thing. The madman turned and looked up the slope at the people, then came across to me.

'Thank you for all the food,' he said. It came true about him being 'Shim's Friend'. He's more; he's my brother-in-law.

David Kossoff
From *The Book of Witness*

'To be born again' means exactly what it says. The emphasis is still on being born: indicative of a process that is still concerned with flesh and blood, i.e. still concerned with concrete problems of this world. But it is still a complete *transformation*; we have still to deal with material things, but we see them now through the eyes of those who are born of the Spirit, and not of those who are born of the will of the flesh. It is this world we are still concerned with; but we see it differently, and do different things about it. We do not deal with new things instead of old things; but with the old things in a new way: indeed all the old 'things' now take on a sacramental significance. 'If any man be in Christ Jesus, he is a new creation. The old things are passed away, *all things are become new*' (Authorised Version, author's italics). The man of business, truly converted, will attend more and not less, to his business, and square up to the problems attendant on the fact that his office has now assumed something of the proportions of a holy place . . . The man of ambition continues to use this attribute of his character (now utterly transformed) for the things of the kingdom. The man of humour has his humour reborn (not garrotted) and cheers up *everyone* – no longer just his self-selected clique. And all forget about haloes and wings, and keep off their coats rather to get into the multifarious activities of converting humanity into Humanity again – not into an anaemic and wholly erroneous imitation of Divinity.

George Macleod
We Shall Rebuild

Proper 8/Ordinary Time 13

Sunday between 26 June and 2 July inclusive

Luke 9:51-62

His eyes saw only his destination.

In one little town, while its market threatened to dwindle away through lack of farmers with any stock to send to it, the march of civilisation was symbolised by pylons striding gigantically over hill and dale to its very doors. Premises were taken in its one street and an electrical showroom opened, whose central attraction was a great oxidised silver fire-basket of the baronial sort filled with a warm glow of make-believe coals, while outside the wind cut along the pinched little thoroughfare, of which the only population seemed to be the knot of unemployed whose gathering-place happened to be just opposite. They stood gazing apathetically across at the luxurious appliance which winked ruddily back at them, while, in between, the plate glass window was like that invisible barrier which starves the world in the midst of its plenty.

They wore a look, those men, which reminded one sharply of the war. One last saw it *en masse* in the faces and attitudes of soldiers about to return to the front. It was the expression of those who had nothing to live for.

Sometimes one met them walking about the country lanes, fecklessly, in the ennui of an eternal Sunday. Once, particularly, I was struck by a contrast. For in front of me went a group of these lads, whose very gesture, even seen from behind, bespoke a lethargic disrelation with their surroundings. They walked each as though his hinder foot did not know why it was being summoned to take another single pace onward, so that they lurched to the side and seemed always to be colliding with one another as they walked, this row of six, like jolted bottles, and vainly their eyes sought the hedge, the trees, for anything to catch their interest. Occasionally they guffawed; one would begin a song on an impulse which wouldn't last till he might finish it, and all the while they whipped their legs idly with green wands they had pulled from the hedge.

Striding from the opposite direction I observed a man, old but not bent, bearded and buskined. He carried a stick – not the limp plaything of the youths, but an ash-pole, shoulder high. He grasped this near the top, and planted it firmly before him at every other step. His steps were straight, neither hurried nor loitering, but continuing regularly. He silently

161

saluted me with a motion of his head as he passed. His face had that stern and steady look of the old but not senile; his eyes saw only his destination, but they were eyes that had absorbed their surroundings – he could have told me whether the oak or the ash were the more forwarder when the hedge beside us had been cut last, or which way the clouds were moving. He was a purposeful part of the place he walked in. The youths he passed were as foreign to it as the tarmac on the road, walking in that light daze of the drug of indolence, swaying with its dull intoxication. They stared aside at him, began to titter. But he passed them as though they were not, and they ceased. I was struck by this crossing of the paths of the old man *who had a destination* [my italics] and the youths who had none. For it seemed to me that the zest for life had died from them, while it had not yet forsaken a man of seventy odd years.

Adrian Bell
The Cherry Tree

Crowds constantly press in upon Jesus. This makes us aware of his body as, like ours, needing space. At times he escapes the crush by fleeing to the desert or the lake. But most often he just accepts it. When the man sick of the palsy is lowered through the roof to bring him before Jesus because there is such a dense crowd round the house that he cannot be got through the door (Mark 2:2-5), the ingenuity and effort this requires makes us aware of Jesus' bodily presence in a way no amount of argument could ever succeed in doing. When the woman touches Jesus and is healed, he suddenly feels 'that virtue had gone out of him' (Mark 5:30 cf. Luke 8:46), and we sense the physical cost of this act of this healing activity. Then too he is always in movement. No OT figure, not even Jacob, is so restless, so continuously on the move. And we do not need a map of Palestine open before us to recognise what this entails, we only need to have used our legs ourselves.

But it is not only his feet which are in motion. It is also his mind. Scholarly attempts to break down the individual chapters into so many periscopes destroy the sense the ordinary reader gets of the sheer tempo and variety of Jesus' debates and arguments. Take chapter 9 of Luke. It begins with Jesus calling his disciples to him and then sending them out to preach and heal the sick. They depart and go 'through the towns, preaching the Gospel, and healing everywhere' (9:6). Then we switch to Herod and his questions to his followers about Jesus: Who is he? John the Baptist come back from the dead? Elijah? The miracle of the loaves and fishes follows, and then Jesus is again alone with his disciples and asks them to tell him who they think he is. Peter answers that he is 'The Christ of God' (20). Jesus prophesies his own death, and this is followed by the Transfiguration, where he is seen talking to Moses and Elijah. Then comes the cure of a possessed youth, and a rebuke to the disciples for not having the faith to cure him. Jesus again tells them about his end. They wish to call down fire from heaven to consume those who will not take Jesus in, but he rebukes them: 'Ye know not what manner of spirit ye are of. For the Son of Man is not come to destroy men's lives, but to save them' (55-60). A man appears and asks to be allowed to follow Jesus. First though he has to go and bury his father. 'Let the dead bury their dead' (60), Jesus says to him; and to another: 'Don't look back; follow me.' So the chapter ends.

Gabriel Josipovici
The Book of God

Verses 57-62 provide three examples of encounters between Jesus and would-be disciples as Jesus moves towards Jerusalem as one who has set his face like a firm stone. A threefold pattern was common to storytelling at that time, even though these may have existed earlier as independent episodes. Matthew 8:19-22 records the first two. The pattern here is: 'I will follow', 'follow me', and again, 'I will follow'. Given the portrayal of Jesus in verse 51, the reader should not expect Jesus to offer easy options. The call for total and primary loyalty is underscored by setting Jesus' demands over against, not the worst or lowest, but the best and the highest loyalties. Anything less would deny his own destiny and the claims of the kingdom of God. There is no reason, then, for the preacher to search for loopholes in Jesus' absolutes. He is on his way to be taken up; shall he deceive his disciples with offers of bargains?

Fred B. Craddock
Preaching Through the Christian Year: 'C'

163

Proper 9/Ordinary Time 14

Sunday between 3 and 9 July inclusive

Luke 10:1-11, 16-20

Keep yourself focused on what is really important, and don't be distracted by issues of little consequence.

When we come across passages like Luke's report of Jesus' commission of the Seventy (10:1-11, 16-20), we are reminded of the need for a historical respect for the narrative, a willingness to let it be an account of the first-century community. The drive for 'instant relevance' becomes a ludicrous, if not dangerous, inclination with a text like this. The directions to 'carry no purse, no bag, no sandals,' even when translated as 'no wallet, no suitcase, no change of clothes,' can be a counsel of irresponsibility if taken literally – not to mention the authority given to the Seventy to tread on snakes and scorpions and not be hurt.

Yet we dare not ignore Jesus' words of commission as if they were a modern embarrassment, merely an outmoded bit of advice for ancient times. The stress on the difficulty of the mission and the need for a spartan style, in fact, seem surprisingly immediate to contemporary disciples, who are called to bear witness in the post-Constantinian world. The increasing experience of the disestablishment of the church makes Jesus' directions amazingly up-to-date . . . We shall highlight three dimensions of Jesus' speech, and then look at his conversation with the Seventy when they return.

What is initially striking is *the subtle but critical call for prayer*. The sequence of a plentiful harvest and a slim work force would suggest a direct appeal for labourers, but instead the text reads, 'Ask the Lord of the harvest to send out labourers into his harvest' (10:2). Later in the narrative, Luke provides more extended instructions about prayer (11:1-13), but here at the outset of the mission, the Seventy are told to beseech the Lord of the harvest for a sufficient number of reapers.

The wording of 10:2 underscores the fact the Lord is not only in charge of the harvest but also in charge of sending the labourers. The authentic workers, those who will get the job done and reap what has been grown, are only those specifically sent by the Lord. This is not a place for self-appointed entrepreneurs, who chart their own course and work as if the outcome depended entirely on themselves. Petitionary prayer clarifies who is in charge and under whose authority one works. The Seventy are obviously part of the chosen work force, because they are immediately told to get on with the job ('Go on your way').

Prayer and a sense of being under commission are important because *the mission is tough*. 'I am sending you out like lambs into the midst of wolves' (10:3). One could hardly have a more vivid picture of the precarious plight of the labourers. No mention here of a shepherd to protect the lambs – only their vulnerability to the wild animals. The declaration of the nearness of God's reign (10:9, 11) is simply not a popular theme everywhere, particularly not amongst those in power, who find its coming a threat to their own stability. They are inclined to react with violence and brutality, because it is the only kind of response they know.

The difficulty of the mission accounts for the detailed instructions about travelling light. When one enters an environment likely to be hostile, one does not want to be encumbered with extra baggage or to risk too much with strangers met on the road. In so many ways 'things' become a hindrance and not a help. Furthermore, one is not to make unnecessary trouble: Declare a 'peace' on every house you enter; don't move from house to house as if searching for a more comfortable spot; eat what is put before you, whether kosher or not. In a word, keep yourself focused on what is really important, and don't be distracted by issues of little consequence.

The warning about the difficulty of the task is in no way meant to detract from *the absolutely critical importance of the mission*. Both to the towns that welcome the Seventy and to the towns that reject them, they are to announce, 'The kingdom of God has come near' (10:9, 11). To one it comes as a word of salvation: the inbreaking of God's rule means deliverance and hope. To the other it comes as a word of judgement, a destiny comparable to Sodom. The stakes are high for those who receive or don't receive the labourers sent into the harvest.

The importance of the mission appears again in 10:16, when through a form of juridical identification both Jesus and God become linked with the labourers. The acceptance or rejection of the labourers becomes an acceptance or rejection of Jesus and God. In declaring God's rule, the Seventy are engaged in a life-or-death business.

According to Luke, the Seventy report a joyous and profitable mission (10:17). Their announcement that even the demons are subject to them evokes from Jesus a theological interpretation and a word of warning. On the one hand,

Jesus sees the exorcisms performed by the Seventy constitute an assault on the heart of the opposition, Satan himself. The rule of the enemy is being overcome. The conflict between the lambs and the wolves is a critical stage in a larger war between God and Satan. On the other hand, Jesus warns that they may not become too preoccupied with their successes, but instead be content to be numbered among God's people. Their identity comes from their inclusion among a great and honoured group.

Beverly R. Gaventa
Texts for Preaching: A Lectionary Commentary Based on the NRSV – Year C

In the glorious summer of 1959 I was sent out from my theological college with three other students with a brief to preach the Gospel in villages and towns along a pre-arranged 750-mile route across England.

We depended on the local people for hospitality, and they mostly gave us a warm welcome. However, I did have two scary experiences which I've never forgotten.

The first came as I preached in the warm sunshine to a crowd of young and old. Suddenly I heard a voice say, 'Let's give him the knife.' I immediately turned to face the voice and saw a teenager with a drawn knife, being urged on by his friend. I carried on preaching as if I were addressing these two lads only. After a while, the knife was put away and they walked off arguing, much to my relief.

The other occasion was when I was confronted by a gang of 'Teddy Boys', all with winkle-picker shoes and what we used to call DA haircuts. One of them was well over six feet tall and cornered me after the service. Leaning right over me he said: 'Will God give me a woman?' After getting over my initial shock at the question, my response was, 'It depends what you want her for'. He laughed and we then had quite a long debate about the meaning of courtship and marriage until, after about twenty minutes, he walked off with some of his mates. As I lay on my makeshift bed in the local church hall I reflected on that conversation and as I did so a most wonderful sense of joy came over me. It made me look forward to passing my exams and offering for the Methodist ministry.

Now that nearly forty years have passed I sometimes wonder what happened to the man with the knife and the 'Teddy' boy with his problem. And as I do so, it makes me appreciate something of what the Seventy experienced as they did in their time what I did in mine, in the name of the same Lord, who sent us out as sheep among wolves.

Ron Dale, 1998

The fall of Satan

I saw Satan fall like lightning from heaven.
(Luke 10:18)

When we think of the fall of Satan, we tend to be more influenced by John Milton than by the Bible. In *Paradise Lost*, Milton describes Satan and his angels being ejected from heaven and falling down to hell back in the primeval past, before the creation of the human race:

> Him the Almighty Power
> hurl'd headlong flaming from th' Ethereal Skie
> with hideous ruin and combustion down
> to bottomless perdition, there to dwell
> in Adamantine Chains and penal Fire,
> who durst defie th' Omnipotent to Arms.

It would be difficult to find biblical authority for this picture, however. The reader of the AV may think of Isaiah 14:12, 'How art thou fallen from heaven, O Lucifer, son of the morning!' And in truth the poetic imagery in which Lucifer's fall is depicted has been borrowed by the traditional concept of the fall of Satan. But Lucifer, son of the morning, is 'Day Star, son of Dawn' (RSV). The prophet is proclaiming the downfall of the king of Babylon, who occupied such a high place in the firmament of imperial power that his overthrow can be compared to the morning star being toppled from heaven. In the Old Testament, Satan, or rather 'the satan' (the adversary), is chief prosecutor in the heavenly court, and when he fills this role he does so in the presence of God and his angels (Job 1:6-2:7; Zechariah 3:1-5).

So when Jesus speaks of seeing Satan's fall from heaven

he is not thinking of an event in the remote past. He is think-ing of the effect of his ministry at the time. He had sent out seventy of his disciples to spread the announcement that the kingdom of God had drawn near, and now they had come back from their mission in great excitement. 'Why,' they said, 'even the demons are subject to us in your name!' To this Jesus replied, 'I watched how Satan fell, like lightning, out of the sky' (NEB). It is implied that he was watching for this when suddenly, like a flash of lightning, it happened; Satan plummeted – whether to earth or down to the abyss is not said.

Jesus may be describing an actual vision which he experi-enced during the mission of the Seventy – not unlike the vision seen by John of Patmos, when, as he says, war broke out in heaven 'and the great dragon was thrown down, that ancient serpent, who is called the Devil and Satan, the deceiver of the whole world' (Revelation 12:9). When Jesus' messengers found that the demons – malignant forces that held men and women in bondage – were compelled to obey them as they commanded them, in Jesus' name, to come out of those people in whose lives they had taken up residence, this was a sign that the kingdom of God was conquering the kingdom of evil. Many of the rabbis held that, at the end of the age, God or the Messiah would overthrow Satan: the report of the Seventy showed that Satan's overthrow had already taken place; and Jesus' vision of his fall from heaven confirmed this. John's Patmos version of Satan being ejected similarly indicates that his downfall was the direct result of Jesus' ministry. So too, when Jesus says in John 12:31, 'Now shall the ruler of this world be cast out', the adverb 'now' refers to his impending passion, which crowned his ministry.

The downfall of Satan may be regarded as the decisive victory in the campaign; the campaign itself goes on. Hence Jesus' further words to the exultant disciples: 'I have given you authority to tread upon serpents and scorpions, and over all the power of the enemy; and nothing shall hurt you' (Luke 10:19). The 'serpents and scorpions' represent the forces of evil: thanks to the work of Christ, his people can trample them underfoot and gain the victory over them. The imagery may be borrowed from Psalm 91:13, where those who trust in God are promised that they 'will tread on the lion and the adder'. Paul uses a similar expression when he tells the Christians in Rome that, if they are 'wise as to what is good and guileless as to what is evil', then the God of peace will soon crush Satan under their feet (Romans 16:19-20). The wording here harks back not so much to Psalm 91 as to the story of man's first disobedience, where the serpent of Eden is told that its offspring will have its head crushed by the offspring of the woman (Genesis 3:15).

Finally, the Seventy are directed not to exult in their spiritual achievements (that way lie pride and catastrophe) but to exult rather in what God has done for them.

> Rejoice not ye that sprites of ill
> yield to your prowess in the fight;
> but joy because your Father God
> hath writ your names elect for life.

To have one's name 'written in heaven' is to have received God's gift of eternal life.

F. F. Bruce
The Hard Sayings of Jesus

Proper 10/Ordinary Time 15

Sunday between 10 and 16 July inclusive

Luke 10:25-37

We must see Jesus first if we are really to see ourselves – the depth of our sin and the hopeless nature of our plight.

From Jerusalem to Jericho

A certain man went down from Jerusalem to Jericho, and fell among thieves, who stripped him of his raiment, and wounded him and departed, leaving him half-dead. (Luke 10:30)

We have been taught recently that the parables are told only to illustrate a single point, and that too much must not be read into the details. This is perhaps true in a general way, though it may leave us asking sometimes, as in the present parable, What is the exact point? In any case, however, it must not be made a slavish rule. Otherwise we shall miss many of the deep lessons which lie in the parables, and which help us to understand their general teaching and its relation to the whole of scripture.

At any rate, we are going to break all the rules today, and turn to just one of the characters in this well-known and well-loved parable, recorded only in St Luke. And I think we shall find in the wounded man, robbed and stripped and half-dead by the wayside, material which will speak directly to our own souls, bring the Gospel itself before us in all its fullness and give real point and power to the command of Christ: 'Go, and do thou likewise.'

Who this man was, his age, his occupation, his background, we do not know. He may have been a real man. Possibly the incident had recently happened, as it often must on that road which wound down through the desolate, brigand-infested hills from Jerusalem to the Jordan valley. Or possibly he was only an invented character. But who he was individually does not greatly matter. It is what this man who fell among thieves has to say to us that matters. And it is from this point of view that he must now claim our attention.

The man, stripped and wounded and half-dead by the roadside, speaks to us first of all of man in general. He is not an individual. He is Everyman. He is held up as a mirror to the world, and in him we see what man is, and what the fate is which has overtaken him, and the situation in which he now finds himself.

He is the man who goes down from Jerusalem to Jericho, from the city of God to the frontier of an alien kingdom. It is not without significance that the journey of this man is a downward journey; and the priest also comes down that way, and so too, presumably, does the Levite. Man is the man who turns his back on God. Man is the man who goes his own way, an easier way, downhill, and therefore he thinks a better way. Man is the man who leaves the house of God as the prodigal did, preferring the ways of the far country to the worship and service of God. Man is the man who was made for Eden but has deliberately chosen the wilderness.

On this supposedly better, downward way, a threefold disaster overtakes him. In the first place, he is waylaid, attacked and robbed by those who, like him, are haunters of this same track. In a more violent form, he meets the same fate as the prodigal, who went out a rich man, but was plundered by his new friends, and came home a beggar. Sin is a hard taskmaster. It promises great rewards, but all its promises are empty. It calls us out full and it sends us back empty: like Naomi, who also made the same disastrous journey from Judah by the fords of Jericho to Moab. When sin has finished its work, it leaves us stripped and naked, not only of our possessions, but also of our gifts, our talents, our health perhaps, our time and opportunities, our qualities, our character. As a sinner, man is only a pale shadow of the man he was created to be: the man who was to have dominion. He has fallen among thieves. *EVERYMAN*

Secondly, he is wounded and dying. And how graphically that speaks to us of the fate of man in the world. We can look at man in many different ways – at his body, mind and soul, at his will, emotion and imagination, at his various purposes, enterprises and activities, at the individual or at the social, political or economic group – and always we shall find that his journey down from Jerusalem to Jericho has brought on him the mortal assault of sin. Everything that he is and has and does is touched by the same scarring and suffering. Everything that he is and has and does stands under the sentence of mortality pronounced in the warning of Eden: 'In the day that thou eatest thereof thou shalt surely die'. Man as he confronts us in the stricken wayfarer from Jerusalem to Jericho is a dying man.

And finally, he is alone. The thieves who attacked and robbed and battered him – his own fellow-travellers on that downward road – have left him. Others who made the same journey have neither the will nor the means to help. Perhaps they feel a momentary compassion – not without a twinge of

We're all wounded physically mentally spiritually by our mortality & we age, we grow old

from children to children

fear – but it is much easier and better to turn away the eyes and shrug the shoulders and press on quickly down the way, busy with their own concerns and problems. Dying and alone, beyond all human help – this is the plight of every man if only he could see it. Even if they have the desire, neither churchmen nor philanthropists, neither politicians nor social reformers, neither educationalists nor commercialists, neither scientists nor medical experts can do anything finally to alleviate this mortal wound. When it comes to the point, there is no help, no saviour – as we are told so plainly in Isaiah 63. Help for the sin-stricken and dying must either come from above, from God, or else there can be no help. The lesser sorrows of the world may to some extent be mitigated. But when we come to the final assault of sin and death and hell, man is helpless and he is alone, quite alone, isolated from all his fellow-travellers, beyond the reach of any help they may extend – shaken, frightened, wounded, dying, and absolutely alone.

The wounded traveller by the roadside speaks to us of man in general – of every man, but that means that first of all he speaks to us of ourselves. Everyman can easily be no man – a generalised humanity. This is how it will always be, of course, when the parable is used merely to commend a vague humanitarianism. But it may also be like this on a more realistic view if we think of this man only in general terms. We have to be prepared for the fact that when we look at this man by the roadside we are looking into a mirror, and the reflection which we see is primarily that of ourselves. The word of Nathan to David, 'Thou art the man', is the word for us in the wounded man on the Jerusalem-Jericho road. Everyman is myself. I am the man who is on the downward journey from Jerusalem to Jericho. I am the man – all of us, whoever we are, even in all our talents or respectability. I am the man who has fallen among thieves. I am the man who has been spoiled of all his actual and potential riches. I am the man who is wounded and half-dead. I am the man who is alone, unable to help himself and beyond the scope of any human help.

But this, of course, is the point at which we rebel. We are perfectly willing to recognise in this wounded man either man generally or other men known or unknown to ourselves. But to be willing to say: 'I am this man; in this man I see myself', is something which runs clean contrary to all our pride and self-sufficiency and self-righteousness. That is why, when we see others who have sunk to the very depths of moral degradation, or even sometimes of physical weakness, with all the sympathy we feel there goes also an almost instinctive feeling of aversion and impatience. Of course, this is not really what the destiny of man should be – to that extent there is a basic justification for the feeling. But the real rub is that this is in fact our destiny, the destiny of all of us as sinners. The healthy are reminded by the sick that this is the way that they, too, must go: the way of weakness and corruption. The upright are reminded by the degraded that this is the logical development of their sin, that there but for the grace of God they, too, would go. It is not surprising that the priest and the Levite are singled out as the ones who pass by, for they of all people are those who do not recognise, who do not want to recognise, that they are on the same downward road and therefore under the same sentence. But there is something of that in us all. It can't happen to us. There must have been something odd about that man. We are different, that is what we are all tempted to say. We want to shut from us that image of utter destitution which, deep down, we know only too well we shall find to be our own image. And only if we let go our pride, only if we let that wounded man, or any other man in need, show us what we ourselves really are, and what will be our fate unless we find the true help in need, can we really begin to be neighbours to our fellow-men. Not as those who patronise them, but as those who, at bottom, are in just the same need ourselves, as those who must find help from them as they find help from us, as those who, with them, are utterly dependent on the same help.

But where is this help to be found? Is there any real help? And if so, what is this help which we must all find and share if there is to be, not just a temporary mitigation, but a real cure for our need? The obvious answer is that the help comes from the Good Samaritan. But there is a less obvious and yet equally true answer which helps to fill out the picture, and that is that the man wounded and half-dead by the roadside himself shows us where true help is to be found. For this man does not speak to us only about man in general. Nor does he speak to us only about ourselves. He speaks to us also about *the* man, the One who is called the Son of Man, the second man, the Lord from heaven. He speaks to us about Jesus Christ. And it is in this Jesus Christ, as seen in this man, that true help is to be found both for ourselves and others.

Jesus Christ is the man who enters on a downward journey to a far country. He left a greater Jerusalem than the city of David (to which, indeed, in his final passion he had to go up). He left a more marvellous Eden than that from which

173

Adam banished himself in his folly. He left a more loving and comfortable home than that from which the prodigal went out in his blindness and self-will. And he came down to a more desolate and hostile land even than the barren and brigand-infested wastes from Jerusalem to Jericho. He came down to Gethsemane and Gabbatha, where human passions were unmasked in all their ultimate ferocity. He came down to Golgotha, the place of a skull, where he was run down and hemmed in by a blood-thirsty, taunting crowd.

But he came down, this man, in obedience to the will of the Father. He came down in the all-surpassing grace of the Father, Son and Holy Spirit. He came down to be one with man, to take his place, the obedient for the disobedient. He came to enter into the judgement of his sin, to bear it away, the just for the unjust. He took the downward journey to reverse the downward journey of man, to catch him before it is too late, to heal his wounds, to give him new life, to grant him new life and health and clothing, to give him a new direction, to set him on the way which leads to eternal blessedness.

Again, Jesus Christ is the man who is attacked and robbed and stripped by the wayside. From his birth in Bethlehem, through his ministry, to the bitter end on the cross, he was ringed round by hostile and jealous opponents. His coming into the world meant that he had to leave behind the unimaginable wealth of his eternal deity. But when he was in the world he did not seek partial compensation in the luxury and splendour of a noble or wealthy home. His birthplace was a stable. The only home he knew was the home of a humble carpenter, or carpenter's widow, at out-of-the-way Nazareth. His were the cattle upon a thousand hills, but he laid claim to none of them. He was content that the proud creature should despoil him of his rights. In the days of his ministry he had no house, no funds. He was dependent upon the ministrations of others. His very name was dragged in the dust. And when his enemies caught up with him, his only sceptre was a reed and his crown a crown of thorns. And then at last on the cross he was stripped even of his clothes: 'They parted my garments among them and for my vesture did they cast lots'. His grave was the gift of Joseph of Arimathea, and the embalming spices those of the women and Nicodemus. His only testament was in his blood. Though he was rich, as Paul puts it, yet for our sakes he became poor. No man has ever been reduced to more hopeless and abject poverty, no man has ever been more ruthlessly and shamelessly despoiled.

Again, Jesus Christ is the man who is wounded and half-dead – no, wholly dead, so that he can be raised to life again only in the life-giving power of the Spirit. Is not this the word of the prophet: 'He was wounded for our transgressions'? Yes, he was genuinely wounded, wounded by sinners, wounded with the wounds of sin. His brow was pricked with thorns. His hands and feet were torn by the nails. His side was thrust through by the spear. And as he was dying, the priests and the Levites, the scribes and the Pharisees, and all the others, even his own disciples, passed by on the other side: 'Is it nothing to you, all ye that pass by?' Yet in the case of this man, it was all of his own will. He willed to be wounded and to die in this way. He willed to take his place with the thieves on the cross, to take the place of the chief of the thieves, the rebel and murderer, Barabbas. And because he willed it, because he identified himself with the wounded man, because he took his place, it is really his image that we see first and foremost when we look at this man, or at any man in trouble. This man is the man whose place has been taken by Jesus Christ, so that it is no longer man in general, or this man, or myself, but Jesus Christ for man, for this man, for me.

And, of course, Jesus Christ is alone. He of all men is really alone. Even his closest friends forsook him and fled. He was despised and rejected by everyone. No earthly help could come to him. No one could share with him the agony of the cross. At other points and in other things the disciples could be with him. But only Jesus Christ could be 'made' sin, because only Jesus Christ was not naturally and necessarily in sin and its condemnation. Only Jesus Christ could be the sin-bearer. But the fact that Jesus Christ is the sin-bearer means that in the proper and deepest sense he is alone on the roadside because he has taken the place of all others. He is there as the one for all others: the representative: the substitute. And he takes the place of others in order that they may be genuinely helped. He takes their place in order that they should not suffer finally, in order that they should be restored and reclothed, and set on their journey back to Jerusalem. He is alone in the bearing of sin in order that others – yes, in order that we ourselves may be able to join him in the new life where there is no more sin, no more despoilment, no more suffering and no more death.

The final and decisive question comes to us then: have *we* seen Jesus – *dare* we see Jesus in that man wounded and half-dead on the road from Jerusalem to Jericho? For we must see Jesus first if we are really to see ourselves – the depth of our sin and the hopeless nature of our plight. We must see Jesus first if we are to see the full extent of the sinfulness and misery of our fellows and the inevitability of their suffering. Seeing Jesus, we will also see this. We will have to see it. And we will also see where help is to be found. We will see the one who took our place, so that when the horror of our position in sin and death breaks upon us we know at once where to turn. We will see the one who took the place of others, so that when we see our fellows – even the most sick, the most crushed, the most sin-sodden – we are reminded of Jesus, of what he was made for us, and we will be moved, not to con-demnation, nor to sentimentality, but to the extending of that genuine help which Jesus made possible, and we will know that ministering even to the vilest wretch in his wretched-ness, we are in a very true sense ministering to Jesus Christ himself. 'Inasmuch as ye have done it unto one of the least of these my brethren, ye have done it unto me.'

To see in that man by the roadside, Jesus the crucified, is a revelation, a promise and a command. It is a revelation of ourselves, of man, of all our fellow-men, as we are shown to be at the cross of Calvary. It is a promise of help, the one help but the genuine help which there is because Jesus Christ has identified himself with man, with us and taken our place. And it is a command to bring this help – and all other help that we can – to our fellow-sufferers, in the name and for the sake of the one who took their place and ours. We have to be prepared for this revelation – otherwise we shall never get more from the parable than pious platitudes. We have to appropriate this promise – apart from Jesus Christ wounded for us we can learn only the lesson of hopelessness and self-despair. We have to fulfil this command, for it is only then that we can enter into the meaning, and therefore the joy and the power, of the 'Go, and do thou likewise'.

Sermon by Geoffrey William Bromily
quoted in *My Way of Preaching*

Proper 11/Ordinary Time 16

Sunday between 17 and 23 July inclusive

Luke 10:38-42

Mary understood and Martha did not.

One of my favourite saints is Mother Julian of Norwich who was born in 1342 and died circa 1420. Even though she lived in turbulent and difficult times, her life was one of wonderful serenity, and I can think of no one else who so captured the spirit of Mary, who was content to sit at the Lord's feet and learn of him.

For me the Mary and Martha story reveals the other side of the coin in Christian living. The parable of The Good Samaritan that precedes Mary and Martha is all about practical help given to a stranger in need. But the Mary and Martha story teaches the importance of 'being', of the contemplative life; the life of listening to the Word of the Lord before doing anything, and there are those scholars who say that the Church of Christ should combine both Mary and Martha in ministering to the world.

Here is an extract from an essay by Anna Maria Reynolds, called 'Woman of Hope', which tells us something of Julian's era and something also of Julian's 'being'.

The close of the Middle Ages was, in fact, throughout Europe a period of violence, cruelty and pessimism. J. Huisinga* declares: 'Calamities and indigence were more afflicting than at present; it was more difficult to guard against them and to find solace. Illness and health presented a more striking contrast . . . Honours and riches were relished with greater avidity and contrasted more vividly with surrounding misery.'

All things presenting themselves to the mind in violent contrasts and impressive forms, lent a tone of excitement and of passion to everyday life and tended to produce that perpetual oscillation between despair and distracted joy, between cruelty and pious tenderness, which characterises life in the Middle Ages.

It is not astonishing that life in such an unstable and violent world should be more inclined to pessimism than to optimism, and so we read: 'At the close of the Middle Ages,

*J. Huisinga, *The Waning of the Middle Ages*

177

a sombre melancholy weighs on people's souls. Whether we read a chronicle, a poem, a sermon, a legal document even, the same impression of immense sadness is produced by them all. It would sometimes seem as if this period had been particularly unhappy, as if it had left behind only the memory of violence, of covetousness and mortal hatred, as if it had known no other enjoyment but that of intemperance, of pride and of cruelty.'

Closely allied with this melancholy was a view of death as something gruesome and dismal, culminating in the macabre idea of 'the dance of death'. Indeed, the dominant thought about death as expressed in the literature, both ecclesiastical and lay, of this period knows but two extremes: the brevity of earthly glory, and jubilation over the salvation of the soul. All else is overshadowed by the over-accentuated and over-vivid representation of death as hideous and threatening – a horrid image of skeletons and worms.

Such are the characteristics of the epoch to which Julian belongs and which projects her as a radiant figure of pure goodness, vibrant with faith, hope and love. The source of the optimism and serenity which Julian diffuses is neither biological – a matter of temperament – nor physical – a matter of feeling good and comfortable in an unchallenging situation, since her situation was, in fact, a desperately challenging one. She repeatedly makes clear that her cheerfulness rests on something outside herself: 'The remedy is that our Lord is with us, keeping us and leading us into the fulness of joy; for our Lord intends this to be an endless joy, that he will be our bliss when we are there (in heaven), is our protector while we are here, our way and our heaven in true love and trust.'

Anna Maria Reynolds
quoted in *Julian, Woman of Our Day*

The clash of temperaments

It would be hard to find more vivid character drawing in greater economy of words than we find in these verses.

(i) They show us *the clash of temperaments*. We have never allowed enough for the place of temperament in religion. Some people are naturally dynamos of activity; others are naturally quiet. It is hard for the active person to understand the person who sits and contemplates and the person who is devoted to quiet times and meditation is apt to look down on the person who would rather be active.

There is no right or wrong in this. God did not make everyone alike. One person may pray,

> 'Lord of all pots and pans and things,
> since I've no time to be
> a saint by doing lovely things,
> or watching late with thee,
>
> or dreaming in the dawnlight,
> or storming heaven's gates,
> make me a saint by getting meals
> and washing up the plates.'

Another may sit with folded hands and mind intense to think and pray. Both are serving God. God needs his Marys and his Marthas too.

(ii) These verses show us something more – they show us *the wrong kind of kindness*. Think where Jesus was going when this happened. He was on his way to Jerusalem – to die. His whole being was taken up with the intensity of the inner battle to bend his will to the will of God. When Jesus came to that home in Bethany it was a great day; *and* Martha was eager to celebrate it by laying on the best the house could give. So she rushed and fussed and cooked; *and that was precisely what Jesus did not want*. All he wanted was quiet. With the cross before him and with the inner tension in his heart, he had turned aside to Bethany to find an oasis of calm away from the demanding crowds, if only for an hour or two; and that is what Mary gave him and what Martha, in her kindness, did her best to destroy. 'One thing is necessary' – quite possibly this means, 'I don't want a big spread; one course, the simplest meal is all I want'. It was simply that Mary understood and that Martha did not.

Here is one of the great difficulties in life. So often we want to be kind to people – but we want to be kind to them *in our way*; and should it happen that our way is not the necessary way, we sometimes take offence and think that we are not appreciated. If we are trying to be kind, the first necessity is to try to see into the heart of the person we desire to help – and then to forget all our own plans and to think only of what he or she needs. Jesus loved Martha and Martha loved him, but when Martha set out to be kind, it had to be her way of being kind which was really being unkind to him whose heart cried out for quiet. Jesus loved Mary and Mary loved him, and Mary understood.

William Barclay
The Daily Study Bible: The Gospel of Luke

Proper 12/Ordinary Time 17

Sunday between 24 and 30 July inclusive

Luke 11:1-13

In the Lord's Prayer we possess a tangible relic of Jesus Christ, and by means of it we touch what was inmost in the person of Jesus.

On the necessity of prayer

Prayer brings the mind into the brightness of the divine light and the will to the warmth of divine love. Nothing else so purges the mind of ignorance and the will of wrong inclinations. It is a fountain which revives our good desires and causes them to bring forth fruit; it washes away the stains of our weaknesses and calms the passion of the heart.

Above all, I would recommend mental prayer, the prayer of the heart; and that drawn from the contemplation of the life and passion of our Lord. If you habitually meditate on him, your soul will be filled with him, you will learn his expression and learn to frame your actions after his example.

He is the light of the world. It is therefore in him, by him and for him that we must be enlightened and illuminated. And so, if we remain close to our Lord, meditating on him and giving heed to his words, we shall gradually by the help of his grace learn to speak, to act and to will like him.

There we must stay, for we can approach God the Father by no other door.

St Francis de Sales

He knows what we want before we ask it. Then why ask? Why, because there may be blessings which only are effectively blessings to those who are in the right condition of mind; just as there is wholesome food which is actually wholesome only to those who are healthy in body. If you give the best beef to somebody in typhoid fever, you do him great harm. The worst of all diseases of the soul is forgetfulness of God; and if everything that we need came to us while we forgot God, we should only be confirmed in our forgetfulness of him, in our sense of independence of him . . . Over and over again, it will happen that, whether or not God can give the blessing which, in his love, he desires to give, will depend on whether or not we recognise the source from which it comes. The way to recognise that he is the source of the blessings, and that we need them, is to ask.

William Temple
Christian Faith and Life

No words ever spoken have taken such a hold on men as those of the Lord's Prayer. It conveys to us the mind of Jesus and no other. Not only does it bear the intrinsic mark of authenticity, but it may fairly be regarded as the best attested of all the utterances of Jesus. His other sayings are preserved to us only by happy accident. He taught informally, and among those who listened to him were sometimes one or two who were impressed by words he said and kept them in their memory. But this prayer was on a different footing from the rest of his teaching. He took care to imprint it on the minds of his disciples. He meant it to be the standard prayer which they would be constantly offering. This they have kept doing from the hour when he first spoke it to the present day. The piety of the Middle Ages was eager above all things to find some tangible relic of Jesus – a fragment of his robe, a cup he had drunk from, a splinter of the Holy Cross. In the Lord's Prayer we actually possess such a relic, and by means of it we touch what was inmost in the person of Jesus. We can feel as we repeat it, that our ears have heard and our hands have handled, his way of life.

E. F. Scott
The Lord's Prayer (adapted)

Proper 13/Ordinary Time 18

Sunday between 31 July and 6 August inclusive

Luke 12:13-21

Jesus called this man a fool because he allowed the means by which he lived to outdistance the ends for which he lived.

And so I came to you this morning to talk about some of the great insights from the scripture in general, and from the New Testament in particular. I want to use as a subject from which to preach: 'Why Jesus called a man a fool.' – '*Why Jesus called a man a fool.*'

I want to share with you a dramatic little story from the Gospel as recorded by Saint Luke. It is a story of a man who by all standards of measurement would be considered a highly successful man. And yet Jesus called him a fool. If you will read that parable, you will discover that the central character in the drama is a certain rich man. This man was so rich that his farm yielded tremendous crops. In fact, the crops were so great that he didn't know what to do. It occurred to him that he had only one alternative, and that was to build some new and bigger barns so he could store all of his crops. And then as he thought about this, he said, 'Then I'm going to do something after I build my new and bigger barns'. He said, 'I'm going to store my goods and fruit there, and then I'm going to say to my soul, "Soul, thou hast much goods, laid up for many years. Take thine ease, eat, drink, and be merry."' That brother thought that was the end of life.

chief end of (life) man

But the parable doesn't end with that man making his statement. It ends by saying that God said to him, 'Thou fool. Not next year, not next week, not tomorrow, but this night, thy soul is required of thee.'

And so it was at the height of his prosperity he died. Look at that parable. Think about it. Think of this man: if he lived in Chicago today, he would be considered 'a big shot'. And he would abound with all of the social prestige and all of the community influence that could be afforded. Most people would look up to him because he would have that something called money. And yet a Galilean peasant had the audacity to call that man a fool.

Now, Jesus didn't call the man a fool because he made his money in a dishonest fashion. There is nothing in that parable to indicate that this man was dishonest and that he made his money through conniving and exploitative methods. In fact, it seems to reveal that he had a modicum of humanity and that he was a very industrious man. He was a thrifty man, apparently a pretty hard worker. So Jesus didn't call him a fool because he got his money through dishonest means.

And there is nothing here to indicate that Jesus called this man a fool because he was rich. Jesus never made a universal indictment against all wealth. It's true that one day a rich young ruler came to him raising some questions about eternal life and Jesus said to him, 'Sell all'. But in that case Jesus was prescribing individual surgery and not setting forth a universal diagnosis. You know, Jesus told another parable about a man who was very rich by the name of Dives, and Dives ended up going to hell. There was nothing indicating that Dives went to hell because he was rich. In fact, when Dives got to hell, he had a conversation with a man in heaven; and on the other end of that long-distance call between hell and heaven was Abraham in heaven. Now, if you go back to the Old Testament, you will discover that Abraham was a real rich man. It wasn't a millionaire in hell talking with a poor man in heaven; it was a little millionaire in hell talking with a multimillionaire in heaven. So that Jesus did not call this man a fool because he was rich.

I'd like you to look at this parable with me and try to decipher the real reason that Jesus called this man a fool. Number one, Jesus called this man a fool because he allowed the means by which he lived to outdistance the ends for which he lived. You see, each of us lives in two realms, the within and the without. Now, the within of our lives is that complex of devices, of mechanisms and instrumentalities by means of which we live. The house we live in, that's part of the means by which we live. The car we drive, the clothes we wear, the money that we are able to accumulate: in short, the physical stuff that's necessary for us to exist.

Now, the problem is that we must always keep a line of demarcation between the two. This man was a fool because he didn't do that.

The other day in Atlanta, the wife of a man had an automobile accident. He received a call that the accident had taken place on the expressway. The first question he asked when he received the call: 'How much damage did it do to my Cadillac?' He never asked how his wife was doing. Now, that man was a fool, because he had allowed an automobile to become more significant than a person. He wasn't a fool because he had a Cadillac, he was a fool because he worshipped his Cadillac. He allowed his automobile to become more important than God.

Somehow in life we must know that we must seek first the kingdom of God, and then all of those other things – clothes, houses, cars – will be added unto us. But the problem is, all too many people fail to put first things first. They don't keep a sharp line of demarcation between the things of life and the ends of life.

And so this man was a fool because he allowed the means by which he lived to outdistance the ends for which he lived. He was a fool because he maximised the minimum and minimised the maximum. This man was a fool because he allowed his technology to outdistance his theology. This man was a fool because he allowed his mentality to outrun his morality. Somehow he became so involved in the means by which he lived that he couldn't deal with the way to eternal matters. He didn't make contributions to civil rights. He looked at suffering humanity and wasn't concerned about it. He may have had great books in his library, but he never read them. He may have had recordings of great music of the ages, but he never listened to (them). He probably gave his wife mink coats, a convertible automobile, but he didn't give her what she needed most: love and affection. He probably provided bread for his children, but he didn't give them any attention; he didn't really love them. Somehow he looked up at the beauty of the stars, but he wasn't moved by them. He had heard the glad tidings of philosophy and poetry, but he really didn't read it or comprehend it, or want to comprehend it. And so this man justly deserved his title. He was an eternal fool. He allowed the means by which he lived to outdistance the ends for which he lived.

Now, number two, this man was a fool because he failed to realise his dependence on others. Now, if you read that parable in the book of Luke, you will discover that this man utters about sixty words. And do you know, in sixty words he said 'I' and 'my' more than fifteen times? This man was a fool because he said 'I' and 'my' so much until he lost the capacity to say 'we' and 'our'. He failed to realise that he couldn't do anything by himself. This man talked like he could build the barns by himself, like he could till the soil by himself. And he failed to realise that wealth is always a result of the commonwealth.

Maybe you haven't ever thought about it, but you can't leave home in the morning without being dependent on most of the world. You get up in the morning, and you go to the bathroom and you reach over for a sponge, and that's even given to you by a Pacific Islander. You reach over for a towel, and that's given to you by a Turk. You reach down to pick up your soap, and that's given to you by a Frenchman. Then after dressing, you rush to the kitchen and you decide this morning that you want to drink a little coffee; that's poured in your cup by a South American. Or maybe this morning you prefer tea; that's poured in your cup by a Chinese. Or maybe you want cocoa this morning; that's poured in your cup by a West African. Then you reach over to get your toast, and that's given to you at the hands of an English-speaking farmer, not to mention the baker. Before you finish eating breakfast in the morning you are dependent on more than half of the world.

And oh, my friends, I don't want you to forget it. No matter where you are today, somebody helped you to get there. It may have been an ordinary person, doing an ordinary job in an extraordinary way.

There is a magnificent lady, with all of the beauty of blackness and black culture, by the name of Marian Anderson. She started out as a little girl singing in the choir of the Union Baptist church in Philadelphia, Pennsylvania. And then came that glad day when she made it. And she stood in Carnegie Hall, with the Philharmonic Orchestra in the background in New York, singing with a beauty that is matchless. Then she came to the end of that concert, singing *Ave Maria* as nobody else can sing it. And they called her back and back and back and back again, and she finally ended by singing *Nobody knows de trouble I seen.* And her mother was sitting out in the audience, and she started crying; tears were flowing down her cheeks. And the person next to her said, 'Mrs Anderson, why are your crying? Your daughter is scoring tonight. The critics tomorrow will be lavishing their praise on her. Why are you crying?' and Mrs Anderson looked over with tears still flowing and said, 'I'm not crying because I'm sad, I'm crying for joy'. She went on to say, 'You may not remember; you wouldn't know. But I remember when Marian was growing up, and I was working in a kitchen till my hands were all but parched, my eyebrows all but scalded. I was working there to make it possible for my daughter to get an education. And I remember one day Marian came to me and said, "Mother, I don't want to see you having to work like this." And I looked down and said, "Honey, I don't mind it. I'm doing it for you and I expect great things of you."'

And finally one day somebody asked Marian Anderson in later years, 'Miss Anderson, what has been the happiest moment of your life? Was it the moment that you had your debut in Carnegie Hall in New York?' She said, 'No, that wasn't it.'

'Miss Anderson, was it the moment that Toscanini said that a voice like yours comes only once in a century?'

'No, that wasn't it.'

'What was it then, Miss Anderson?'

And she looked up and said quietly, 'The happiest moment in my life was the moment that I could say, "Mother, you can stop working now"'. Marian Anderson realised that she was where she was because somebody helped her to get there.

Martin Luther King
A Knock at Midnight

Assets – a poem for three voices

'I have four big lollies.'
'Ten were given to me.'
'I will show you
where blackberries grow
if you'll come and see.'

'I have twenty fireworks.'
'I've got sixty-three.'
'I know a place
where the sunset and moon
reflect in the sea.'

'I can shout the loudest.'
'Just listen to me.'
'I share a space
that is full of quiet
with a willow tree.'

'I've got the bomb and a country.'
'I rule over three.'
'I have the birds
and the curving sky,
and *all* that is free.'

Cecily Taylor

The parable calls covetousness folly. It could also have said it was a violation of the law of Moses (Exodus 20:17) and of the teachings of the prophets (Micah 2:2). Even so, it seems to have been a widespread problem in the Church (Romans 1:29; Mark 7:22; Colossians 3:5; Ephesians 5:5; 1 Timothy 6:10). This craving to hoard not only puts goods in the place of God (in Pauline theology, covetousness is idolatry: Romans 1:25; Colossians 3:5) but is an act of total disregard for the needs of others. The preacher will want to be careful not to caricature the farmer and thus rob the story of the power of its realism. There is nothing here of graft or theft; there is no mistreatment of workers or any criminal act. Sun, soil, and rain join to make him wealthy. He is careful and conservative. If he is not unjust, then what is he? He is a fool, says the parable. He lives completely for himself, he talks to himself, he plans for himself, he congratulates himself. His sudden death proves him to have lived as a fool. 'For what does it profit a man if he gains the whole world and loses or forfeits himself?' (9:25).

We have known since Mary sang of the reversal of fortunes of the full and the empty (1:53) that Luke would again and again raise the seductive and difficult subject of possessions. He will hold up as the standard for disciples the voluntary sharing of one's goods. This, says Luke, was the message of John the Baptist (3:10-14) and of Jesus (6:30; 16:19-31) and was the practice of early Christians (Acts 4:34-37).

Fred B. Craddock
Luke

There are few areas in the lives of modern Christians where help is needed more than in the matter of material possessions. Members of congregations may be familiar with stewardship appeals during the particular season of the year when pledges are solicited, but they very rarely find themselves confronted with the other passages in the Bible that speak to the threat and temptation that material possessions pose. The fact that many North American congregations have greatly benefited from the gifts of the wealthy makes ministers a bit reluctant to tackle the ominous texts that raise serious questions about the amassing of riches. What if the big givers are offended by what the Bible says?

Yet it is also true that many church members want help in discerning how they earn, invest, and spend their money. They live in a capitalistic culture that thrives on the profit motive and puts a high premium on expansion and growth. At the same time, they read in their Bibles about the condemnation of avarice, one of the seven deadly sins. How does one distinguish the profit motive from greed? Or how does one function (that is, earn a living, raise a family, live responsibly) in a society that values people in terms of what they possess, and where the accumulation of money is the quickest access to power? The latter question becomes a particularly urgent issue when one is faced with the loss of a job and the accompanying sense of failure and valuelessness. Both this Sunday and next, the assigned Gospel lessons provide occasions for reflection on the meaning of possessions, and it is particularly appropriate to do so in the context of thinking about the larger issue of discipleship (one of the thematic foci of Luke's travel narrative). The Gospel texts are not immediately addressed to the broader culture, to provide a blueprint for an economic system that is peculiarly Christian. They in fact are addressed to disciples and would-be disciples, who have little or no leverage to change economic patterns but who want to live faithfully to their calling as believers. Jesus' words make sense only in the circle of faith where the intrusion of God into the lives of people (as with the rich man in the parable) is taken seriously.

The manner in which the nameless person in the crowd interrupts Jesus to asks that he adjudicate a family dispute over inheritance is abrupt (Luke 12:13). In an instant the topic changes from solemn encouragement to disciples to remain steadfast in their confessions of faith (12:4-12) to what seems like a trivial concern – except that Jesus makes it more than trivial. Though he refuses to be the arbitrator, Jesus warns the person who made the request of two things (constantly be on guard against all kinds of greed and know that your life does not consist of what you possess), and then tells a forceful parable.

The initial warnings are indirect. The person asking for arbitration is not immediately condemned for being greedy, nor is he chided for having abruptly changed the subject. Instead, he is instructed to set up a perpetual watch against the variety of ways greed operates in human life. (The imperative 'Be on guard' is a present tense.) Greed (*pleonexia*, literally 'the yearning to have more') is insidious and results in idolatry (see Colossians 3:5). Furthermore, life is more than possessions. As a divine gift it is valued in other ways than by the size of bank accounts and stock portfolios.

The parable is powerful and needs little explanation. It pushes the whole issue of possessions a step farther by depicting the tragedy of trusting in false security. The rich fool is not guilty of greed; his acreage simply produces a bumper crop. His problem is the misguided illusion that his prosperity has secured the future. He feels amply supplied 'for many years'. But then in the midst of a conversation he is having with himself, God interrupts to inform him that death is on its way. One whose whole speech has been delivered in the first person ('I will do this and that') is left with the rhetorical question, 'And the things you have prepared, whose will they be?'

Now the text does not prescribe specific answers to our questions about possessions. It does not provide rules that define how much is 'enough' and what people should do with their wealth if they have some. The reader hunts in vain for a guideline, a principle, a quantifiable definition of greed that will tell one whether he or she has stepped over the line. The text does not offer a new law, but it does confront the reader with eloquent language and powerful symbols that continue to prod the imagination. To be constantly on guard against greed, to be reminded that life is a gift of God and not a hard-earned acquisition, to be warned vividly against the presumption that affluence can secure the future – these are more than rules.

Charles B. Cousar
Texts for Preaching: A Lectionary Commentary Based on the NRSV – Year C

Proper 14/Ordinary Time 19

Sunday between 7 and 13 August inclusive

Luke 12:32-40

One's attitude towards wealth and one's actions with the money he or she has are part of the disciple's readiness and watchfulness.

The Gospel lesson for last Sunday (Proper 13) came from a critical chapter in Luke's narrative dealing with the devastating effects of wealth. It issued pointed warnings against greed and the presumption that by material possessions one can secure the future. The lection for Proper 14 continues the instruction about possessions, this time setting the issue in an eschatological context and offering more specific guidance about how one can act responsibly.

First, a word about the literary structure of the section. Following the parable of the rich fool (Luke 12:16-21), Jesus tells the disciples not to become preoccupied with even the basic necessities of life – food and clothing. Their one concern is to pursue zealously God's rule and to be assured that God will care for them. If God can feed the ravens and clothe the fields with lovely lilies, then God will not ignore their need for life's essentials. These are words of comfort for disciples who will be called to risk a lot for the kingdom (12:22-34).

The concluding paragraph of this counsel to avoid anxiety (verses 32-34) is assigned as the starting point for today's lesson and is coupled with the next section, including Jesus' words about being prepared for the coming of the Son of man (verses 35-40). The linkage between directions about possessions and calls for preparedness for the return of Jesus at an unexpected time, presents a dynamic context for reflection.

Three dimensions of the text can guide our considerations about possessions. First, the presupposition for any talk about what to do with wealth is the reality of God's reign. Paradoxically, disciples are told to *strive* for the divine kingdom (verse 31) and at the same time to be comforted that God is delighted to *give* them the kingdom (verse 32). The striving is set over against the temptation to strive for food and clothes. The giving reassures them that the world is controlled not by fate or by the demonic forces of disorder and confusion, but by a caring parent ('your Father'), whose kindly gift is to the 'little flock.'

Whose will prevails in the world makes a great difference when one begins to think about possessions. If one believes that the divine rule has begun with the advent of Jesus and the present is orientated to the completion of that reign in Jesus' return, then one has reason to bring God into any discussion about money. If, however, what makes the world go round is chance or human aggressiveness or a demonic force, then Jesus' words make little sense. The presence of God's rule is the only justifiable reason for a carefree attitude towards life's necessities and a willingness to share one's possessions with the poor.

Second, in light of God's gift of the divine rule, disciples are told to sell their possessions and give to the poor. They are beginning to discover what the rich fool should have done with his abundant crops. Instead of deluding himself into thinking that his prosperity guaranteed his future, he could have eased the immediate burdens of those whose crops had been devastated by drought.

Furthermore, there is a clear affirmation that taking a carefree stance towards one's personal needs and giving alms to the poor result in heavenly treasure. A reward is promised, but one that demands the rejection of the strategy of the rich fool and his ilk, who store up treasures for themselves (12-21). To be sure, the pursuit of wealth has its rewards, but they are ephemeral, fleeting, and at the mercy of the acquisitiveness of others more greedy, in contrast to purses 'that do not wear out' and treasures 'unfailing.'

The theme of almsgiving is, of course, persistent in Luke (14:33; 18:22) and paves the way for the picture of the ideal community in Acts 2:45; 4:34-37, where a regularised programme of caring for the needy is instituted. The Christian community cannot contemplate the meaning of discipleship apart from considering how it will serve the poor and less fortunate. It lies at the heart of faithfulness.

Third, the section of Luke 12:35-40 talks about perpetual readiness for the Son of man, adding a new dimension to the importance of almsgiving. The initial vignette depicts a master returning from a wedding feast and finding alert servants, immediately opening the door on his arrival. The master is so delighted at their watchfulness that he exchanges roles with them, like another master (*kyrios*) we know, becomes their servant (see 22:27). The second vignette describes an unfortunate homeowner whose house has been broken into. Had he known when the thief was coming, he would certainly have prepared for him.

All life is lived in the expectation of the Son of Man's return. The time of the arrival is unknown, but the coming is sure. This eschatological anticipation sets the talk about possessions in a new context. One's attitude toward wealth and its enticements and one's actions with the money he or she has are not trivial matters. They are part of the disciples' readiness and watchfulness.

Charles B. Cousar
Texts for Preaching: A Lectionary Commentary Based on the NRSV – Year C

Proper 15/Ordinary Time 20

Sunday between 14 and 20 August inclusive

Luke 12:49-56

There are some things a man cannot afford to put off; above all, making his peace with God.

To those who were learning to regard Jesus as the Messiah, the anointed one of God, these words would come as a bleak shock. They regarded the Messiah as conqueror and king, and the Messianic age as a golden time.

(i) In Jewish thought, fire is almost always the symbol of *judgement*. So then, Jesus regarded the coming of his kingdom as a time of judgement. The Jews firmly believed that God would judge other nations by one standard and themselves by another; that the very fact that a man was a Jew would be enough to absolve him. However much we may wish to eliminate the element of judgement from the message of Jesus, it remains stubbornly and unalterably there.

(ii) The Authorised Version and the Revised Standard translate verse 50, 'I have a baptism to be baptised with'. The Greek verb *baptizein* means to dip. In the passive it means to be submerged. Often it is used metaphorically. For instance, it is used of a ship sunk beneath the waves. It can be used of a man submerged in drink and therefore dead-drunk. It can be used of a scholar submerged (or sunk, as we say) by an examiner's questions. Above all it is used of a man submerged in some grim and terrible experience – someone who can say, 'All the waves and billows are gone over me'.

That is the way in which Jesus uses it here. 'I have,' he said, 'a terrible experience through which I must pass; and life is full of tension until I pass through it and emerge triumphantly from it.' The cross was ever before his eyes. How different from the Jewish idea of God's King! Jesus came, not with avenging armies and flying banners, but to give his life as ransom for many . . .

(iii) His coming would inevitably mean division; in point of fact it did. That was one of the great reasons why the Romans hated Christianity – it tore families in two. Over and over again a man had to decide whether he loved better his kith and kin or Christ. The essence of Christianity is that loyalty to Christ has to take precedence over the dearest loyalties of this earth. A man must be prepared to count all things but loss for the excellence of Jesus Christ.

The Jews of Palestine were weatherwise. When they saw

the clouds forming in the west, over the Mediterranean Sea, they knew rain was on the way. When the south wind blew from the desert they knew the sirocco-like wind was coming. But those who were so wise to read the signs of the sky could not, or would not, read the signs of the times. If they had, they would have seen that the kingdom of God was on the way.

Jesus used a very vivid illustration. He said: 'When you are threatened with a law-suit, come to an agreement with your adversary before the matter comes to court, for if you do not you will have imprisonment to endure and a fine to pay.' The assumption is that the defendant has a bad case which will inevitably go against him. 'Every man,' Jesus implied, 'has a bad case in the presence of God; and if he is wise, he will make his peace with God while yet there is time.'

Jesus and all his great servants have always been obsessed with the urgency of time. Andrew Marvell spoke of ever hearing 'time's wingéd chariot hurrying near'. There are some things a man cannot afford to put off; above all, making his peace with God.

William Barclay
The Daily Study Bible: The Gospel of Luke

I include this poem because for me, it tells of a lady who did not recognise the time of her ardent lover's visitation, since the poem ends with no mention of any response from her.

To his coy mistress

Had we but world enough, and time,
this coyness, Lady, were no crime.
We would sit down, and think which way
to walk, and pass our long love's day.
Thou by the Indian Ganges' side
shouldst rubies find: I by the tide
of Humber would complain. I would
love you ten years before the Flood:
and you should, if you please, refuse
till the conversion of the Jews.
My vegetable love should grow

vaster than empires, and more slow.
An hundred years should go to praise
thine eyes, and on thy forehead gaze.
Two hundred to adore each breast:
but thirty thousand to the rest.
An age at least to every part,
and the last age should show your heart.
For, Lady, you deserve this state;
nor would I love at lower rate.

But at my back I always hear
time's wingéd chariot hurrying near:
and yonder all before us lie
deserts of vast eternity.
Thy beauty shall no more be found;
nor, in thy marble vault, shall sound
my echoing song: then worms shall try
that long preserved virginity:
and your quaint honour turn to dust;
and into ashes all my lust.
The grave's a fine and private place,
but none I think do there embrace.

Now therefore, while the youthful hue
sits on thy skin like morning dew,
and while thy willing soul transpires
at every pore with instant fires,
now let us sport us while we may;
and now, like amorous birds of prey,
rather at once our time devour
than languish in this slow-chap't power.
Let us roll all our strength, and all
our sweetness, up into one ball:
and tear our pleasures with rough strife
through the iron gates of life.
Thus, though we cannot make our sun
stand still, yet we will make him run.

Andrew Marvell

Proper 16/Ordinary Time 21

Sunday between 21 and 27 August inclusive

Luke 13:10-17

The house is divided; the adversaries are put to shame; the crowd rejoices. Such is the effect of the presence of Jesus and the inbreaking of God's reign over satanic forces.

Sunday

My mother's strongest religious feeling
was that Catholics were a sinister lot;
she would hardly trust even a lapsed one.
My father was a lapsed Catholic.

Yet we were sent to Sunday school.
Perhaps in the spirit that others
were sent to public schools. It
might come in useful later on.

In Sunday school a sickly adult
taught the teachings of a sickly lamb
to a gathering of sickly children.

It was a far cry from that brisk person
who created the heaven and the earth in
six days and then took Sunday off.

The churches were run by a picked crew
of bad actors radiating insincerity.
Not that one thought of them in that way,
one merely disliked the sound of their voices.
I cannot recall one elevated moment in church,
though as a choirboy I pulled in a useful
sixpence per month.

Strange, that a sense of religion should
somehow survive all this grim buffoonery!
Perhaps that brisk old person does exist,
and we are living through his Sunday.

D. J. Enright

Pain

Greek thought, to which Christian theology is heir, insisted that God was above pain and suffering. According to it, whenever God entered into the human situation in order to relieve pain or suffering, in order to bring succour to the anxious or distressed, he came from outside. The *deus ex machina* of Greek drama was a true representation of Greek thought.

The Hebrew conception was more realistic. It perceived the fact that in actual experience there was no *deus ex machina*: and that the God/man relationship was really one of mutual involvement. Pain and suffering, anxiety and distress would always be there with this difference: that there would be the experience of relief and remission, the experience of succour and courage to bear, the experience of God's presence and power whereby every situation pointed beyond itself to God, in whom was the resolution of and victory over man's present predicament.

In the book of Job is the picture of a man refusing to accept every form of consolation which his friends seek to bring him in his pain and sorrow. The consolations are too superficial. Job also rejects all the explanations which his friends offer him for his condition. These explanations are spurious. Ethics, religion, metaphysics – all are set aside as throwing no real light on Job's situation. On the other hand, Job seeks an answer from God himself. He hurls his questions in the face of God, only to be met by the divine silence; while in his own heart he begins to wonder whether he will understand even if God answers. Can it be that the whole thing is only make-believe and that the truth is simply that there is no God? The answer of Job is 'No'. 'I know,' he says, 'that my Redeemer lives, and that he will stand upon the earth.' *There are no explanations that really explain. There are no consolations that really console. There are no answers that come to the questions which are asked. But God remains* [my italics]. And I know that here and now, in the midst of my situation whatever it be, I shall find him as my Redeemer. 'He will stand upon the earth.'

How does he stand? What does Immanuel mean, when God who is affirmed as 'with us' is 'with us' because of his kenosis and only as a result of it? What does it mean to God that he is man's God? The answer of Christian faith is in terms of the pain of God. *The pain of God is God's answer to the pain of man* [my italics]. God's true response to it; and man's response to his own pain is to make it the pathway by which he enters into the pain of God. God's pain is the measure of his concern for his whole creation. It is also the consequence of his involvement with creation in its struggle with sin and evil, and in its cry for redemption. Besides, God is not just Creator: he has also given himself to his creation in order to be part of it. He is the source of its new birth.

First of all then, God is *concerned with man*. It grieves him when men destroy themselves through rebellion or idolatry. His grief is like the grief of a father whose son has denied or betrayed the love of his home. His grief is like the grief of a husband whose wife has become a prey of other men. His grief is like the grief of a friend whose friendship has been spurned. There is pain in the heart of God when his purpose for creation is thwarted.

But the pain of God is more than pain on account of man. He is also *involved with man* – involved with him in his struggle with sin, in his contest with evil, in his groping for holiness, in his search for community, in his cry for wholeness. God is a participant in the whole movement of life. Indeed there would be no movement if not for him. The leaves on the tree would like to be still, but the wind keeps blowing. God engages man and is engaged with man in the pilgrimage of life.

There is more to it even than that. For God suffers also *as part of man*. When there is pain in the human body, it is an indication that the resources of life are resisting and attacking the causes of ill-health. Pain is the symptom which shows that health is actively present. Similarly, it is the active presence of God as part of man which causes both the pain of man and the pain of God. Sin and evil would not cause pain but death, were not God actively present.

D. T. Niles
A Testament of Faith

The preacher who has been following the Gospel lessons from Luke, especially 9:51 since about two months ago, may by this time begin to feel what the listeners are feeling: these demands of discipleship are heavy. Recall some phrases from those texts: set his face to go to Jerusalem; leave the dead to bury the dead; whoever puts the hand to the plough and looks back; carry no purse, no bag, no sandals; shake the dust off your feet; go and do likewise; one thing is necessary; beware of all covetousness; sell your possessions and give alms; be ready, for the Son of Man is coming at an unexpected hour; I came to cast fire upon the earth, not peace but division. If there is a sense of an accumulated burden, then let the preacher welcome this story of a healing. However, for all its refreshing promise, it, too, is not without strong tension and controversy. In fact, this is Luke's last reference to Jesus teaching in a synagogue, and the scene is prophetic of what awaits Jesus in Jerusalem. To alert the reader further about dark days ahead Luke again mentions Jerusalem (verse 22) and has Herod Antipas reappear in the story (verse 31), this time threatening Jesus' life.

We cannot locate this healing geographically; it has already become clear that Jesus' journey to Jerusalem, beginning at Luke 9:51, is *theological* and *pedagogical*, not *geographical* [my italics]. The story recalls a similar incident at 6:6-11 as well as the tension in the synagogue at Nazareth (4:16-30). It was Jesus' custom to attend the synagogue on the Sabbath (4:16); his ministry was inside, not outside, the worship and common life of Israel. To be in the synagogue on the Sabbath was to be at the heart of Judaism in its most prevalent and in many ways its strongest form.

Apparently the stooped woman came to worship, although the synagogue leader spoke to the crowd about coming on the Sabbath for healing (verse14). Notice that the woman does not approach Jesus, makes no request of him, and reveals no faith in him. Once healed, she praises God (verse 13), but the initiative for the healing belongs totally to Jesus. In this respect, her recovery is through an act of radical grace. The leader's reprimand is directed to the people as accessories in Sabbath violation, but indirectly it is an attack on Jesus. Jesus' response is not to the people but directly to the leader and his associates, whose application of Sabbath law is hypocritical. The key words are 'bound' and 'set free'. The leaders permit a bound (tethered) animal to be loosed for watering on the Sabbath, but they forbid this woman, a daughter of Abraham, and not an animal, who has been bound by Satan for eighteen years, from being set free from her infirmity on the Sabbath.

Jesus' argument, from the lesser to the greater, is incontrovertible. The house is divided: the adversaries are put to shame; the crowd rejoices. Such is the effect of the presence of Jesus and the inbreaking of God's reign over satanic forces. A crisis is created; but if setting a woman free shatters an unhealthy peace, then crisis it has to be.

Fred B. Craddock
Preaching Through the Christian Year: 'C'

Proper 17/Ordinary Time 22

Sunday between 28 August and 3 September inclusive

Luke 14:1, 7-14

Humility has always been one of the characteristics of greatness.

Mrs Malone

Mrs Malone
lived hard by a wood
all on her lonesome
as nobody should.
With her crust on her plate
and her pot on the coal
and none but herself
to converse with, poor soul.
In a shawl and a hood
she got sticks out-o'-door,
on a bit of old sacking
she slept on the floor,
and nobody, nobody
asked how she fared
or knew how she managed,
for nobody cared.
  Why make a pother
  about an old crone?
  What for should they bother
  with Mrs Malone?

One Monday in winter
with snow on the ground
so thick that a footstep
fell without sound,
she heard a faint frostbitten
peck on the pane
and went to the window
to listen again.
There sat a cock-sparrow
bedraggled and weak,
with half-open eyelid
and ice on his beak.
She threw up the sash
and she took the bird in,
and mumbled and fumbled it
under her chin.

'Ye're all of a smother,
ye're fair overblown!
I've room fer another,'
said Mrs Malone.

Come Tuesday while eating
her dry morning slice
with the sparrow a-picking
('Ain't company nice!')
she heard on the doorpost
a curious scratch,
and there was a cat
with its claw on the latch.
It was hungry and thirsty
and thin as a lath,
it mewed and it mowed
on the slithery path.
She threw the door open
and warmed up some pap,
and huddled and cuddled it
in her old lap.
　'There, there, little brother,
　ye poor skin-an'-bone,
　there's room fer another,'
　said Mrs Malone.

Come Wednesday while all of them
crouched on the mat
with a crumb for the sparrow,
a sip for the cat,
there was wailing and whining
outside in the wood,
and there sat a vixen
with six of her brood.
She was haggard and ragged
and worn to a shred,
and her half-dozen babies
were only half-fed,
but Mrs Malone, crying
'My! ain't they sweet!'
happed them and lapped them
and gave them to eat.
　'You warm yerself, mother,
　ye're cold as a stone!
　There's room fer another,'
　said Mrs Malone.

Come Thursday a donkey
stepped in off the road
with sores on his withers
from bearing a load.
Come Friday when icicles
pierced the white air,
down from the mountainside
lumbered a bear.
For each she had something,
if little, to give –
'Lord knows, the poor critters
must all of 'em live.'
She gave them her sacking,
her hood and her shawl,
her loaf and her teapot –
she gave them her all.
    'What with one thing and t'other
    me fambily's grown,
    and there's room fer another,'
    said Mrs Malone.

Come Saturday evening
when time was to sup
Mrs Malone
had forgot to sit up.
The cat said meeow,
and the sparrow said peep,
the vixen, she's sleeping,
the bear, let her sleep.
On the back of the donkey
they bore her away,
through trees and up mountains
beyond night and day,
till come Sunday morning
they brought her in state
through the last cloudbank
as far as the Gate.
    'Who is it,' asked Peter,
    'you have with you there?'
    And donkey and sparrow,
    cat, vixen and bear

exclaimed, 'Do you tell us
up here she's unknown?
It's our mother, God bless us!
It's Mrs Malone,

whose havings were few
and whose holding was small
and whose heart was so big
it had room for us all.'
Then Mrs Malone
of a sudden awoke,
she rubbed her two eyeballs
and anxiously spoke:
'Where am I, to goodness,
and what do I see?
My dears, let's turn back,
this ain't no place fer me!'
But Peter said, 'Mother,
go into the Throne.
There's room for another
one, Mrs Malone.'

Eleanor Farjeon

Jesus chose a homely illustration to point an eternal truth. If a quite undistinguished guest arrived early at a feast and annexed the top place, and if a more distinguished person then arrived, and the man who had usurped the first place was told to step down, a most embarrassing situation resulted. If, on the other hand, a man deliberately slipped into the bottom place, and was then asked to occupy a more distinguished place, his humility gained him all the more honour.

Humility has always been one of the characteristics of greatness. When Thomas Hardy was so famous that any newspaper would gladly have paid enormous sums for his work, he used sometimes to submit a poem, and always with it a stamped and addressed envelope for the return of his manuscript should it be rejected. Even in his greatness he was humble enough to think that his work might be turned down.

. . . How can we retain our humility?

(i) We can retain it by realising the facts. However much we know, we still know very little compared with the sum of total knowledge. However much we have achieved, we still have achieved very little in the end. However important we may believe ourselves to be, when death removes us or when we retire from our position, life and work will go on just the same.

(ii) We can retain it by comparison with the perfect. It is when we see or hear the expert that we realise how poor our own performance is. Many a man has decided to burn his clubs after a day at golf's Open Championship. Many a man has decided never to appear in public again after hearing a master musician perform. Many a preacher has been humbled almost to despair when he has heard a real saint of God speak. And if we set our lives beside the life of the Lord of all good life, if we see our unworthiness in comparison with the radiance of his stainless purity, pride will die and self-satisfaction will be shrivelled up.

William Barclay
The Daily Study Bible: The Gospel of Luke

Verses 12-14 address the host, and again Jesus is not giving lessons on social graces. The point is, hosting can be a way of making others feel they are in your debt, so they in turn will reciprocate when preparing their guest lists. The cycle of seeking a return on one's behaviour toward others repeats itself. For common sense dictates that self-interest does not offer self or goods to persons who cannot repay. In the kingdom, however, God is always host, and we extend God's invitation to those who cannot repay. After all, who can repay God? Jesus, therefore, is calling for behaviour that lives out this conviction about the kingdom; that is, inviting to table (quite different from sending food to) those who have neither property nor place in society. Luke's fourfold list (the poor, the maimed, the lame and the blind, verse 13) is repeated in the next story (beyond our lection). In that passage containing the parable of the banquet (verses 15-24), these people from the fringes are guests at the banquet, replacing those who failed to attend because they had other things to do. From the Song of Mary (1:46-55) to the end of his Gospel, Luke is careful to remind us that these, too, are kingdom people.

Fred B. Craddock
Preaching Through the Christian Year: 'C'

Proper 18/Ordinary Time 23

Sunday between 4 and 10 September inclusive

Luke 14:25-33

For prospective disciples, the willingness to make full commitment is the one needed resource. Without that, all other resources are insufficient.

The assigned lection for this Sunday from the travel section of Luke's Gospel specifically reminds us of the theme of discipleship that pervades the section. It is not an easy passage, because of the rash and exclusive way statements are made, but just for this reason it is important for contemporary audiences. It confronts us with hard choices and jars any notion that being a Christian leads to social enhancement or personal betterment. While there are texts that comfort the disturbed, this one disturbs the comfortable.

The location of the passage in the narrative is critical. The preceding parable of the great banquet (Luke 14:15-24) depicts previously invited guests who offer excuses for their refusal to attend the party and then relates the host's persistence in seeing that his dining hall is filled and his meal eaten. Two groups are recruited (1) the poor, the crippled, the blind, and the lame, and (2) those in the countryside. It is a remarkable story of the divine grace, which reaches beyond traditional bounds to include those otherwise excluded.

But it is easy to be presumptuous about grace. The three who send excuses for their absence illustrate just how easy it can be to take lightly God's gracious invitations, and there is no reason to think that the outsiders brought in at the last minute are going to be any less vulnerable to such presumptuousness. Therefore, to the 'large crowds' who 'were travelling with him', Jesus delivers these sharp words about the demands and priorities of discipleship. If they are contemplating being more than hangers-on and intend to be regular diners at Jesus' table, they need to know what they are getting into and to decide whether they can sign on for the long haul.

The passage is cleanly structured. The introductory verse (14:25) is followed by three parallel statements about the nature of discipleship (verses 26, 27, and 33). The middle one provides the clue for understanding the first and last. In between the second and third statements are two analogies (building a tower, waging a war) that raise the question whether would-be disciples can follow through on their initial commitments (verses 28-32).

How are we to understand 14:26? It includes a piece of Semitic hyperbole that Matthew has softened a bit ('Whoever loves father or mother more than me . . . and whoever loves son or daughter more than me is not worthy of me', Matthew 10:37). Jesus is clearly not telling the crowds to hate their parents and abandon their children. He is sharply confronting them with the priority of their commitments and implicitly pointing them to the new surrogate family they join as they become disciples. It is a note repeatedly sounded in Luke's narrative (Luke 8:19-21; 12:52-53; 21:16) and needing to be heard in a society that talks much about family values.

The second statement about discipleship is the familiar word about cross-bearing (14:27). By putting the verb 'carry' in the present tense, Luke tends to stress the everydayness of this identification with Jesus (compare 9:23). By including 'one's own cross' (not clearly rendered in the NRSV), Luke underscores the need for a personal acknowledgement of such an identification.

The third statement about discipleship, with its inclusive 'all', reiterates another Luke theme (14:33). Material possessions have a seductive appeal that can turn them quickly from being servants to being masters (12:13-34; 18:18-25; 19:8). They become excess baggage that makes the journey with Jesus difficult to negotiate. Thus, at the outset, choices have to be made. 'You cannot serve God and wealth' (16:13).

The intervening analogies of assessing resources before building a tower and doing feasibility studies before going to war vividly argue the case for a commitment that is made with eyes wide open to the cost (14:28-32). A hasty or casual decision leaves one vulnerable to ridicule and defeat. The warning is not meant to encourage a calculating wariness about discipleship (which would certainly seem incongruous with the daring, risk-laden calls to follow Jesus), but a sober realism about what it entails.

In light of the hardness of the text and the overwhelming demands made, one is tempted to give the two analogies a further twist. In answer to the questions, 'Which of you would fail to make an assessment before building a tower? Which of you would bypass reconnaissance before starting a war?' the responder of course says, 'None of us'. But then neither would God! God has counted the cost. God knows what it takes to build a tower. God knows how strong the enemy's forces are. The rule God has inaugurated will not be left unfinished. It may have a rather unpromising beginning, but do not be deceived: God means to win. It is just this certain and conclusive cause we are called to join.

Charles B. Cousar
Texts for Preaching: A Lectionary Commentary Based on the NRSV – Year C

Luke provides a transition from the semiprivate conversation of Jesus in 14:1-24 to Jesus' re-entry into the public arena. Verse 25 tells us two things about the teachings that follow: they are addressed to the crowds, and they will be in response to the hearers enthusiastically joining the company of Jesus and his disciples. Jesus speaks here to those who come to him (verse 26), not to those called out from the crowd to join him. In other words, we have a repeat of the situation in Luke 9:57, where a volunteer comes to Jesus saying, 'I will follow you wherever you go'. It is important to read what follows as Jesus responding to the enthusiasm of those who seem unaware that he is moving toward the cross and that his disciples are not exempt from their leader's burden.

The structure of our text is as follows: verse 25 is transitional and introductory; verses 26-27 state the demands of discipleship, paralleled in Matthew 10:37-38 as part of the charge to those being sent out; verses 28-32 contain twin parables; and verse 33 repeats in digest verses 26-27. In fact, the unit is built on a refrain: 'whoever does not . . . cannot be my disciple' (verse 26), repeated in verse 27, and after the parables repeated again in verse 33. The negative form of this refrain expresses the caution and warning to the hasty volunteers who may be caught up in the movement toward Jerusalem as though it were a march or a parade. To persons already cautious, Jesus has already spoken his word: drop everything and come immediately (Luke 9:59-62).

The repeated call to cross-bearing (verse 27; earlier at Luke 9:23; Mark 8:34-35) is here joined to the unusual demand that one hate one's own life (verse 26). The key to understanding this teaching is the word 'hate'. It is a Semitic way of expressing detachment, turning away from. It is not the emotion-filled word we experience in the scream, 'I hate you'. Were that the case, verse 26 alone would shatter all the calls to love, to understand, to forgive, to care for others, especially one's own family (1 Timothy 5:8), found throughout both Testaments. Hating one's own life is not a call to self-loathing, to throw one's body across the doorway and beg the world to trample on it as though it were a doormat. Paul labelled as valueless such 'self-imposed piety, humility, and severe treatment of the body' (Colossians 2:23). Rather, what Jesus is calling for is that those who follow him understand that loyalty to him can and will create tensions within the self and between oneself and those one loves; and in such a conflict of loyalties, he requires primary allegiance.

The two parables that follow (verses 28-32) say, in effect, 'Now sit down and decide if that price is more than you will pay'. The first parable is drawn from rural life and the building of a tower in the vineyard from which to watch for destructive animals and thieves. The second is from the royal capital where decisions of war, peace, and compromise are made. But with peasant or king, the same fear of embarrassment should create caution. No one should take on more than can or will be carried though to completion. The questions are two: 'Do I have the resources?' And, 'Will I commit them fully to this purpose?' For prospective disciples, the willingness to make full commitment is the one needed resource. Without that, all other resources are insufficient.

Fred B. Craddock
Preaching Through the Christian Year: 'C'

Proper 19/Ordinary Time 24

Sunday between 11 and 17 September inclusive

Luke 15:1-10

The healing laughter of redemption . . . is the joy of new birth. Has God not 'found' us in Jesus Christ?

Lost and found in love

An unforgettable experience of my life was being a house-guest for a week in the home of the former prime minister of Rhodesia, Garfield Todd, in 1961. This man of marvellous bearing, mental superiority, and spiritual sensitivity served as a Christian missionary for more than twenty years. Then he went into politics, believing that he could accomplish more for native Africans in this role. He was so successful that the white people did not send him back to office.

Among the many episodes shared with me, this phenomenal man recalled the most frightening experience of his life – that of being lost in the jungle and walking alone all night. It was just after World War II and fencing wire was scarce. He had heard of used wire for sale at a distant ranch and went to examine it. He arrived late in the afternoon, found the wire fence and started following it, examining its condition and estimating the cost of removing it, prior to submitting a bid.

The time was later than he realised and almost suddenly he was enveloped in darkness. In following the circuitous path of the fence, he lost his sense of direction. Although he walked and walked, he had only moved deeper and deeper into the jungle. To survive, he realised he had to follow the fence and keep walking, for he could hear animals pursuing him. He also reasoned that at some point the fence would probably reach a clearing and there perhaps he could gain his bearings. Furthermore, if he could find a road in the clearing, he would be rescued by his wife whom he knew would be circling the jungle in her car.

After the most horrendous night imaginable, at about dawn he stumbled into a clearing, then to a road. Shortly thereafter he saw lights from a car and his wife Grace appeared. Garfield Todd, exhausted, half-frozen, clothes in tatters, body bleeding, dropped at her feet. There was tender rejoicing.

Love had persisted all night. While love was trying to find its way out of darkness, love was also diligently searching for the one in darkness. Both were lost, and found, in love!

G. Curtis Jones and Paul H. Jones
500 Illustrations: Stories from Life for Preaching & Teaching

211

God and laughter

The finding of the lost coin and the lost sheep resulted in a communal celebration which no doubt would have included joy and laughter, so here is a piece on the theme of laughter. It is taken from a sermon by George A. Buttrick and called 'God and Laughter'. (George A. Buttrick was a former pastor of Madison Avenue Presbyterian Church in New York City and a minister to the University at Harvard. He died in 1980 at the age of 88).

But there is another kind of laughter, the healing laughter of redemption. It is not a child's laughter, and it is not a man's dilemma-laughter. It is the joy of new birth. Francis knew child's laughter in his earliest years in Assisi; and he knew adult laughter when as an unruly youth in that city he was the 'life of the party' not without knowing and giving some real happiness; but the third laughter he did not know until with vows of poverty he gave himself to God before a high altar. Then and there joy was born in him by which he preached to the sparrows and danced in the village square. This laughter is the laughter of childlikeness beyond childishness. Perhaps our life is a pilgrimage from childish laughter through the laughter of our guilty dilemma, to the childlike laughter that comes of God's forgiving and renewing grace. Many a man lives and dies only in the ruefulness of that middle term.

Can we find any parable of this best laughter? The small boy decided to run away from home: 'I do not like this nasty house.' Always we rebel against the walls of creaturehood. His mother told him that she was sorry for his desire but that she would help him pack. The lad was plucky: he left, scarcely able to lift the luggage. Where to go? When he reached the sidewalk, he sat there on the step between the garden path and the sidewalk. Where *shall* we go, where *can* we go, when we try to leave our humanness? His parents watched from behind window curtains. Soon he returned, saving face cheerfully: 'I've been away a long time.' They agreed: 'Was it a nice journey?' But, oh, the joy of the homecoming for them and for him! 'Even so, I tell you, there is joy before the angels of God over one sinner who repents.' This is the word of Christ. This is the joy that he revealed to our world. The bells of heaven ring whenever a man turns from his perverted skills and his insensate pride, from his poor attempts to live an animal life, to trust in the Power and the Love – the God who can lift him when he cannot lift himself.

Another parable, since here story is far better than argument. In the sequel to *The Pilgrim's Progress,* Christiana (Pilgrim's wife), her children, and a friend called Mercy follow him to the

Celestial City. Christiana asks Mercy: 'What was the matter that you did laugh in your sleep tonight? I suppose you was in a dream.' Yes, Mercy had dreamed. She saw herself bemoaning the hardness of her heart, with people about her who were impatient of her complaint: 'At this, some laughed at me, some called me fool, and some began to thrust me about' – the earthly answer to those ill-content with merely an earthly life. Then an angel came: 'Mercy, what aileth thee?' As if she knew! Only angels know! 'Peace be to thee!' Then she saw herself clothed in silver and gold, led by the angel through the skies to a throne, which was not 'derision', for he who sat there said gently: 'Welcome, daughter.' Said Mercy: 'So I woke . . . but did I laugh?' She laughed and cried, with tears no longer bitter but rather childlike and at peace. 'When the Lord turned again the captivity of Zion, we were like them that dream. Then was our mouth filled with laughter, and our tongue with singing.'

Even the laughter of our dilemma is still laughter, as if we knew unawares that the dilemma is always held in light. To the portent of laughter Christian faith gives the Christ-event, the historical drama of uncoercive love. So we may now choose how to laugh. We can laugh because life despite its darkness is good: 'Glad that I live am I.' That is basic laughter, and sadness may wait its turn. We can laugh too loud: that is dilemma-laughter, its loudness confessing its insecurity. We can laugh ruefully, with realism for man's failures, yet with kindly judgement since we also are 'in the same condemnation', well knowing that adult laughter is never far from tears. Are there not two faces over the proscenium arch of the theatre, which portray our mortal life – a laughing face and a weeping face?

But if we will, we may laugh in the midst of the storm in 'unmixed' laughter. We can 'become as little children', in a new childlikeness, beyond childishness and beyond the adulthood that has known too many roads and too many doors. We can laugh even in an atomic age, even in the storm that we have raised by our own unruliness:

> Well roars the storm to those that hear
> a deeper voice across the storm.
> (Tennyson, *In Memoriam*)

'Be of good cheer, I have overcome the world.' 'Be of good cheer: laugh!' Beyond the clinging doubt and beyond the unruly deed – God. Has he not 'found' us in Jesus Christ? So *that* door is always open – into laughter.

George Buttrick
Sermons Preached in a University Church

Proper 20/Ordinary Time 25

Sunday between 18 and 24 September inclusive

Luke 16:1-13

The children of the world pursue the trivial as though it were eternal; the Christian too often pursues the eternal as though it were quite trivial.

Learning from the enemy

> *The children of this world are in their generation wiser than the children of light.* (Luke 16:8)

This might well be called 'the problem parable'. At first sight it simply bristles with difficulties. It upsets so many preconceived ideas. It is apparently a panegyric on worldly prudence: but isn't that terribly unlike Jesus? Isn't it very strange that this rogue of a man in the story should be held up for eulogy? Can we conceive such a commendation of evil coming from Christ? In the attempt to get over the difficulty, scores of ingenious interpretations have been suggested. One German critic has actually tried to cut the knot by declaring that it can't be an authentic parable of Jesus at all.

The trouble of course is that Jesus, when he chose, could be so daring in his originality. Some of the commentators, not noticeable for originality themselves, become quite flustered when it thrusts itself into their path, as it does here. Clothe old truths in new and unaccustomed phraseology, and there will always be some who will grow uneasy, and suspect doctrinal unsoundness. Well, Jesus was not afraid of that. Let us be clear about this: you can't get Jesus to talk platitudes. The one thing he will not do is be dull and trite and obvious. You never know what he is going to say next. He electrifies with his dramatic unexpectedness.

Take this parable. Here is how it ought to have ended, in verse 8: 'And the Lord condemned the unjust steward to outer darkness'. That is what all the audience were sure was coming. And here is what did come – the very opposite – 'the Lord commended the unjust steward, because he had done shrewdly'. That's startling! And the thought in many minds is, 'That is not what Jesus ought to have said!' In fact, this whole picture is not the kind of picture he ought to have used – it is too motley in its characters, too lively in its keen-humoured wit, too unorthodox in its way of pointing a moral. Can this be Jesus?

If we experience that difficulty, may it not be that in a perfectly sincere but mistaken kind of reverence we have been allowing our mental picture of Jesus to become too formal, too stilted, too conventionalised in the halo that it wears? Of course this is Jesus! The very daring of it is the surest sign and seal of the Master's authentic touch.

Just look at it again. You will get the sense of it best if you retranslate these words 'the lord' and 'the steward' as 'the laird' and 'the factor': for that is exactly what it means. Here was this factor administering the laird's estate. He began (as we would say) to 'feather his own nest'. He began to juggle with the accounts. Then one day his embezzlements were discovered. Dismissal, ruin, stared him in the face. But swiftly his astute mind went to work. 'What shall I do when I am turned out of house and home, thrown out on to the streets? I can't dig: I haven't the physique for that. I can't beg: for I won't demean myself to that. But here's an idea! Why shouldn't I make friends of all the laird's tenants! Suppose I halve their rents!'

And it was no sooner thought of than done. 'How much do you owe the laird? Fifty pounds? Take your voucher and write down twenty-five!' And so he went right round. And when it was finished, 'Ha! now,' he said, 'when I'm thrown out, there will be plenty open doors to welcome me! I won't lack a bed or a meal!' And, says the story, the laird commended – please notice, it is the laird who commends him, not Jesus the teller of the story – the laird commended his unjust factor – not meaning, of course, that he approved the man's morals (we'd have to be painfully solemn literalists to interpret it like that), but meaning that he couldn't help admiring the fellow's sheer impudent resourcefulness and effrontery!

'My word,' he said, 'you are an astute and daring rascal! For barefaced coolness, you have got us all beaten hollow!' And there, abruptly, the story ends.

Now, once again, I beg you to remember the basic principle for interpreting all the parables of Jesus. It is this: each parable, unlike an allegory, was meant by Jesus to convey one cardinal truth, and that therefore it is essential in every case to disentangle this salient truth in Jesus' mind from the details of the story, the picturesque ornament and drapery in which the story is clothed.

So here in the story before us. Half our trouble comes from persisting in asking – quite gratuitously – who do these characters – the laird, the factor, the tenants – represent? The answer is: They don't represent anyone – except three sets of people such as might be encountered in Galilee or anywhere else. The biggest mistake of all is the one we persist in making the most – our tacit assumption that the laird – the lord, as the story calls him – must stand for God. It is safe to say that nothing was further from Jesus' intention. The laird is *not* God: he is just any easy-going, slightly cynical man of the world – nothing else.

And do let me emphasise again that it is not the factor's morals or his methods that are being approved – but only the man's resourcefulness, foresight and acumen. That is the one highlight of the whole story.

In other words, here is what Christ is fixing on, here is the one salient truth he is after: *God's people might well take an occasional lesson from God's enemies – the saint has something to learn from the sinner.* For the children of this world are sometimes wiser in their generation – more resourceful and far-seeing and inventive and purposeful – than the children of light are for theirs. Or, to put it differently, if all God's people would bring to the service of God's kingdom the superb, magnificent concentration, determination and resourcefulness that are so often given to the affairs of this world, what strides that kingdom would make! That, then, is the challenge; and we dare not pass it by.

So, now, we've got to ask this question. In what respects are Christ's people to take a lesson from those outside? The parable itself suggests three.

For one thing, the children of this world might teach the children of light something about *definiteness of aim*.

Take this factor in the story. He knew exactly what he was after. Money, comfort, security – that was his all-absorbing quest. He saw his goal, and bent all his energies towards it. He could have said, quite sincerely, 'This one thing I do'.

That is characteristic of the children of this world. They work to plan. They see their goal, and go 'all out' to reach it. We have witnessed an illustration of that on a gigantic scale in our generation. Think of the people who are simply possessed, in body, mind and soul, by the totalitarian idea – the glorification of the state. *They* have no vagueness in their creed. *They* know what they are after, and what they mean to get.

Have we anything like that definiteness of aim in our service of Christ? Take the Church. Isn't there a danger of the Church getting side-tracked into non-essentials, frittering away on secondary things the time and strength that ought to be given to the one thing that justifies the Church's existence – namely, the bringing of men and women into a saving relationship to God through Jesus Christ? Take the evidence of history. The great days of the Church, the days when the tides of the evangel rose to the flood and swept the world and broke through the barricades, have always been days when the Church has gone crusading with one thought in her mind – the all-sufficient Saviourhood of Christ; and one passion in her heart – the passion for the souls of men.

Men and women, we want to recapture that definiteness of aim. We are not a society existing to carry on a score of unrelated activities. We are not a debating club for the discussion of anything that happens to be topical at the moment. We are not a device for the multiplication of meetings and machinery. We are the community of Christ, charged with one commission – the winning of the world for God.

And I beg you to make no mistake about this, that in this day of rampant new religions, Caesarisms and Communisms and deified materialisms, creeds that are absolutely definite in their aims and categorical about the path that they pursue, it is no use playing about with a religion that is vague and nebulous and woolly and not quite sure of what it is after. The worldly-minded materialist believes the world to be of great importance: do we Christians give the impression of believing that the kingdom of God is as commandingly important? It is no use setting up a 'C3' Christianity to meet an 'A1' paganism. 'The children of this world are wiser in their generation than the children of light.'

But if the Church can recapture that decisiveness of touch that has always been hers in her greatest days – or rather, let me put it like this (for I don't want to speak of the Church as an abstract thing, seeing that the Church is just the men and women who compose it), if you and I as Christians can live the dedicated life, in which the interests of God's kingdom matter more than any personal interests, in which those truly terrific truths – the sovereignty of God, the eternity of right, the Redeemership of Christ – have gripped us like a passion, then, then only, we can beat the world at its own game; and even through the darkness of these days, God's kingdom will go marching on.

Can't we learn a lesson from the children of the world? They pursue the trivial as though it were eternal; the Christian too often pursues the eternal as though it were quite trivial.

I've known a man keen enough on golf to spend hours correcting a slice or practising with a putter; absolutely absorbed in it – as he is quite right to be, if he wants to. But just compare that absorbed devotion to something which in the long run is utterly trivial, with our lackadaisical Christian attitude to things that matter as supremely as the Bible, and prayer, and the knowledge of God! A man will steep himself in Stock Exchange statistics, and if that is his job he is

217

entitled to concentrate on it. But the searching question is – are we Christians as keen to steep ourselves in the things of God?

That is one challenge to us of this parable. May the Holy Spirit give to us, as Christians, such clear definiteness of aim. I pass to another thing. Don't you think the children of this world can sometimes teach the children of light a lesson about *inventiveness and resource?*

Take this factor in the story. He may have been defective in morals, but he certainly had plenty of wits. How fertile his imagination! How prolific his plans! Why, even the master he defrauded couldn't help congratulating him on his ingenuity!

The question is – have we anything like that enterprising spirit, that ingenious resourcefulness, in our service of Christ? There was a characteristic prayer that Professor A. B. Bruce often used at the opening of his classes in New College: 'Lord, give us a fearless inventiveness in thy service.' Have we got that, when we take counsel together concerning the things of the kingdom – a fearless inventiveness in the service of Jesus?

What does it mean? Listen to what it meant for Paul the Apostle: 'I have become all things to all men, that I might by all means save some.' There obviously was a man you simply couldn't confine in any ecclesiastical rut! There was a man who refused to jog along the beaten tracks of precedent and tradition. 'I am become all things to all men'. Of course, he was criticised for it, and furiously misunderstood. But what matter? Christ blessed that fearless inventiveness of Paul's, that consecrated fertility of resource. And he waits to bless it still.

Surely, of all people, the children of light should be wide awake! Surely they, the sons of the morning, ought to have nothing to learn from the sons of night about the exhilaration of the spirit of adventure! It is a thoroughly bad idea that when a man comes to Jesus, he is supposed to leave his imagination at home. It is a thoroughly mischievous notion which suggests that to 'get religion' means to have all his individual excrescences smoothed out, to be cut to a standard stereotyped pattern, and to be doomed to walk in a groove for the rest of his days. If there *is a* religion like that, it is not *Christ's* religion.

Was there ever a mind so fearlessly inventive, so daringly creative, as the mind of Jesus? And are we not to pray, 'Let that mind which was in Christ be also in us'?

> *Lord, give us the spirit of enterprise and discovery,*
> *and the spirit of the pioneer who strikes out into the*

unknown. Don't let it be said of the children of light
that they were less resourceful for Christ's ends than
the children of darkness are for the Devil's ends.
Give us a fearless inventiveness in thy service!

I pass to the final thing. I have spoken of definiteness of aim, and inventiveness of resource. But don't you think the children of this world can also teach the children of light something about foresight and vision for the future?

Take this factor in the story. When he saw his fortunes threatening to tumble about him like a house of cards, what did he do? He might have thrust disturbing thoughts of a possible dismissal away. He might have said, 'Why worry myself with what hasn't yet happened? The present is good enough for me!' But no! His one thought was – 'I must look ahead. I must devise means not to be left homeless and penniless when the crash comes. There's not a moment to lose. The time is short. If I act now, I may just manage it. Now is the accepted time!'

Well, what of the children of light? Stretching away in front of us the vast expanses of eternity – have we as much thought for that, as much foresight envisaging that, as the children of this world have for the narrow little sphere of this hectic earthly existence? In short, do we believe in our infinitely greater tomorrow as vividly and intensely as the world believes in the tomorrows for which it hopes and plans?

Mark you, I am not suggesting that religion ought to operate with prudential motives. I am not preaching that a man ought to give his life to God, simply to secure a blissful hereafter: that kind of spiritual feathering of our nest would be a travesty of the Gospel of Christ. But I am saying that if the basic assertions of our Christian faith are true; if you and I are really immortal with God's own immortality; if this world is a passing show, and only the spiritual things have any permanent validity; if weak things like beauty, truth, goodness, love, are destined to go lasting on when mighty things like the proud tyrannies of today are levelled in the dust and their very names forgotten; if these brief transient years on earth are big for us with eternal issues; if our true citizenship *is* in heaven – if all that is true (and Christ is the guarantee that it *is* true), then isn't it lamentable that any who profess a faith like that should simply drift through life with loins ungirt and lamps unlit and slumber in their souls? The children of this world are wiser in their generation – they have more foresight, look further ahead – than the children of light!

But ringing down the years comes Christ's challenge to our souls – 'Behold, I come quickly! Behold, the years are hastening on! Behold your swift days are drawing ever nearer to the goal! Pause and consider. O make room in your life for thought, for prayer, for the incorruptible eternal things, for the living breath of God. You who are an immortal spirit, don't scorn your immortality!'

That is Christ's own summons to all the children of men.

> *He hath sounded forth the trumpet that shall never*
> *call retreat;*
> *he is sifting out the hearts of men before his*
> *judgement seat;*
> *O, be swift my soul to answer him; be jubilant,*
> *my feet!*
> *Our God is marching on.*

James S. Stewart
Walking with God

Proper 21/Ordinary Time 26

Sunday between 25 September and 1 October inclusive

Luke 16:19-31

In a state of arrogance, we are all about us.

For the period of the Gilded Age – roughly from the mid-1870s to the early 1900s – brought the deepest and fiercest class conflict America had ever experienced. The North's victory in the Civil War unified America politically, but not socially. The explosion of the great railway strikes of 1877, which spread from West Virginia to Pittsburgh, erupted into near class war in Chicago, and paralysed freight and communications in the Midwest, left a scar of death and destruction; this was only the prelude to thirty years of unrest, in which American workers forged the links of class solidarity against the boss, the Pinkerton, the scab, the hired militias, the corrupt judges, and the bought police force. Never had the gulf between rich and poor been wider or more bitterly felt. But if in these years American labour was creating an unprecedented mutual strength, so was American capital: for the Gilded Age earned its name by becoming a time of unassailable and mutually interlocking trusts, combines, and cartels, of rampant money acting under laws it wrote for itself in an orgiastic monopolisation of American resources. The new financial barons took over the Republican party, turning it into the instrument of big business and high tariffs. When labour organised and resisted them, they struck back with fury. More and more power lay in fewer and fewer hands. Nowhere was the adage that 'behind every great fortune lies a great crime' truer than in the United States. 'Get rich,' wrote Mark Twain sardonically, 'dishonestly if we can, honestly if we must.' From this culture of Promethean greed arose the primal names of American business: Rockefeller (oil), Carnegie and Frick (steel), Vanderbilt (railroads), the Goulds, Astors, Fisks, and, towering over them all, J. Pierpont Morgan, the real power behind the Vanderbilt lines, who by 1900 controlled forty-nine thousand miles of track directly and another fifty thousand indirectly, and thus dominated the entire communications and long-range transport system of the continent on the eve of the automobile age.

Through such men, Americans lost all vestiges of their Puritan inhibitions about the display of wealth. Their cultural ideology was consistent with their principles, such as they were: it revolved around a belief in trusteeship and patronage. God had made the rich man rich so that he could discharge his will on earth. He would not fail them. Greed was public service: how could the poor or the middling classes be expected to manage money with equal responsibility? In the words of Samuel Tilden to a room of magnates at a dinner for Junius Morgan, J. P. Morgan's father:

While you are scheming for your own selfish ends, here is an over-ruling and wise Providence directing that the most of all you do should inure to the benefit of the people. Men of colossal fortunes are in effect, if not in fact, trustees for the public.

How to bridge the chasm between their business doings and this delusive piety? Some felt no need to: they remained social Darwinists, red like Nature itself in tooth and claw – vile brutes with coffers full of bonds. But for other and more reflective money barons, the Protestant ethic enjoined a sense of obligation, released in philanthropy and public works: the creation of libraries, schools, university colleges, concert halls, parks, museums, and other amenities, which would inspire gratitude in the labouring masses and defuse their resentments, while creating around their donors the aura of Maecenas.

Robert Hughes
American Visions: the Epic History of Art in America

God's grace to the arrogant

My reflection has continually stricken me with the image of Dives and Lazarus as presented in the Gospel of Luke. It is a chilling story.

The story tells of a rich man and his friends whose daily food intake might have fed a whole village if everyone had eaten reasonable portions and had been willing to share the abundance. A poor man from the village lay at the rich man's gate daily. The gate was a long way from the main house, but this poor man, whose name was Lazarus, could still smell the food being prepared and served each and every day.

He was sick, and he had no money for medical care. The

ancestors of contemporary American lawmakers were the government leaders of Lazarus' day; Medicaid had been de-funded, and Medicare had gone bankrupt. No hospitals treated indigent people. Lazarus had sores all over his body, but nobody knew why; and there were no treatments for his infirmities that he could have afforded anyway.

The Bible says that, as Lazarus lay there day by day at the gate of the rich man (who is never named in the Biblical account, though legend has called him Dives), he 'longed to satisfy his hunger with what fell from the rich man's table' (Luke 16:21a). Evidently, he never asked for anything; he never begged in any overt manner. His situation was obvious: he could have used the food, and he hoped that some-one who went in and came out of there regularly in a chauffeur-driven chariot would be compassionate and offer a few scraps from one of the legendary luncheons. The poor man didn't imagine that he might have any of the delicacies served to the socialites and the dignitaries at the banquet table; the most that he could hope for was a scrap or two, such as bread bits the rich folk used as napkins to wipe their hands and faces before dropping them on the floor for the pets to eat or the servants to clean up. No one ever gave him a thing – no one offered to get him to a physician. Lazarus waited there until, finally, he died a miserable death – likely from a number of complications, with starvation near the top of the list of causes of death.

Immediately, Lazarus was in the heavenly places with Father Abraham. His pain was relieved. He was at peace.

Soon after Lazarus' death, and entirely unexpectedly, the rich man died. He might have died from overeating or from a related illness. At any rate, he was immediately in hell or Hades or whatever you want to call the place of torment.

Even on the other side, the rich man believed that he was still in a position to give orders and have others follow without question. He essentially demanded that Abraham demonstrate mercy to him – given his plight – and send Lazarus from heaven into hell for the express purpose of getting him something cool and wet to quench his thirst.

Abraham was amazed that the rich man didn't see the irony of the scene he had created. He said, 'Hey there, Mr Rich Man, things don't work on this side the same way they worked for you on earth. I'm not your genie, and Mr Lazarus is not your lackey! If you're going to get your thirst satisfied at all, you'll have to figure out a way to do it down there. And that's not likely to happen because, as you have discovered, water is in mighty short supply where you're living! Besides, even if we were willing, we're not able. We can talk to you from here, but we can't get to you regardless of how much we might want to.'

The rich man said, 'Well, if that's the way things are, I'm begging you now, Father Abraham, send that beggar to do something worthwhile for a change, an honest day's work. Send him to my five brothers to warn them what's going to happen to them if they don't change their ways.'

'Wouldn't do a bit of good,' Abraham insisted. 'They haven't listened to the clear word they have in scripture. They're surely not going to pay any attention to a ghost!'

Arrogant in life, the rich man remained arrogant in his place of torment. His arrogance desensitised him to the needs of real people who became, for him, nothing more than a blemish on the landscape. Indeed, he preferred his arrogance to the kind of gratitude before God that would have made him compassionate and concerned about the well-being of all God's children.

When we lose our ability and our inclination to be humble in taking note of what we have – not the riches and the frills, but the basics for a good and fulfilling life – we become arrogant. In a state of arrogance, we are all about *us*. We no longer have any regard for the care of those who are in need, who don't have the resources to provide for themselves that are readily available to us. We no longer demonstrate any appreciation for God's wondrous creation.

David A. Farmer
Teaching Sermons on the Love and Grace of God: Unmerited Favour

Dives and Lazarus

As it fell out upon a day,
rich Dives he made a feast,
and he invited all his friends,
and gentry of the best.

Then Lazarus laid him down and down,
and down at Dives' door:
'Some meat, some drink, brother Dives,
bestow upon the poor.'

'Thou art none of my brother, Lazarus,
that lies begging at my door;
no meat nor drink will I give thee,
nor bestow upon the poor.'

Then Lazarus laid him down and down
and down at Dives' wall:
'Some meat, some drink, brother Dives
or with hunger starve I shall.'

'Thou art none of my brother, Lazarus,
that lies begging at my wall;
no meat nor drink will I give thee,
but with hunger starve you shall.'

Then Lazarus laid him down and down
and down at Dives' gate:
'Some meat, some drink, brother Dives,
for Jesus Christ his sake.'

'Thou art none of my brother, Lazarus,
that lies begging at my gate;
no meat nor drink will I give thee.
for Jesus Christ his sake.'

Then Dives sent out his merry men,
to whip poor Lazarus away;
they had no power to strike a stroke,
but flung their whips away.

Then Dives sent out his hungry dogs,
to bite him as he lay;
they had no power to bite at all,
but licked his sores away.

As it fell out upon a day,
poor Lazarus sickened and died;
then came two angels out of heaven
his soul therein to guide.

'Rise up, rise up, brother Lazarus,
and go along with me;
for you've a place prepared in heaven,
to sit on an angel's knee.'

As it fell out upon a day,
rich Dives sickened and died;
then came two serpents out of hell,
his soul therein to guide.

'Rise up, rise up, brother Dives,
and go with us to see
a dismal place, prepared in hell,
from which thou canst not flee.'

Then Dives looked up with his eyes,
and saw poor Lazarus blest:
'Give me one drop of water, brother Lazarus,
to quench my flaming thirst.

'Oh had I as many years to abide
as there are blades of grass,
then there would be an end, but now
hell's pains will ne'er be past.

'Oh was I now but alive again,
the space of one half hour!
Oh that I had my peace secure!
Then the devil should have no power.'

Anonymous

Proper 22/Ordinary Time 27

Sunday between 2 and 8 October inclusive

Luke 17:5-10

The small faith already ours can put us in touch with the power of God.

There is a story by a French writer in which a retired acrobat had gone to finish his life as a lay brother in a monastery; one day the monks passing the chapel saw him doing an acrobatic turn in front of an image of the Madonna. It was all that he had to offer her.

It might seem that acrobatics have little to do with religion or service to God. But that view would be wrong. Working at a machine or in an office, singing in a theatre or doing the housework at home are all services, which, like acrobatics, can be offered in a spirit which will satisfy our duty to God and will make others happier.

We hold our accomplishments in trust from God to offer them in his service, and that service on earth is, as Christ taught us so thoroughly, to bring happiness and well-being to our fellow-men.

Sir Stafford Cripps
God in Our Work

Verse 5 functions as a transition from the subject of forgiveness (verses 3-4) to that of faith. If one sees verses 5-6 as having a contextual meaning, then very likely the apostles' request for increased faith is an expression of their sense of inadequacy in the face of the unusual demands of caring for weaker members of the community (verses 1-2) and forgiving repeatedly the offending brother or sister (verses 3-4). In other words, 'Lord, make us adequate for discipleship'. Jesus' response, 'If you had faith . . .' deserves careful examination. The Greek language has basically two types of 'if', or conditional, clauses: those that express a condition contrary to fact ('if I were you'); and those that express a condition according to fact ('if Christ is our Lord'). The conditional clause of verse 6 is the second type. One could translate it 'if you have faith (and you do)'. In other words, Jesus' response is not a judgement on an absence of faith but an indirect affirmation of the faith they have and an invitation to live and act in that faith. The apostles request an increase of faith, and Jesus says that even the small faith you have is effective and powerful beyond your present realisation. The possibilities opened up by faith cancel out such words as 'impossible' (a tree being uprooted) and 'absurd' (planting a tree in the sea). The small faith already theirs could put them in touch with the power of God.

. . . The parable in verses 7-10 opens in a fashion common in Luke: 'Will any one of you?' or 'Who among you?' (11: 5-7; 14:23, 31; 15:4, 8). This story concerns a slave who does double duty, serving in the fields and in the master's house. The slave/master relationship is without analogy in our employee/employer society, and so the preacher is well advised not to draw social and economic lessons from the parable. The rather simple thrust of the story is that the slave's time and labour belong to the master, and, therefore, the slave has no claim on the master, even after a period of obedient service. There is no point of fulfilled duty beyond which the servant can expect special favours in return. There is no ground for boasting (Romans 3:27), no work of supererogation, no balance of merit after obligation is paid. Disciples of Jesus live by faith, even if it be as small as a mustard seed, but the life of trust is new each day. Like the manna in the wilderness, there is no surplus for tomorrow, no time in which there is more than enough for today. Disciples of Jesus live in obedience, but that, too, is new each day. One does not ever say, 'Now that I have completed all the duties of love, it is my turn to be served'. Such calculations are foreign to life in the kingdom of God.

Fred B. Craddock
Preaching Through the Christian Year: 'C'

Proper 23/Ordinary Time 28

Sunday between 9 and 15 October inclusive

Luke 17:11-19

Few of us in the end satisfy the debt of gratitude we owe.

It is hard to say what effect the tenth leper's response had on Jesus. Something happened, because all of a sudden he started asking questions. 'Weren't there ten lepers here a minute ago? Where are the other nine? Is this foreigner the only one who knows how to say thank you?' he said, and then turned to the tenth leper. 'Rise and go your way,' he said; 'your faith has made you well.' Or straight from the Greek, 'Your faith has saved you'. Once you stop to think about it, this is all very odd. Didn't Jesus tell all ten to go show themselves to the priests? And didn't nine do what they were told? Didn't this one, in fact, not do what he was told, and even flaunt his disobedience with a great sloppy show of emotion? And weren't all ten healed? Then how come this one got special treatment, got told his faith had made him well? Weren't all ten made well? What is going on here?

Ten were healed of their skin diseases, but only one was saved. Ten were declared clean and restored to society, but only one was said to have faith. Ten set out for Jerusalem to claim their free gifts as they were told, but only one turned back and gave himself to the Giver instead. Ten behaved like good lepers, good Jews; only one, a double loser, behaved like a man in love. There is a lot going on here.

. . . But that was a long time ago now, and what has become apparent in the meantime is that I know how to be obedient but I do not know how to be in love. It does not seem to be an ability I can command, like reflective listening or public speaking. And so I do what I know how to do, and I do it as well as I know how. I read my Bible, say my prayers, pay my pledge. And there is nothing wrong with that, nothing at all. It is that kind of steady, law-abiding discipleship – the discipleship of the nine lepers – that has kept the great ship of the Church afloat for thousands of years. I am one of the nine, but it is the tenth leper that interests me – the outsider, the double loser, who captures my imagination – the one whose disease I fear, whose passion confounds me, whom I may not see at all because he does not need a priest to certify his cure.

'Where are the nine?' Jesus asks, but I know where they are. 'Where is the tenth leper?' That is what I want to know. Where is the one who followed his heart instead of his instructions, who accepted his life as a gift and gave it back again, whose thanksgiving rose up from somewhere so deep inside him that it turned him around, changed his direction, led him to Jesus, made him well? Where are the nine? Where is the tenth? Where is the disorderly one who failed to go along with the crowd, the impulsive who fell on his face in the dirt, the fanatical one who loved God so much that obedience was beside the point? Where did that one go?

Not that I am likely to go after him. It is safer here with the nine – we know the rules and who does what. We are the ones upon whom the institution depends. But the missing one, the one who turned back, or was turned away, or turned against – where did he go? Who is he, and whom is he with, and what does he know that we do not know? Where are the nine? We are here, right here. But where, for the love of God, is the tenth?

Barbara Brown Taylor
The Preaching Life

The Rarity of Gratitude

Jesus was on the border between Galilee and Samaria and was met by a band of ten lepers. We know that the Jews had no dealings with the Samaritans; yet in this band there was at least one Samaritan. Here is an example of a great law of life. A common misfortune had broken down the racial and national barriers. In the common tragedy of their leprosy they had forgotten they were Jews and Samaritans and remembered only they were men in need. If flood surges over a piece of country and the wild animals congregate for safety on some little bit of higher ground, you will find standing peacefully together animals who are natural enemies and who at any other time would do their best to kill each other. Surely one of the things that should draw all men together is their common need of God.

The lepers stood far off (cf. Leviticus 13:45, 46; Numbers 5:2). There was no specified distance at which they should stand, but we know that at least one authority laid it down that, when he was to windward of a healthy person, the leper should stand at least fifty yards away. Nothing could better show the utter isolation in which lepers lived.

No story in all the Gospels so poignantly shows man's ingratitude. The lepers came to Jesus with desperate longing; he cured them; and nine never came back to give thanks. So often, once a man has got what he wants, he never comes back.

(i) Often we are ungrateful to our parents. There was a time in our lives when a week's neglect would have killed us. Of all living creatures man requires longest to become able to meet the needs essential for life. There were years when we were dependent on our parents for literally everything. Yet the day often comes when an aged parent is a nuisance; and many young people are unwilling to repay the debt they owe. As King Lear said in the day of his own tragedy: 'How sharper than a serpent's tooth it is to have a thankless child!'

(ii) Often we are ungrateful to our fellow men. Few of us have not at some time owed a great deal to some fellow-man. Few of us at the moment, believed we could ever forget; but few of us in the end satisfy the debt of gratitude we owe. It often happens that a friend, a teacher, a doctor, a surgeon does something for us which it is impossible to repay; but the tragedy is that we often do not even try to repay it.

> 'Blow, blow, thou winter wind,
> thou art not so unkind
> as man's ingratitude.' (King Lear)

(iii) Often we are ungrateful to God. In some time of bitter need we pray with desperate intensity; the time passes and we forget God. Many of us never even offer a grace before meat. God gave us his only Son and often we never give to him even a word of thanks. The best thanks we can give him is to try to deserve his goodness and his mercy a little better. 'Bless the Lord, O my soul, and *forget not all his benefits*' (Psalm 103:2).

William Barclay
The Daily Study Bible: The Gospel of Luke

If anyone would tell you the shortest, surest way to all happiness and all perfection, he must tell you to make it a rule to yourself to thank and praise God for everything that happens to you. For it is certain that whatever seeming calamity happens to you, if you thank and praise God for it, you turn it into a blessing. Could you therefore work miracles, you could not do more for yourself than by this thankful spirit; for it heals with a word spoken, and turns all that it touches into happiness.

William Law
quoted in *Gathered Together*

Proper 24/Ordinary Time 29

Sunday between 16 and 22 October inclusive

Luke 18:1-8

God can be counted on to vindicate the oppressed. God won't turn a deaf ear to our prayers.

Human rights

The American novelist John Grisham has a story about a murder in the Deep South. Sam Cayhall, a member of the Ku Klux Klan, has just murdered a black man called Joe Lincoln. Sam's daughter describes the arrival of the sheriff on the scene: 'He and Sam talked for a bit. Sam showed him Joe's shotgun and explained how it was a simple matter of self-defence. Just another dead nigger.

"He wasn't arrested?" asked her nephew.

"No, Adam. This was Mississippi in the early fifties. I'm sure the sheriff had a good laugh about it, patted Sam on the back, and told him to be a good boy, and then left. He even allowed Sam to keep Joe's shotgun."'

The most devastating expression of racism in the Deep South in the fifties was that black people did not hope for justice from the courts.

The most devastating expression of racism in de Klerk's South Africa was that black people could not hope for justice from the courts. Perhaps the most interesting thing about the O. J. Simpson trial was that most white people, both in America and in Britain, thought he should be convicted and most black people, both in America and in Britain, thought he should be acquitted. The explanations of that curious fact are various and deep: but at least they suggest that there are huge problems for a legal system when large numbers of the community assume that it is arrayed against them instead of for them.

Andrew R. C. McLellan
Preaching for These People

233

The delightful and humorous story of the persevering widow and the ruthless judge provides enough clues within itself to its own meaning. Yet it is set in a literary context in Luke's narrative that gives it even greater depth and urgency. For example, the parable is made a part of the preceding discourse about the eschatological crisis (17:22-37). Jesus warns the disciples about the frantic days just prior to the coming of the Son of Man, days comparable to the days of the Flood and the judgement on Sodom. In the meantime, the parable directs the disciples to pray and leaves them with the question: 'When the Son of Man comes, will he find faith on earth? (18:8).

The inclusion of the parable in the larger discourse provides a new definition of faith – fervent and persistent prayer.

. . . When the early Christians repeated this story of the widow and the judge to one another, the accent sometimes fell on one character and sometimes on the other. Sometimes they paid special attention to the widow, with whom they felt they could empathise rather easily. They knew how she felt in her defenceless predicament. She had no clout in the community. She did not know the mayor of the town or any of the county commissioners who might pull strings for her to get her case on the docket. All she could do was to go back time and again to hound the judge. She turned up regularly at the gates of the city where he held court, and pursued him on the streets and in the shops. She would not let him rest until he granted her justice. Finally, exasperated, the judge gave in: 'Otherwise this widow will keep after me until she gives me a black eye!'

The widow became a model for the early Christians, to teach them 'to pray always and not to lose heart' (18:1). She was a reminder in days of crisis and moments of despair to continue to pray. Prayer was not a last resort when all the plans and programmes and power plays had failed; prayer was, rather, the first and primary task of Christians. Her prayerful pursuit of justice became an expression of deep faith, the kind of faith the Son of Man seeks.

. . . The early Christians thought about the judge. Look, they reasoned, if an unscrupulous person like this heartless judge gave in to the unceasing pleas of the widow, how much more will God listen to his people as they cry day and night for justice in the world? God can be counted on to vindicate the oppressed. God won't turn a deaf ear to our prayers.

The unjust judge in many ways parallels the begrudging

neighbour who refuses to help his friend at midnight until he realises the shame he might otherwise bring on himself (Luke 11:5-8). They both represent contrasting types for God. By their unsavoury characters they call attention to the opposite attributes of God – one to be trusted, one responsive to requests, one who sees that justice is carried out. Their stinginess and reluctance to help is more than matched by the lavish generosity of God.

But the two characters (widow and judge) also belong together. Persistence in prayer is rooted in the character of God. There is no reason to continue to pray unless the one who prays has at least an inkling of confidence (no more than a mustard seed?) that the one who hears prayers will answer them. Otherwise, exhortations to persevere can result only in frustration and discouragement.

Moreover, the character of God – just, holy, merciful, responsive – determines the answer to persistent prayer. The widow only asks for justice (18:3) and what God grants is justice (18:7, 8). The parable is not a commitment that God will give us whatever we want, unless what we want is in line with the character of God. What more could we want?

Charles B. Cousar
Texts for Preaching: A Lectionary Commentary Based on the NRSV – Year C

The old order changeth, yielding place to new,
and God fulfils himself in many ways.
More things are wrought by prayer
than this world dreams of. Wherefore, let thy voice
rise like a fountain . . .
For what are men better than sheep or goats
that nourish a blind life within the brain,
if, knowing God, they lift not hands of prayer
both for themselves and for those who call them friend?
For so the whole round earth is every way
bound by gold chains about the feet of God.

Alfred, Lord Tennyson
Morte d'Arthur

Proper 25/Ordinary Time 30

Sunday between 23 and 29 October inclusive

Luke 18:9-14

The tax collector has done the one thing that God requires of those who seek access to him: he has faced the truth about himself and cast himself on God's compassion.

The Pharisee and the Tax Collector

The person telling the parable enters the stage and pronounces sentence. Jesus introduces his judgement with weighty solemnity: 'I tell you . . .' Here Jesus is speaking in the name of God himself. This is a shock that shatters even the language of the parable. In the first place, no one can know what two people prayed in the temple except the God to whom they prayed. Secondly, Jesus' 'I tell you' follows directly on the tax collector's cry, 'God, be merciful to me a sinner'. It is the divine 'I' that Jesus uses and that utters itself through his words. And what does this divine judgement say?

It declares the tax collector and sinner to be righteous 'rather than' the just Pharisee. 'This man went down to his house justified rather than the other.' Some manuscripts leave out 'rather than the other' altogether. Then the pronouncement sounds harsher still. The tax collector went down to his house justified. The Pharisee is not even worth talking about anymore. What does this mean?

Jesus declares that, in God's eyes, right is on the side of the tax collector, not the Pharisee. Jesus declares that the tax collector is not merely granted the grace he prayed for. 'God, be *merciful* to me a sinner' was what he asked for. He went down to his house *justified* – that is the response. The answer is far greater than the request. If Jesus had only wanted to say how inconceivably good God can be, then he would merely have had to say: the Pharisee went to his house justified, and God had mercy on the tax collector. Then each of them would have received his due, and Jesus would have been as 'well balanced' as we are always being told today. And everyone would have been quite content – including ourselves.

But the radical from Nazareth turns everything upside down: the sinner goes home justified, while to the righteous man God is not even gracious. This is hard for all the 'good' people – and extremely surprising for the 'bad' ones. If we appeal to the importance of good and bad in the social order, we might even say that it menaces society.

. . . Jesus' justifying judgement brings out a splendid

inward and outward deliverance. God condemns the good person who I want to be, but am not, and accepts the bad person who I do not want to be, but am.

Jurgen Moltmann
The Power of the Powerless

Two men went into the temple to pray, but only one of them prayed. Prayer must be addressed to God, and the Pharisee was not really interested in God, but only in himself. All the verbs are in the first person. His prayer is a catalogue of negative virtues and minor pieties. Where a humble man is content to put his trust in God, this man's trust is in his own righteousness and religious achievement, and the inevitable result is that he despises those who fail to reach his own standard. Not all Pharisees were like this, but the Pharisaic emphasis on merit and legal observance must always have carried with it the danger of spiritual pride. Rabbinic literature provides enough parallels to show that Jesus' portrait was no caricature. An old prayer from the Jewish Prayer Book runs: 'Blessed art Thou, O Lord our God, King of the universe, who hast not made me a Gentile. Blessed art thou . . . who hast not made me a slave. Blessed art thou . . . who hast not made me a woman' (cf. Galatians 3:28). It is reported also in the Talmud (Berakoth 28b) that Rabbi Nehunia ben Hakeneh used to pray daily on leaving the rabbinical school: 'I give thanks to thee, O Lord my God, that thou hast set my portion with those who sit in the house of instruction, and thou hast not set my portion with those who sit in street corners, for I rise early and they rise early, but I rise early for words of torah and they rise early for frivolous talk; I labour and they labour, but I labour and receive a reward and they labour and do not receive a reward; I run and they run, but I run to the life of the world to come and they run to the pit of destruction.' No man can genuinely place himself in the presence of the holy God and still congratulate himself on his own piety; and this means that piety can become a barrier between man and God.

The tax collector, with all his faults and follies, has thought only for God; and because his mind is on God, he knows himself to be a sinner. He has lived a disreputable life, and can find no help for his condition but in God; and he finds also that such honest humility is the one sure way into the divine presence. He rather than the Pharisee is justified, declared righteous; not that he is good and the other bad – this is not the case – but because he has done the one thing that God requires of those who seek access to him: he has faced the truth about himself and cast himself on God's compassion. Whether his repentance was deep or shallow we are not told; God can use even the first traces of a nascent faith.

G. B. Caird
taken from *The Pelican New Testament Commentaries:
The Gospel of Saint Luke*

Proper 26/Ordinary Time 31
Fourth Sunday before Advent

Sunday between 30 October and 5 November inclusive

Luke 19:1-10

A testimony is utterly worthless unless it is backed by deeds which guarantee its sincerity.

On Zacchaeus

Me thinks, I see, with what a busy haste,
Zacchaeus climb'd the Tree: But O, how fast,
How full of speed, canst thou imagine (when
Our Saviour call'd) he powder'd down agen!
He ne'er made trial if the boughs were sound
Or rotton; nor how far 'twas to the ground:
There was no danger fear'd; at such a Call,
He'll venture nothing, that dare fear a fall;
Needs must be down, by such a Spirit driven,
Nor could he fall unless he fall to Heaven.
Down came Zacchaeus, ravisht from the tree;
Bird that was shot ne'er dropt so quick as he.

Francis Quarles

Jericho was a very wealthy and a very important town. It lay on the Jordan valley and commanded both the approach to Jerusalem and the crossings of the river which gave access to the lands east of Jordan. It had a great palm forest and world-famous balsam groves which perfumed the air for miles around. Its gardens of roses were known far and wide. Men called it 'The City of Palms'. Josephus called it 'a divine region', 'the fattest in Palestine'. The Romans carried its dates and balsam to worldwide trade and fame. All this combined to make Jericho one of the greatest taxation centres in Palestine.

Zacchaeus was a man who had reached the top of his profession; and he was the most hated man in the district. There are three stages in his story.

(i) Zacchaeus was wealthy but he was not happy. Inevitably he was lonely, for he had chosen a way that made him an outcast. He had heard of this Jesus who welcomed

239

tax collectors and sinners, and he wondered if he would have any word for him. Despised and hated by men, Zacchaeus was reaching after the love of God.

(ii) Zacchaeus determined to see Jesus, and would let nothing stop him. For Zacchaeus to mingle with the crowd at all was a courageous thing to do, for many a man would take the chance to get a nudge or kick, or push at the little tax collector. It was an opportunity not to be missed. Zacchaeus would be black and blue with bruises that day. He could not see – the crowd took an ill delight in making sure of that. So he ran on ahead and climbed a fig-mulberry tree. A traveller describes the tree as being like 'the English oak, and its shade is most pleasing. It is consequently a favourite way-side tree . . . It is very easy to climb, with its short trunk and its wide lateral branches forking out in all directions.' Things were not easy for Zacchaeus but the little man had the courage of desperation.

(iii) Zacchaeus took steps to show all the community that he was a changed man. When Jesus announced that he would stay that day at his house, and when he discovered that he had found a new and wonderful friend, immediately Zacchaeus took a decision. He decided to give half his goods to the poor; the other half he did not intend to keep to himself but to use to make restitution for the frauds of which he had been self-confessedly guilty.

In his restitution he went far beyond what was legally necessary. Only if a robbery was a deliberate and violent act of destruction was a fourfold restitution necessary (Exodus 22:1). If it had been ordinary robbery and the original goods were not restorable, double the value had to be repaid (Exodus 22:4, 7). If voluntary confession was made and voluntary restitution offered, the value of the original goods had to be paid, plus one-fifth (Leviticus 6:5; Numbers 5:7). Zacchaeus was determined to do far more than the law demanded. He showed by his deeds that he was a changed man.

Dr Boreham has a terrible story. There was a meeting in progress at which several women were giving their testimony. One woman kept grimly silent. She was asked to testify but refused. She was asked why and she answered, 'Four of these women who have just given their testimony owe me money, and I and my family are half-starved because we cannot buy food.'

A testimony is utterly worthless unless it is backed by deeds which guarantee its sincerity. It is not a mere change of words which Jesus Christ demands, but a change of life.

The story ends with the great words, 'the Son of Man came

to seek and to save that which was lost'. We must always be careful how we take the meaning of this word 'lost'. In the New Testament it does not mean damned or doomed. It simply means *in the wrong place*. A thing is lost when it has got out of its own place into the wrong place; and when we find such a thing, we return it to the place it ought to occupy. A man is lost when he has wandered away from God; and he is found when once again he takes his rightful place as an obedient child in the household and the family of his Father.

William Barclay
The Daily Study Bible: The Gospel of Luke

All Saints' Day

Sunday between 30 October and 5 November or, if this is not kept as All Saints' Sunday, on 1 November itself.

Luke 6:20-31

Those who live in the expectation of faith live the experience of faith.

Let your light so shine before men, that they may see your good works, and glorify your Father which is in heaven. (Matthew 5:16 KJV)

In our conventional reading of the Beatitudes we frequently yield to two temptations. The first is to regard them as a set of principles, a collection of rules or aphorisms. They are, in this sense, thought of as a happier and much improved version of that earlier set of rules and ethics known as the Ten Commandments. Human progress is indicated here, we are told, for rather than being forbidden by a stern succession of 'thou shalt nots,' we are encouraged, indeed, even rewarded, with a state of beatitude, happiness, if we do the right thing. 'Carrot' theology rather than 'stick' theology, we might say, and it has proven attractive. Usually compared with the tortuous theology of Paul and the rigidities of Jewish law, the Beatitudes of Jesus are the spiritual ancestors of Dale Carnegie, Dr Peale and Dr Schuller, for they tell us not only how to win friends and influence people but how to gain eternal happiness in the bargain. These ethical rules are so popular and useful that they acquire a life beyond that of their teachers, and in certain understandings of the Beatitudes as rules for ethical living, Jesus himself is quite superfluous. We have patented the formula for making people good, and we no longer require the services of the inventor. The Pythagorean theorem works quite well without the interfering personality of Pythagoras.

We humans require and respect the stability of principles, the security of rules, laws, and theorems. We may not obey or understand them but it gives us enormous comfort to know that they are there. The most erratic of modern musicians and artists honour the conventional rules of harmony and colour, for it gives them all the more joy and power when they ignore them, and in some sense is this not the appeal and mystery of science, at least to the non-scientist? That there are dependabilities and immutabilities, and if we discover them, control them, and codify them we shall have peace, power, and perfection? Principles and rules are important to us whether or not we obey them, and I suspect it is for that reason, among others, that we like the Beatitudes, for here is a recipe for virtue, and if we read it right, use the right ingredients and in the right proportions, we can all cook like Julia Child, [or, for British readers, Delia Smith] and who will then need Julia Child? Here's the rub, however.

We have all been invited to dinner parties prepared by people who were tutored over the television by Julia Child but somehow, we admit in our heart of hearts, despite all of the creamery butter, the leeks, and that French copper paraphernalia, the meal is not quite the same without Julia in the kitchen. Once all is said and done, there is more personality than principle to cooking; and there is more personality than principle in the Beatitudes.

What makes the Beatitudes worthy of notice is not their abstract virtue, their essential correctness; on the face of it they make no sense at all. The thought of the meek inheriting the earth is as ludicrous now as it was then, and there is little happiness in mourning or joy in persecution. No, as in cookery, the power of the teaching is in the magic between teacher and taught. The 'personality' of the Beatitudes, and hence their so-called authority, rests in the person, the life of Jesus, and in the persons and lives of those people who hear, believe, and act. These principles without the person of their author and the persons to whom they are addressed mean nothing at all. As one commentary notes: 'It is not the Christian ethic which makes Christian men and women, it is Christian men and women who can live the Christian life'; and, we might add, they cannot do so without Christ. So the first step in our effort to rehabilitate the Beatitudes is to remember that they are concerned with ordinary people, and not simply with abstract principles.

I have said that there are two temptations to which we are inclined concerning the Beatitudes, and the second is that we postpone them into the future; the good part always comes later. When I was a child I was always told to eat all of my carrots for they would improve my eyesight, and to eat all of my beets for they would make my hair curly. I suppose one out of two is not a bad average, but every child knows they are expected to eat awful vegetables now for some postponed future happiness, and since most of us don't believe it, we neither eat our carrots nor have our sight improved. The radical power of Jesus' extraordinary message to his ordinary hearers is that now, in this moment, in your mourning you have happiness, and in your persecution you have joy. Now, as you eat your carrots, you see.

The various English translations of the New Testament Greek do not do justice to this meaning, for the Beatitudes are rendered as statements: 'Blessed are the poor in spirit, for theirs is the kingdom of heaven,' but the Greek states them as exclamations, ecstatic utterances of present reality, literally: 'Now happiness and the kingdom of heaven for those poor in spirit!'; 'Now mercy for those who are merciful!'

Do you see what has happened? Tomorrow has become today, the kingdom that is to come is already here; that which we seek, we have, that which we would be, we are! This is not to say, as many do, that this is all there is, or 'What you see is what you get'. It is, rather, to say that in some real sense those who live in the expectation of faith live the experience of faith. The happiness of the Gospel is not hope deferred but the consequence of hope experienced here and now by you and by me, and the wonder of it all is that this extraordinary message is for us ordinary people, who of ourselves can accomplish nothing, but who with Christ can indeed overcome the world. Is that not something for which to be grateful? Is that not sufficient reason to shine and glow and give glory to God in all that we say and do? Does not this add zest to life, and light to those who sit in darkness? That is what the fifth chapter of Matthew is all about, and the New Testament with it, and that is why we are here . . . Our Christian lives are meant to shine before the world, and our good works to give glory to our Father who is in heaven.

How then may we do this, if we want to? What must we do to let our light shine, we ordinary people? Well, in the first place, it is not what we do but who we are that counts; it is not in doing but in being, and that is a hard lesson for such achievement-oriented souls as we. Phillips Brooks reminded us that preaching is 'truth though personality', and that means that what a person is speaks so loudly that we cannot hear what the person says. 'Being' comes from within; the light shines out, not in. When Saul went down among the sons of Jesse to find a new king for Israel he was first attracted to Eliab, who was handsome and comely, and Samuel thought, 'Surely, the Lord's anointed is before him'. The Lord, however, said to Saul, 'Do not look on his appearance or on the height of his stature, because I have rejected him; for the Lord sees not as man sees: man looks on the outward appearance, but the Lord looks on the heart.' So the search continued until David was found, whose heart was pleasing to God. What David did in his life was not always pleasing to God but who he was, his being, always was, and that is why, flaws and all, he is counted the greatest among the sons of God, for who he was was greater than what he did, and in his best moments he made his name a blessing among the nations.

All of us have had, in our time, light shed upon our path, and not necessarily by the famous or the powerful or those who get their names in the paper. A teacher here, a friend there, and sometimes by someone who will never be aware of the extent of their influence for good upon us but who at the right time and the right place was the bearer of light in a dark or difficult time. What is always amazing to me is that these bearers of light are almost always ordinary people, men and women like you and me, with no special claim upon the world but upon whom God has placed a claim which by his grace he shares with the world and with us. My mother was always suspicious of saints; anybody who had that much time just to be good probably wasn't doing what needed to be done, she thought. She would not want to be thought of as a saint, and she wasn't one, thank God. She was more than that for me and for countless others known and unknown to me, a vehicle by which God's grace shone in the world. In that ordinary life God shone with extraordinary brightness, and for that I thank God.

The philosopher William James, on the underestimated power of the ordinary, modest, and simple, said:

I am done with great things and big things, great institutions and big success; and am for those tiny, invisible molecular moral forces that work from individual to individual through the crannies of the world, like so many rootlets, or like the capillary oozing of water, yet which, if you give them time, will rend the hardest moments of man's pride.

So, what is this all about? The Gospel of Jesus Christ comes down to a rather simple proposition for ordinary people like you and like me: if God is to be known, that knowledge will be in the lives of ordinary people who are redeemed by his extraordinary message of love. What the world knows of God it will know through us; for better or for worse we are the good news, the Gospel; we are the light of the world. You don't need to finish your PhD or your [DD], or even the *Sunday Times* to let your light shine. We do not have to postpone the blessedness of Christ into some ever-retreating future, and we dare not wait for more qualified Christians, better prayers, or better rules to come along and do our shining for us. No, the work of God awaits our hands, the love of God awaits our hearts, and the people of God await our fellowship here and now, ordinary and imperfect though we may be. Therefore, undergraduates, graduates, townfolk and gownfolk, brothers and sisters, strong and weak, let your light so shine in the world that all may see your good works, and give glory to your Father which is in heaven.

Peter J. Gomes
Sermons: Biblical Wisdom for Daily Living

Proper 27/Ordinary Time 32
Third Sunday before Advent

Sunday between 6 and 12 November inclusive

Luke 20:27-38

Death may put an end to physical existence, but not to a relationship that is by nature eternal.

The question with which the Sadducees thought to ridicule Jesus was based on the law of Levirate marriage (Deuteronomy 25:5-6), the object of which was to provide a legal heir for a man who died childless. In the time of Jesus the law had fallen into abeyance, so that the question was a somewhat academic one. The Sadducees, no doubt, would have argued that, since the commandment was in the Torah, and since it made belief in resurrection absurd, therefore the Torah excluded belief in an afterlife. Jesus, however, did not hold the naive view of resurrection they attributed to him. He had simply to state, therefore, that in an existence which has no place for death, marriage as a means of propagating the species or assuring a legal succession becomes irrelevant.

Once again, however, Jesus takes the question more seriously than the questioner, and turns to the important assumptions that underlie it. By a quotation from Exodus 3:6 he argues that the Torah does imply a belief in eternal life, so that even on their own premise the Sadducees are wrong. The argument runs as follows: inanimate things may have a Creator, but only the living can have a God. When God says to Moses, 'I am the God of Abraham . . .' this implies that Abraham is still alive. In form the argument is typically rabbinic, relying as it does on the precise wording of the sacred text, and, as Luke tells us, the scribes were impressed by it. But the substance of the argument has a deeper validity, and is capable of being expressed in a form more congenial to the modern mind. Jesus is saying, in effect: all life, here and hereafter, consists of friendship with God, and nothing less is worthy of the name of life. Abraham was the friend of God, and it is incredible that such friendship should be severed by death. Death may put an end to physical existence, but not to a relationship that is by nature eternal. Men may lose their friends by death, but not God.

G. B. Caird
taken from *The Pelican New Testament Commentaries: The Gospel of Saint Luke*

The Christian belief is that after death, individuality will survive, that you will still be you and I will still be I. Beside that, we have to set another immense fact. To the Greek the body could not be consecrated. It was matter, the source of all evil, the prison-house of the soul. But to the Christian the body is not evil. Jesus, the Son of God, has taken this human body upon him and therefore it is not contemptible because it has been inhabited by God. To the Christian, therefore, the life to come involves the total man, body and soul.

Now it is easy to misinterpret and to caricature the doctrine of the resurrection of the body. Celsus, who lived about AD 200, a bitter opponent of Christianity, did this very thing long ago. 'How can those who have died rise with their identical bodies?' he demands. 'Really it is the hope of worms! For what soul of a man would any longer wish for a body that had rotted?' It is easy to cite the case of a person smashed up in an accident or dying of cancer.

But Paul never said that we would rise with the body with which we died. He insisted that we would have a spiritual body. What he really meant was that a man's *personality* would survive. It is almost impossible to conceive of personality without a body, because it is through the body that the personality expresses itself. What Paul is contending for is that after death the individual remains. He did not inherit the Greek contempt for the body but believed in the resurrection of the whole man. He will still be himself; he will survive as a person. That is what Paul means by the resurrection of the body. Everything of the body and of the soul that is necessary to make a man a person will survive, but at the same time, all things will be new, and the body and spirit will alike be very different from earthly things, for they will alike be divine.

William Barclay
The Letter to the Corinthians, volume 1

Proper 28/Ordinary Time 33
Second Sunday before Advent

Sunday between 13 and 19 November inclusive

Luke 21:5-19

Come earthquakes, come famines, come plagues, come great signs from heaven, we are to hold on to one another – we are to endure in that – because that is how we hold on to our Lord.

Portents and signs

As the end of the last millennium drew near, stranger and stranger things happened. Survivalists took to the woods with their stockpiles of weapons. More passive types committed mass suicide in hopes of escaping to another planet. Even the most placid among us may have checked the sky from time to time, just to make sure everything was where it is supposed to be.

It is easy enough to see why some people think history is drawing to a close. All you have to do is hold a newspaper in one hand and Luke's Gospel in the other. 'Nation will rise against nation, and kingdom against kingdom.' Check. 'There will be great earthquakes.' Check. 'In various places famines and plagues.' Check, check. 'Dreadful portents and great signs from heaven.' Does a gaping hole in the ozone layer count? Check.

'They will arrest you and persecute you.' Well, no, not yet, or at least not here. In Central America, yes, in South Africa, maybe, as well as in the Middle East; but it is hard to read the part about being brought before kings and governors without thinking of the second-century Church, and the third, for whom martyrdom was a fact of daily life. Church history began with those who were burned at the stake or beheaded or fed to the lions.

So this frightening passage not only looks forward; it also looks back, to the many times before now when Christians experienced all these things and believed their world was coming to an end, only it did not. This inexplicable delay in the coming of the Lord is one of the stickiest problems the Christian Church has ever had to face. Jesus himself did not seem to know the answer. 'Truly, I tell you, this generation will not pass away until all things have taken place,' he said, almost two thousand years ago (Luke 21:32).

He says it as part of his last public teaching on earth. He has done everything he knows how to do. He has said everything he knows how to say. He has come to Jerusalem knowing full well he will collide with the authorities there, and he is sitting in the temple talking with his disciples when some of them begin to admire the place out loud, commenting on how beautiful the stone is, how grand the gifts dedicated to God, when Jesus reminds them that it will all be rubble some day soon.

He does not say it to be cruel. He is simply telling them the truth – that the things of this world will not last – that even some place as stunning and holy as the temple will become a ruin when the old world collapses in upon itself, which is becoming as clear to him as his own death. It is the kind of news that shrinks your heart and ties your stomach in knots. It is the kind of news that makes you start collecting canned goods in the basement and looking around for someone who can save you – someone who seems to have access to God's calendar and who will tell you exactly when the ship starts to sink so that you can make it to the lifeboats in time.

Only Jesus does not recommend that course of action. He warns against it, in fact. 'Beware that you are not led astray,' he tells those gathered around him; 'for many will come in my name and say, "I am he!" and "The time is near!" Do not go after them. When you hear of wars and insurrections, do not be terrified; for these things must take place first, but the end will not follow immediately.'

Do not go after them. Do not be terrified. When the sky is falling? When the world is coming to an end? That is right. Do not go after them. Do not be terrified.

I will tell you the most interesting thing about this passage for me. When I read the newspaper or tune into the five o'clock news on the radio – when I hear of wars and insurrections, and holes in the ozone layer, and rising interest rates, and unemployment figures, and all the other symptoms of a world in deep distress, I start wondering where God has gone. I wonder if God had something important to do in some other corner of the universe and forgot about us here, or just got tired of bailing us out and decided to let the human experiment come to an end.

I read the signs of the times as signs of God's absence, in other words, but according to Luke's Gospel they are not signs of God's absence at all but signs of God's sure and certain presence. Nothing is going on that is unknown to God – not the things in the newspaper or the things in our own lives; God foresaw them long ago and encouraged us not to be terrified. Because to become terrified is to become part of the problem, you see, which is not what God has in mind for us. God has something else in mind for us, something Jesus calls endurance.

'These things happen,' he said. 'These things must take place. When all that is lovely to you, when all that is holy looks as if it may soon be reduced to rubble, do not lose heart. I never promised to lead you around the trouble in the world; I only promised to lead you through. Do not be terrified, little flock. Hold on to one another and follow me through. Not a hair of your head will perish, not ultimately. By your endurance you will gain your souls.'

According to the newspaper, the mainline Church is one of the many things in the world that is falling apart. We read that we are losing members. We read that we are torn by schism and scandal, and that it is hard to tell what the Church stands for anymore. With all of this in mind, I and several members of the congregation recently attended the annual meeting of our denomination in Atlanta. We went to remember that we are not a solitary outpost of believers in northeast Georgia but that we are connected to a worldwide communion of faith who remember us when they say their prayers the same way we remember them. We went to take our places in the greater body of Christ of which we are all a part, and some of us went with concerns about the health of that body.

Our presiding bishop was with us, and we spent all day Saturday talking with him about the issues confronting the Church and the world: the hamstrung economy, family values, human sexuality, the growing number of poor people, the challenges faced by our youth. We talked honestly and from the heart. We expressed vast differences. We listened carefully to one another. No one booed anyone else, and there was a lot of applause. A sense of mutual respect for one another pervaded our long day of dialogue – perhaps because we prayed together morning, noon, and night – and I think it is fair to say that we all came away with a sense that God was with us, and is with us, in all our differences and struggle.

There is a time-honoured saying in the Anglican Church, that schism is worse than heresy. What that means is that it is okay for us to disagree, and it is even okay for some of us to be way, way out of line as far as orthodox theology is concerned, but what is not okay is for us to let go of one another. Staying in communion with one another – holding on to one another through all the stormy blasts that blow us around – that is how we know that God is still with us, no matter what the headlines say. Come earthquakes, come famines, come plagues, come great signs from heaven, we are to hold on to one another – we are to endure in that – because holding on to one another is how we hold on to our Lord.

I had a very wonderful old lady for a friend until she died several years ago at the age of 97. The newspaper headlines changed a lot over the course of her lifetime. When she was born, in 1894, there were no airplanes, no televisions, no automobiles to speak of. Russia was ruled by a czar and China by an emperor. The only way to get to Europe was by boat.

As she got older, her short-term memory got worse, but her long-term memory got better, and one day as I sat by her bed she told me about a summer's day from her childhood, when she and some of her girlfriends hitched up their long skirts and climbed Mount Washington in the White Mountains of New Hampshire. They went too far and stayed too long, she said, and before they knew it the beautiful sunset they were watching had turned into a foggy dusk so that they could not see their hands in front of their faces.

No one had a flashlight – flashlights had not been invented yet and no one knew for sure which way was down, but they agreed they would all hold hands and that they would not, under any circumstance, let go of one another. So that is how they did it – one girl at the front, picking her way down the mountain one step at a time and all the rest of them strung out behind her, holding onto each other's wrists so that they made a living human chain. Every now and then someone would want to argue about which way to go and the others would listen, but what none of them did was let go.

'Sometimes,' my friend said, 'all I knew or could see of the world was the hand ahead of me and the one behind. Sometimes my arms ached so badly I thought I would cry out loud, but that is how we made it at last. We found our way home by holding on to one another.'

'Do not be terrified,' he said, 'for all these things must take place. But lo, I am with you always, even unto the end of the age.' Amen.

Barbara Brown Taylor
God in Pain: Teaching Sermons on Suffering

Proper 29/Christ the King

Sunday between 20 and 26 November inclusive

Luke 23:33-43

*King of the Jews.
Yes, verily, and
more, God's King,
God's Anointed
and Appointed
King over all; and
so that cross is
seen as the throne
of imperial and
eternal Empire!*

*And when they came unto the place that is called
The Skull, there they crucified him.*

'The place that is called The Skull'; I do not know whether
we have gained much by translating there. The *King James
Version* reads, 'which is called Calvary'. The Greek word is
Kranion, of which *Calvaria* is the Latin equivalent, and *Golgotha*
the Hebrew. Whether the Greek word *Kranion*, or the Latin
Calvaria, or the Hebrew *Golgotha*, each means the place of a
skull. The word Calvary has taken a very definite place in
the language of the Church. It only occurs once in the Bible,
and now it has gone in the Revised. The actual place so
named is not positively known. I personally believe that the
traditional hill is not the place at all, and that General Gordon found the true site. It was evidently at the time the place
of execution, outside the city wall, a hillock, in the shape of a
skull. There 'they crucified him'.

Now listen to the voices. The first that we hear is the
voice of Jesus: 'Father, forgive them; for they know not what
they do.'

That is humanity at its greatest. Men have their conceptions of human nature, and of what things make for greatness therein. These conceptions are very many and very
varied. I submit that humanity has never been seen greater
than in the man Jesus, when he said: 'Father, forgive them;
for they know not what they do.'

In the soul of Jesus there was no resentment, no anger, no
lurking desire for punishment upon the men who were mal-
treating him. Men have spoken in admiration of the mailed
fist. When I hear Jesus thus pray I know that the only place
for the mailed fist is in hell.

If that is humanity at its greatest, it is also an unveiling of
the deepest fact in God. 'God willeth not the death of a sinner, but rather that all should turn to him, and repent.'
What does the cross mean? 'Father, forgive them; for they
know not what they do.'

As I read that story, I ask myself this question, 'Was that
prayer answered?' There can be but one answer, they were

253

forgiven unquestionably. That does not mean necessarily that the forgiven men entered into right relationship with God, but it does mean that there was forgiveness for every man, in answer to that cry of Jesus Christ. Legendary lore has been busy with this matter. We cannot depend upon legendary lore, except that we know that at the back of every legend there is some element of truth struggling to express itself; often failing to do it by over-emphasis and grotesque emphases. I do not know, I have no evidence; but nothing would surprise me less when I reach the land beyond, than to meet the men who drove the nails into the hands of Jesus, those who brought about his death. At any rate, the prayer was heard. Forgiveness was provided. I cannot listen to that first cry coming out of the perfected humanity of Jesus, and therefore revealing the deepest will and purpose and passion of God, without being perfectly certain that it was heard, that it was answered, and that there was forgiveness for all men.

Now let me read on, and we shall hear other voices:

'And the rulers also scoffed at him, saying, "He saved others; let him save himself, if this is the Christ of God, his Chosen."'

What I hear in the scoffing mockery of these rulers is their test of Messiahship. What was their test? What did they say? If he is really the Messiah, if he is really the Chosen of God, let him save himself. It did not enter into their minds for a moment that the meaning of Messiahship was not the saving of himself, but the saving of others. Their whole conception of Messiahship had become blunted, materialised, blasted; and when they saw him on the cross they said: That ends it, he is no Messiah, or he would never be there; he would save himself. But still he hung there, and so right before their eyes was the supreme evidence of Messiahship. The thing they said was true. He saved others, himself he could not save. That is Messiahship. He could not save himself. Why not? Because he would save others. He can save others. Why? Because he would not save himself.

Again:

'And the soldiers also mocked him.'

They did not say anything about Messiahship. They did not know anything about Messiahship. They did not care anything about Christ as the Chosen of God. That is not the point with the soldiers. That is not the concern of the empire. They said, 'If thou art the King of the Jews, save thyself.'

Here we see their test of kingship: ability to take care of himself. They did not see that the true function of the king was to take care of his kingdom and all those who were members of it. How could they? They were soldiers of Rome. What did they know of an emperor who had no power to take care of himself. If a Roman Caesar failed to take care of himself they had no more use for him as Imperator. The qualification for a king was his ability to break men, and rule over them, and subdue them. So the soldiers mocked him, and said: 'If you are King of the Jews, save yourself.'

Thus, whether it is the voice of the religious rulers, or the voice of Empire represented in the soldiers, we see human life hell-inspired, with its one motto, 'Look after yourself', and mastered by that conception of greatness, whether for Messiahship or kingship. And yet, by the suffering, dying Saviour, Messiahship is demonstrated, in the fact that he will not save himself, but that he will save others; and kingship is assured for ever, by that selfsame fact of determination still to empty and humble himself, that he may exalt and fill humanity.

And the last thing is the superscription:

'There was also a superscription over him, THIS IS THE KING OF THE JEWS.'

Observe the truth of it, and the limitation of it. He was the King of the Jews. He told Pilate that he was. When Pilate put that question to him, he said, 'Thou sayest.' He was the glory and the crown of God's purpose in Israel. Through all the process of their history, at last, here is the one who fulfilled the divine purpose, and whose right it is to reign, King of the Jews in very deed.

And yet how limited the superscription, and how it fails. That is chapter 23. Go back to chapter one. Among other things there recorded is the announcement which the angel made to the Virgin Mother concerning the coming of Jesus:

'Thou shalt call his name Jesus. He shall be great, and shall be called the Son of the Most High; and the Lord God shall give unto him the throne of his father David; and he shall reign over the house of Jacob for ever.'

All that was said, but more: 'And of his kingdom there shall be no end.'

No end, *telos*, that is, no limit. It describes the uncircumscribed kingdom of Jesus. King of the Jews. Yes, verily, and more, God's King, God's Anointed and Appointed King over all; and so that cross is seen as the throne of imperial and eternal Empire!

G. Campbell Morgan
The Gospel According to Luke

Today

Remember me, when you get to your kingdom.

The thief hanging by his side was the only one who still believed that he was dying beside a king. For him, even though he couldn't read, that mocking inscription nailed above the cross – *Jesus of Nazareth, king of the Jews* – was truly a royal standard. The thief thought that his companion's kingdom would be a big garden with towers, fountains and fragrant wines. A paradise of open coffers where everything could be stolen with a clear conscience while you looked passers-by cheerfully in the eye because there'd be no guards. And the streets where he, as always, would sleep would be touched with the golden warmth of the sun and the night would know no winter. When he'd arrive up there, possibly in an ivory chariot, would the king be so kind as to remember him amid the bowing and scraping of his ministers?

Why should he *remember* him? What did being *remembered* mean to him? That highway robber was no sentimentalist. Did he perhaps mean that in the ditch where they would surely throw him graces and prayers might pour down on him? And what did grace and prayer mean? And then in what aspect would his friend remember him? As a bloodthirsty malefactor with his knife at his victim's throat and his hand on his purse? Or as he was now, hanging next to him, with his ugly bloodstained face and his great hairy belly? He didn't know and it didn't concern him. All he wanted was a little corner in Christ's memory – 'remember me'. If he'd had some little portrait he'd have shown it to him – as simple people do who strike up warm friendships on railway journeys.

The other thief was cursing, like the people down below. He was a furious blasphemer, but with a trace of cunning ('If you're the Christ, save yourself and us'.) Perhaps – you never knew – if he abused that gentleman who had worked miracles, a miracle would result. Abuse – that was what was needed. And then the good thief rediscovered his violence (he'd have knifed him well and truly if his hands had been free) and addressed a last attack to his former accomplice: 'Aren't you even afraid of God, though you're undergoing the same punishment? It's only justice that we should suffer for our crimes, but he hadn't done any harm.'

Yes, the one crucified between them was Christ. But the good thief didn't ask for a miracle, he didn't feel he had any right to be saved. He, who had lived on greed and robbery, was a crystal of total disinterestedness within himself.

Jesus answered: 'Today you'll be with me in paradise.' The hardened evil-doer was accustomed to long years of waiting; five years condemned to the galleys, ten to the mines. But now those long periods were over. Jesus wasn't satisfied with wiping out all that man's stains. He hastened to assure him that immediately, today, he'd enter that garden without policemen where you sleep on warm streets.

'Forgive them because they don't know what they're doing,' Christ asked. But the good thief could be absolved more easily: he knew what he was doing.

Luigi Santucci
Wrestling with Christ

Alex's death

As almost all of you know, a week ago last Monday night, driving in a terrible storm, my son Alexander – who to his friends was a real day-brightener, and to his family 'Fair as a star when only one is shining in the sky' – my 24-year-old Alexander, who enjoyed beating his old man at every game and in every race, beat his father to the grave.

Among the healing flood of letters that followed his death was one carrying this wonderful quote from the end of Hemingway's *Farewell to Arms*: 'The world breaks everyone, then some become strong at the broken places.' My own broken heart is mending, and largely thanks to so many of you, my dear parishioners; for if in the last week I have relearned one lesson, it is that love not only begets love, it transmits strength.

Because so many of you have cared so deeply and because obviously I've been able to think of little else, I want this morning to talk of Alex's death, I hope in a way helpful to all.

When a person dies, there are many things that can be said, and there is at least one thing that should never be said. The night after Alex died I was sitting in the living room of my sister's house outside of Boston, when the front door opened and in came a nice-looking middle-aged woman, carrying about eighteen quiches. When she saw me she shook her head, then headed for the kitchen, saying sadly over her shoulder, 'I just don't understand the will of God'.

Instantly I was up and in hot pursuit, swarming all over

her. 'I'll say you don't, lady!' I said. (I knew the anger would do me good, and the instruction to her was long overdue.) I continued, 'Do you think it was the will of God that Alex never fixed that lousy windshield wiper of his, that he was probably driving too fast in such a storm, that he probably had had a couple of "frosties" too many? Do you think it is God's will that there are no streetlights along that stretch of road, and no guardrail separating the road and Boston Harbor?'

For some reason, nothing so infuriates me as the incapacity of seemingly intelligent people to get it through their heads that God doesn't go around this world with his finger on triggers, his fist around knives, his hands on steering wheels. God is dead set against all unnatural deaths. And Christ spent an inordinate amount of time delivering people from paralysis, insanity, leprosy and muteness. Which is not to say that there are no nature-caused deaths (I can think of many right here in this parish in the five years I've been here), deaths that are untimely and slow and pain-ridden, which for that reason raise unanswerable questions, and even the spectre of a Cosmic Sadist – yes, even an Eternal Vivisector. But violent deaths, such as the one Alex died – to understand those is a piece of cake. As his younger brother put it simply, standing at the head of the casket at the Boston funeral, 'You blew it, buddy. You blew it.' The one thing that should never be said when someone dies is 'It is the will of God'. Never do we know enough to say that. My own con- solation lies in knowing that it was not the will of God that Alex die; that when the waves closed over the sinking car, God's heart was the first of all our hearts to break.

I mentioned the healing flood of letters. Some of the very best, and easily the worst, came from fellow reverends, a few of whom proved they knew their Bibles better than the human condition. I know all the 'right' biblical passages, including 'Blessed are those who mourn', and my faith is no house of cards; these passages are true, I know. But the point is this: while the words of the Bible are true, grief renders them unreal. The reality of grief is the absence of God – 'My God, my God, why hast thou forsaken me?' The reality of grief is the solitude of pain, the feeling that your heart is in pieces, your mind's a blank, that 'there is no joy the world can give like that it takes away' (Lord Byron).

That's why immediately after such a tragedy people must come to your rescue, people who only want to hold your hand, not to quote anybody or even say anything, people who simply bring food and flowers – the basics of beauty and life – people who sign letters simply, 'Your broken-hearted sister'. In other words, in my intense grief I felt some of my fellow reverends – not many, and none of you, thank God – were using comforting words of scripture for self-protection, to pretty up a situation whose bleakness they simply couldn't face. But like God herself, scripture is not around for anyone's protection, just for everyone's unending support.

And that's what hundreds of you understood so beautifully. You gave me what God gives all of us – minimum protection, maximum support. I swear to you, I wouldn't be standing here were I not upheld.

After the death of his wife, C. S. Lewis wrote, 'They say, "the coward dies many times"; so does the beloved. Didn't the eagle find a fresh liver to tear in Prometheus every time it dined?'

When parents die, as did my mother last month, they take with them a large portion of the past. But when children die, they take away the future as well. That is what makes the valley of the shadow of death seem so incredibly dark and unending. In a prideful way it would be easier to walk the valley alone, nobly, head high, instead of – as we must – marching as the latest recruit in the world's army of the bereaved.

Still there is much by way of consolation. Because there are no rankling unanswered questions, and because Alex and I simply adored each other, the wound for me is deep, but clean. I know how lucky I am! I also know that this day-brightener of a son wouldn't wish to be held close by grief (nor, for that matter, would any but the meanest of our beloved departed), and that, interestingly enough, when I mourn Alex least I see him best.

Another consolation, of course, will be the learning – which better be good, given the price. But it's a fact: few of us are naturally profound; we have to be forced down. So while trite, it's true:

I walked a mile with Pleasure,
she chattered all the way;
but left me none the wiser
for all she had to say.

I walked a mile with Sorrow
and ne'er a word said she;
but oh, the things I learned from her
when Sorrow walked with me.

Robert Browning Hamilton

Or, in Emily Dickinson's verse,

By a departing light
we see acuter quite
than by a wick that stays.
There's something in the flight
that clarifies the sight
and decks the rays.

And of course I know, even when pain is deep, that God is good. 'My God, my God, why hast thou forsaken me?' Yes, but at least, 'My God, my God'; and the psalm only begins that way, it doesn't end that way. As the grief that once seemed unbearable begins to turn now to bearable sorrow, the truths in the 'right' biblical passages are beginning, once again, to take hold: 'Cast thy burden upon the Lord and he shall strengthen thee'; 'Weeping may endure for a night, but joy cometh in the morning'; 'Lord, by thy favour thou hast made my mountain to stand strong'; 'For thou hast delivered my soul from death, mine eyes from tears, and my feet from falling'; 'In this world ye shall have tribulation, but be of good cheer; I have overcome the world'; 'The light shines in the darkness, and the darkness has not overcome it'.

And finally I know that when Alex beat me to the grave, the finish line was not Boston Harbor in the middle of the night. If a week ago last Monday a lamp went out, it was because, for him at least, the Dawn had come.

So I shall – so let us all – seek consolation in that love which never dies, and find peace in the dazzling grace that always is.

William Sloane Coffin
The Courage to Love

Index of Authors and Translators

Acknowledgements

The Publishers wish to thank all those who have given their permission to reproduce copyright material in this publication. The readings listed below are all in copyright and the addresses of the copyright owners are given at the end of this section.

First Sunday of Advent

A tourist wandering . . . (H.L. Gee), extract from *Telling Tales* © 1962 Epworth Press. Used by permission of Methodist Publishing House.

The response put into . . . (John B, Taylor), taken from *Preaching on God's Justice*, 1994 Mowbray, an imprint of Continuum. Used by permission.

Can we come to any . . . (William Barclay), taken from *Great Themes of the New Testament*, published by T & T Clark Ltd, 1979. Used by permission.

Second Sunday of Advent

The introduction to the song . . . (Fred B. Craddock), taken from *Preaching Through the Christian Year: 'C'*, © 1994 Fred B. Craddock, John H. Hayes, Carl R. Holliday, Gene M. Tucker. Reproduced by permission of Trinity Press International, USA.

He shall not judge . . . (Andrew R.C. McLellan), taken from *Preaching for These People*, published by Mowbray, an imprint of Continuum, 1994. Used by permission.

Third Sunday of Advent

Kaj Munk was a pastor . . . (Allan Boesak), taken from *Walking with Thorns: The call to Christian Discipleship* © 1984 WCC Publications, Geneva. Used by permission.

Into this world of lyrical poetry . . . (Walter Brueggemann), taken from *The Threat of Life*, published by Augsburg Fortress Publishers. Used by permission.

God's attitude to sin . . . (N.H. Snaith), taken from *A Theological Word Book of the Bible*, Edited by Alan Richardson DD, Published by SCM Press, 1950. World rights.

Fourth Sunday of Advent

Describing a local farmer . . . (Laurie Lee), taken from *Cider with Rosie*, published by Hogarth Press 1959. Used by permission of Random House Group Ltd.

I wish you joy . . . (Katie Mitchell) quoted in *For all Occasions*. © Copyright Control.

Stanford in G . . . (Eric James), taken from *A Time to Speak*, published by SPCK Publishing, 1997. Used by permission.

Christmas Day – First Proper

There is nothing like . . . (G. Curtis Jones & Paul H. Jones), taken from *500 Illustrations: Stories from Life for Preaching & Teaching*, published by Abingdon Press, 1998. Used by permission.

Christmas Day – Second Proper

Let me tell you . . . (Eric James), taken from *A Time to Speak*, published by SPCK Publishing, 1997. Used by permission.

Christmas Day – Third Proper

Shadowlands – the play . . . (Eric James), quoted in *A Time to Speak*, published by SPCK Publishing, 1997. Used by permission.

First Sunday of Christmas

Oh, vicar, thank you . . . (S.J. Forrest), taken from *What's the Use?* © Copyright Control.

Jesus now claims . . . (Fred B. Craddock), taken from *Preaching Through the Christian Year: 'C'*, © 1994 Fred B. Craddock, John H. Hayes, Carl R. Holliday, Gene M. Tucker. Reproduced by permission of Trinity Press International, USA.

Second Sunday of Christmas

In the year . . . (Hans Kung), taken from *On Being a Christian*, published by Harper-Collins Publishers, London, 1977. (Rights now reverted to author).

Jesus apparently cannot . . . (Hans Kung), taken from *On Being a Christian*, published by HarperCollins Publishers, London, 1977. (Rights now reverted to author).

Christian living is . . . (D.T. Niles), taken from *The Power at Work Among Us* © 1968 Epworth Press. Used by permission of Methodist Publishing House.

The Epiphany

The Bible contains two . . . (F. W. Boreham), taken from *Daily Readings from F.W. Boreham*, 1976, reproduced by permission of Hodder and Stoughton Limited.

Towards the end . . . (F. W. Boreham), taken from *Arrows of Desire*, © Epworth Press. Used by permission of Methodist Publishing House.

First Sunday of Epiphany/The Baptism of the Lord /Ordinary Time 1

The third and last . . . (Fred B. Craddock), from *Luke* (Interpretation Series) © 1990 Westminster John Knox Press. Used by permission.

Second Sunday of Epiphany/Ordinary Time 2

But how could Jesus . . . (J. Paterson Smyth), taken from *A Boys' and Girls' Life of Christ*, © Copyright Control.

A man was talking . . . (Frank Pagden) taken from *Laughter and Tears*, © Frank Pagden. Published by Monarch Publications. Used by permission.

Third Sunday of Epiphany/Ordinary Time 3

Just as he told . . . (Fred B. Craddock), from *Luke* (Interpretation Series) © 1990 Westminster John Knox Press. Used by permission.

Fourth Sunday of Epiphany/Ordinary Time 4

Wanted – for sedition . . . (Hans Kung), taken from *On Being a Christian*, published by HarperCollins Publishers, London, 1977. (Rights now reverted to author).

His whole way . . . (Hans Kung), taken from *On Being a Christian*, published by Harper-Collins Publishers, London, 1977. (Rights now reverted to author).

I seek thee . . . (G. Vermes), taken from *The Dead Sea Scrolls in English*, Allen Lane (The Penguin Press), 1962 (Fourth edition 1995). © G. Vermes 1962, 1965, 1968, 1975, 1995 and 1997. Used by permission of Penguin UK.

In the New Testament, . . . (Alan Richardson), taken from *A Theological Word Book of the Bible*, published by SCM Press, 1950. World rights.

Fourth Sunday of Epiphany/Ordinary Time 4

There was no Jew . . . (Fred B. Craddock), taken from *Preaching Through the Christian Year: 'C'*, © 1994 Fred B. Craddock, John H. Hayes, Carl R. Holliday, Gene M. Tucker. Reproduced by permission of Trinity Press International, USA.

The text that provides . . . (Fred B. Craddock), taken from *Preaching Through the Christian Year: 'C'*, © 1994 Fred B. Craddock, John H. Hayes, Carl R. Holliday, Gene M. Tucker. Reproduced by permission of Trinity Press International, USA.

Fifth Sunday of Epiphany/Proper 1/Ordinary Time 5

The famous sheet . . . (William Barclay), taken from *The Daily Study Bible: The Gospel of Luke*, published by The Saint Andrew Press, 1994. Used by permission.

On my very first visit . . . (Ron Dale), © Ron Dale.

Sixth Sunday of Epiphany/Proper 2/Ordinary Time 6

Towards the end . . . (Ron Dale), © 1998 Ron Dale.

It is not only . . . (Walter J. Burghardt), taken from *Preaching the Just Word*, published by Yale University Press, 1996. Used by Permission.

Psalm 23 in a new . . . (Ron Dale), © Ron Dale.

Seventh Sunday of Epiphany/Proper 3/Ordinary Time 7

At the end of the . . . (T. Wingfield Heale), taken from *Crossing the Border*, © Copyright Control.

What then is forgiveness . . . (D. T. Niles), taken from *The Power at Work Among Us*, © 1968 Epworth Press. Used by permission of Methodist Publishing House.

One day I . . . (Ron Dale), © 1998 Ron Dale.

Eighth Sunday of Epiphany/Second Sunday before Lent/Ordinary Time 8

The *Des Moines Tribune* . . . (G. Curtis Jones and Paul H. Jones), taken from *500 Illustrations: Stories from Life for Preaching & Teaching*, published by Abingdon Press, 1998. Used by permission.

Goodmanham was the . . . (John Hillaby), taken from *Journey Home*, published by Granada Publishing Ltd, 1983.

The Military Police . . . (Ron Dale), © Ron Dale.

Eighth Sunday of Epiphany/Second Sunday before Lent/Ordinary Time 8

Who are you? . . . (Peter J. Gomes), taken from *Sermons: Biblical Wisdom for Daily Living*, © 1998 Peter J. Gomes. Used by permission of HarperCollins Publishers, Inc., New York.

Ninth Sunday of Epiphany

Jewish People . . . (G. Curtis Jones and Paul H. Jones), taken from *500 Illustrations: Stories from Life for Preaching & Teaching*, published by Abingdon Press, 1998. Used by permission.

I once visited . . . (Ron Dale), © 1998 Ron Dale.

The central character . . . (William Barclay), taken from *The Gospel of Luke*, published by The Saint Andrew Press, 1994. Used by permission.

This story opens . . . (Fred B. Craddock), from *Luke* (Interpretation Series) © 1990 John Knox Press. Used by permission of Westminster John Knox Press.

Last Sunday of Epiphany/Sunday next before Lent/Transfiguration Sunday

Earlier in this chapter . . . (Beverly R. Gaventa), taken from *Texts for Preaching – Year C*, by Charles B. Cousar, Beverly R. Gaventa, J. Clinton McCann and James D. Newsom. © 1994 Westminster John Knox Press. Used by permission.

Dare I suggest . . . (Eric James), taken from *A Time to Speak*, Published by SPCK Publishing, 1997. Used by permission.

First Sunday in Lent

In his 'Two Standards' . . . (Gerard Hughes), taken from *God of Surprises*, © 1985 and 1996 Darton, Longman and Todd Ltd. Used by permission of the publishers.

Second Sunday in Lent

Every sermon preached . . . (Elizabeth Achtemeier), taken from *Preaching from the Old Testament*, © 1989 Elizabeth Achtemeier. Used by permission of Westminster John Knox Press.

Luke 13:31-35 is especially . . . (Fred B. Craddock), taken from *Preaching Through the Christian Year: 'C'*, © 1994 Fred B. Craddock, John H. Hayes, Carl R. Holliday, Gene M. Tucker. Reproduced by permission of Trinity Press International, USA.

The chapter in Matthew's . . . (F. F. Bruce), taken from *The Hard Sayings of Jesus*, 1983, reproduced by permission of Hodder and Stoughton Limited.

Third Sunday in Lent

The world is a violent place . . . (Clive Marsh and Gaye Ortiz), taken from *Explorations in Theology and Film*, published by Blackwell Publishers Limited, 1997. Used by permission.

265

Just over four years ago . . . (Ron Dale), © Ron Dale.

Here is a parable . . . (William Barclay), taken from *The Daily Study Bible: The Gospel of Luke*, published by The Saint Andrew Press, 1994. Used by permission.

Fourth Sunday in Lent

There was a man . . . (Beverly R. Gaventa), taken from *Texts for Preaching – Year C*, by Charles B. Cousar, Beverly R. Gaventa, J. Clinton McCann and James D. Newsom. © 1994 Westminster John Knox Press. Used by permission.

The fact that Jesus' . . . (Gabriel Josipovici), taken from *The Book of God*, published by Yale University Press, 1988. Used by permission.

Fifth Sunday in Lent

No one notices . . . (Barbara Brown Taylor), taken from *Bread of Angels*, © Barbara Brown Taylor, published by Cowley Publications, 1997. Used by permission.

All four Gospels . . . (Fred B. Craddock), taken from *Preaching Through the Christian Year: 'C'*, © 1994 Fred B. Craddock, John H. Hayes, Carl R. Holliday, Gene M. Tucker. Reproduced by permission of Trinity Press International, USA.

Palm/Passion Sunday

I once had the privilege . . . (Ron Dale), © Ron Dale.

We have, in the course . . . (Gabriel Josipovici), taken from *The Book of God*, published by Yale University Press, 1998. Used by permission.

In his book *Messengers of God* . . . (Barbara Brown Taylor), taken from *God in Pain: Teaching Sermons on Suffering*, published by Abingdon Press, 1998. Used by permission.

Easter Day

To suggest in the . . . (Thomas Lynch), taken from *The Undertaking*, published by Vintage, 1998. Used by permission of Random House Group Ltd.

Like the world of . . . (Frederick Buechner), taken from *Telling the Truth: The Gospel as Tragedy, Comedy & Fairy Tale*, © 1977 Frederick Buechner. Reprinted by permission of Harper-Collins Publishers, Inc., New York.

Second Sunday of Easter

My grandfather who . . . (Kahlil Gibran), taken from *Jesus the Son of Man*, published by Oneworld Publishing, 1993.

Thomas, after the . . . (Giovanni Papini), taken from *Life of Christ*, published by Dell Publishing Co. Inc., 1957.

Third Sunday of Easter

On the whole, . . . (Barbara Brown Tayor), taken from *Gospel Medicine*, © Barbara Brown Taylor, published by Cowley Publications, 1995. Used by permission.

Fourth Sunday of Easter

It was the feast . . . (R.H. Strachan), taken from *The Fourth Gospel*, published by SCM Press, revised edition 1941. World rights.

One of my favourite names . . . (Barbara Brown Taylor), taken from *The Preaching Life*, © Barbara Brown Taylor. Published by Cowley Publications, 1993. Used by permission.

Fifth Sunday of Easter

France, 1861 . . . (Alessandro Baricco), extract from *Silk*. Translated by Guido Waldman. First published by Rizzoli, Milan in 1996. First published in Great Britian in 1998 by Harvill. © R.C.S Libri & Grandi Opere, Milan, 1996. English translation © The Harvill Press, 1996. Reproduced by permission of The Harvill Press.

It may seem a bit . . . (Charles B. Cousar), taken from *Texts for Preaching – Year C*, by Charles B. Cousar, Beverly R. Gaventa, J. Clinton McCann and James D. Newsom. © 1994 Westminster John Knox Press. Used by permission.

Sixth Sunday of Easter

We must reflect . . . (Clive Marsh & Gaye Ortiz), taken from *Explorations in Theology and Film*, published by Blackwell Publishers Ltd, 1997. Used by permission.

The preach*er* who . . . (Fred B. Craddock), taken from *Preaching Through the Christian Year: 'C'*, © 1994 Fred B. Craddock, John H. Hayes, Carl R. Holliday, Gene M. Tucker. Reproduced by permission of Trinity Press International, USA.

Seventh Sunday of Easter

Verses 20-26 . . . (Gerard Sloyan), taken from *John* (Interpretation Series) by Gerard S. Sloyan. © 1988 Westminster John Knox Press. Used by permission.

We believe in one . . . (Subir Biswas), quoted in *Liturgy of Life*, 1995, reproduced by permission of the National Christian Education Council.

Pentecost

There is no mechanical . . . (Francis Schaeffer), taken from *True Spirituality*, pp. 87-88, © 1971 by Tyndale House Publishers, Inc. Used by permission. All rights reserved.

Creativity and spirituality . . . (Choan-Seng Song), taken from *Third Eye Theology*, published by The Lutterworth Press, 1980. Used by permission.

We cannot overlook . . . (Hans Kung), taken from *On Being a Christian*, published by HarperCollins Publishers, London, 1977. (Rights now reverted to author).

Trinity Sunday

Here is a young man . . . (D.W. Cleverley Ford), taken from *New Preaching from The New Testament*, published by Mowbray, an imprint of Continuum, 1977. Used by permission.

Human parents know . . . (William D. Watley), taken from *Are You the One?* Published by Abingdon Press, 1997. Used by permission.

I answered, . . . (Nicholas Motovilov), taken from *Valentine Zander St. Seraphim of Sarov*, published by SPCK Publishing. Used by permission.

Proper 4 /Ordinary Time 9

The central character . . . (William Barclay), taken from *The Daily Study Bible: The Gospel of Luke*, published by The Saint Andrew Press, 1994. Used by permission.

Proper 5/Ordinary Time 10

'Hold still, . . . (William Langland), taken from *The Vision of Piers Ploughman*, translated by R. Tamplin, published by Penguin UK, 1963. Used by permission.

In the mid-eighties . . . (Ron Dale), © 1988 Ron Dale.

Proper 6/Ordinary Time 11

This story is so . . . (William Barclay), taken from *The Daily Study Bible: The Gospel of Luke*, published by The Saint Andrew Press, 1994. Used by permission.

One of the deepest . . . (Peter G. Van Breeman, SJ), taken from *As Bread that is Broken*, published by Dimension Books © 1974.

Proper 7/Ordinary Time 12

You are surprised . . . (David Kossoff), taken from *The Book of Witness*, published by HarperCollins Publishers, London, 1971.

To be born again . . . (George Macleod), taken from *We Shall Rebuild*, © Copyright Control.

Proper 8/Ordinary Time 13

In one little town, . . . (Adrian Bell), taken from *The Cherry Tree*, published by Oxford University Press, 1985. © The Estate of Adrian Bell. Used by permission.

Crowds constantly . . . (Gabriel Josipovici), taken from *The Book of God*, published by Yale University Press, 1988. Used by permission.

Verses 57-62 . . . (Fred B. Craddock), taken from *Preaching Through the Christian Year: 'C'*, © 1994 Fred B. Craddock, John H. Hayes, Carl R. Holliday, Gene M. Tucker. Reproduced by permission of Trinity Press International, USA.

Proper 9/Ordinary Time 14

When we come . . . (Beverly R. Gaventa), taken from *Texts for Preaching – Year C*, by Charles B. Cousar, Beverly R. Gaventa, J. Clinton McCann and James D. Newsom. © 1994 Westminster John Knox Press. Used by permission.

In the glorious summer . . . (Ron Dale), © 1998 Ron Dale.

When we think . . . (F. F. Bruce), taken from *The Hard Sayings of Jesus*, 1983, reproduced by permission of Hodder and Stoughton Limited.

Proper 10/Ordinary Time 15

We have been taught . . . (Geoffrey William Bromily), quoted in *My Way of Preaching*, © Copyright Control.

Proper 11/Ordinary Time 16

The close of the . . . (Anna Maria Reynolds), taken from *Julian: Woman of our Day*, edited by Robert Llewelyn, published and copyright 1985 by Darton, Longman and Todd Ltd, and used by permission of the publishers.

It would be hard . . . (William Barclay), taken from *The Daily Study Bible: The Gospel of Luke*, published by The Saint Andrew Press, 1994. Used by permission.

Proper 12/Ordinary Time 17

He knows what . . . (William Temple), taken from *Christian Faith and Life*, published by SCM Press, 1931. World rights.

No words ever spoken . . . (E. F. Scott), taken from *The Lord's Prayer*, published by Charles Scribner & Sons, 1971 (an imprint of Simon & Schuster Inc., New York). Used by permission.

Proper 13/Ordinary Time 18

And so I came . . . (Martin Luther King), taken from *A Knock at Midnight*, 1999, used by permission of Laurence Pollinger Ltd on behalf of the Estate of Martin Luther King.

I have four big lollies . . . (Cecily Taylor), from the anthology *Liturgy of Life*, published

by the National Christian Education Council, 1995. Reprinted by permission of the author.

The parable calls . . . (Fred B. Craddock), taken from *Luke* (Interpretation Series) © 1990 Westminster John Knox Press. Used by permission.

There are few areas . . . (Charles B. Cousar), taken from *Texts for Preaching – Year 'C'*, by Charles B. Cousar, Beverly R. Gaventa, J. Clinton McCann and James D. Newsom. © 1994 Westminster John Knox Press. Used by permission.

Proper 14/Ordinary Time 19

The Gospel lesson . . . (Charles B. Cousar), taken from *Texts for Preaching – Year C*, by Charles B. Cousar, Beverly R. Gaventa, J. Clinton McCann and James D. Newsom. © 1994 Westminster John Knox Press. Used by permission.

Proper 15/Ordinary Time 20

To those who . . . (William Barclay) taken from *The Daily Study Bible: The Gospel of Luke*, published by The Saint Andrew Press, 1994. Used by permission.

Proper 16/Ordinary Time 21

My mother's strongest . . . (D.J. Enright), quoted in *The Sun Dancing*, published by Penguin UK, 1982.

Greek thought, to . . . (D. T. Niles), taken from *A Testament of Faith*, © 1970 Epworth Press. Used by permission of Methodist Publishing House.

The preacher who . . . (Fred B. Craddock), Taken from *Preaching Through the Christian Year: 'C'*, © 1994 Fred B. Craddock, John H. Hayes, Carl R. Holliday, Gene M. Tucker. Reproduced by permission of Trinity Press International, USA.

Proper 17/Ordinary Time 22

Mrs Malone . . . (Eleanor Farjeon), taken from *Silver Sand and Snow*, published by Michael Joseph. Used by permission of David Higham Associates.

Jesus chose a homely . . . (William Barclay), taken from *The Daily Study Bible: The Gospel of Luke*, published by The Saint Andrew Press, 1994. Used by permission.

Verses 12-14 address . . . (Fred B. Craddock), taken from *Preaching Through the Christian Year: 'C'*, © 1994 Fred B. Craddock, John H. Hayes, Carl R. Holliday, Gene M. Tucker. Reproduced by permission of Trinity Press International, USA.

Proper 18/Ordinary Time 23

The assigned lection . . . (Charles B. Cousar), taken from *Texts for Preaching – Year C*, by Charles B. Cousar, Beverly R. Gaventa, J. Clinton McCann and James D. Newsom. © 1994 Westminster John Knox Press. Used by permission.

Luke provides a . . . (Fred B. Craddock), taken from *Preaching Through the Christian Year: 'C'*, © 1994 Fred B. Craddock, John H. Hayes, Carl R. Holliday, Gene M. Tucker. Reproduced by permission of Trinity Press International, USA.

Proper 19/Ordinary Time 24

An unforgettable . . . (G. Curtis Jones and Paul H. Jones), taken from *500 Illustrations: Stories from Life for Preaching and Teaching*, published by Abingdon Press, 1998. Used by permission.

The finding of the . . . (George Buttrick), taken from *Sermons Preached in a University Church*, published by Abingdon Press. Used by permission.

Proper 20/Ordinary Time 25

This might well . . . (James S. Stewart), taken from *Walking with God*, published by The Saint Andrew Press, edited by Gordon Grant. Used by permission of the editor.

Proper 21/Ordinary Time 26

For the period . . . (Robert Hughes), extract from *American Visions*. First published in 1997 by Alfred A. Knopf and Random House, Canada. First published in Great Britain by Harvill in 1997. © Robert Hughes, 1997. Reproduced by permission of The Harvill Press.

My reflection has . . . (David A. Farmer), taken from *Teaching Sermons on the Love and Grace of God: Unmerited Favour*, published by Abingdon Press, 1997. Used by permission.

Proper 22/Ordinary Time 27

There is a story . . . (Sir Stafford Cripps), taken from *God in Our Work*, © Copyright Control.

Verse 5 functions . . . (Fred B. Craddock), taken from *Preaching Through the Christian Year: 'C'*, © 1994 Fred B. Craddock, John H. Hayes, Carl R. Holliday, Gene M. Tucker. Reproduced by permission of Trinity Press International, USA.

Proper 23/Ordinary Time 28

It is hard to say . . . (Barbara Brown Taylor), taken from *The Peaching Life*, © Barbara Brown Taylor, published by Cowley Publications, 1993. Used by permission.

Jesus was on the . . . (William Barclay), taken from *The Daily Study Bible: The Gospel of Luke*, published by The Saint Andrew Press, 1994. Used by permission.

Proper 24/Ordinary Time 29

The American novelist . . . (Andrew R.C. McLellan), taken from *Preaching for These People*, published by Mowbray, an imprint of Continuum, 1997. Used by permission.

The delightful and . . . (Charles B. Cousar), taken from *Texts for Preaching – Year C*, by Charles B. Cousar, Beverly R. Gaventa, J. Clinton McCann and James D. Newsom. © 1994 Westminster John Knox Press. Used by permission.

Proper 25/Ordinary Time 30

The person telling . . . (Jurgen Moltmann), taken from *The Power of the Powerless*, published by SCM Press, 1983. World rights outside US and Canada.

Proper 26/Ordinary Time 31
Fourth Sunday before Advent

All Saints' Day

Proper 27/Ordinary Time 32
Third Sunday before Advent

Proper 28/Ordinary Time 33
Second Sunday before Advent

Proper 29/Christ the King

Addresses of copyright owners

Abingdon Press, 201 Eighth Avenue South, Nashville, TN 37203, USA.

Augsburg Fortress, PO Box 1209, Minneapolis, MN 55440-1209, USA.

Blackwell Publishers Ltd, 108 Cowley Road, Oxford, OX4 1JF.

T & T Clarke Ltd, 59 George Street, Edinburgh, EH2 2LQ.

The Continuum International Publishing Group Ltd, Wellington House, 125 Strand, London, WC2R 0BB.

Cowley Publications/Barbara Brown Taylor, 28 Temple Place, Boston, Massachusetts 02111, USA.

Darton Longman & Todd, 1 Spencer Court, 140-142 Wandsworth High Street, London, SW18 4JJ.

Dell Publishing Co. Inc., 261 Fifth Avenue, New York 10036-4094, USA.

Dimension Books Inc., PO Box 811, Denville, New Jersey 07834, USA.

Fleming H. Revell Co., 158 Fifth Street, New York 10036-4094, USA.

Granada Publishing Ltd, 8 Grafton Street, London,W1X 3LA.

HarperCollins Publishers, 77-85 Fulham Palace Road, London, N1 1RD.

HarperCollins Publishers, 10 East 53rd Street, New York, NY 10022-5299, USA.

The Harvill Press Ltd, 2 Aztec Row, Berners Road, London, N1 0PW.

David Higham Associates Ltd, 5-8 Lower John Street, Golden Square, London, W1R 4HA.

Hodder & Stoughton Publishers, 338 Euston Road, London, NW1 3BH.

The Lutterworth Press, PO Box 60, Cambridge, CB1 2NT.

Method Publishing House, 20 Ivatt Way, Peterborough, PE3 7PG.

Monarch Publications, The Broadway, Crowborough, East Sussex, TN6 1HQ.

National Christian Education Council, 1020 Bristol Road, Selly Oak, Birmingham, B29 6LB.

Oneworld Publications, 185 Banbury Road, Oxford, OX2 7AR.

Penguin UK, 29 Wrights Lane, London, W8 5TZ.

Laurence Pollinger Ltd, 18 Maddox Street, Mayfair, London, W1R 0EU.

Random House Group Ltd, 20 Vauxhall Bridge Road, London, SW1V 2SA.

The Saint Andrew Press, 121 George Street, Edinburgh, EH2 4YN.

SCM Press, 9-17 Albans Place, London, N1 0NX.

Simon & Schuster Inc., 1230 Avenue of the Americas, New York, NY 10020, USA.

SPCK Publishing, Holy Trinity Church, Marylebone Road, London, NW1 4DU.

Tyndale House Publishers Inc., PO Box 80, Wheaton, IL 60189-0080, USA.

Trinity Press International, 4775 Linglestown Road, Harrisburg, PA17112, USA.

Westminster John Knox Press, 100 Witherspoon Street, Louisville, Kentucky, 40202-1396, USA.

World Council of Churches, 150 Route De Ferney, PO Box 2100, 1211 Geneva 2, Switzerland.

Yale University Press, 23 Pond Street, London, NW3 2PN.